Foreign Capital
in Latin America

José Antonio Ocampo and Roberto Steiner
Editors
FEDESARROLLO,
Santa Fe de Bogotá, Colombia

Published by the Inter-American Development Bank
Distributed by The Johns Hopkins University Press

Washington, D.C.
1994

The views and opinions expressed in this publication are those of the authors and do not necessarily reflect the official position of the Inter-American Development Bank.

Foreign Capital in Latin America

© Copyright 1994 by the Inter-American Development Bank

Inter-American Development Bank
1300 New York Avenue, N.W.
Washington, D.C. 20577

Distributed by
The Johns Hopkins University Press
2715 North Charles Street
Baltimore, Maryland 21218-4319

Library of Congress Catalog Card Number: 94-78311
ISBN: 0-940602-77-6

AUTHORS

Agosin, Manuel R.
Director of Graduate Studies in Economic and Administrative Science, Universidad de Chile, Santiago.

Barrera O., Felipe
Researcher, Fundación para la Educación Superior y el Desarrollo (FEDESARROLLO), Santa Fe de Bogotá.

Cárdenas S., Mauricio
Researcher, FEDESARROLLO, Santa Fe de Bogotá.

Damill, Mario
Researcher, Centro de Estudios Estado y Sociedad (CEDES), Buenos Aires.

Fanelli, José María
Researcher, CEDES, Buenos Aires.

Fuentes, J. Rodrigo
Professor of Research, Economic and Administrative Science Department, Universidad de Chile, Santiago.

Letelier, Leonardo
Professor of Research, Economic and Administrative Science Department, Universidad de Chile, Santiago.

Ocampo, José Antonio
Researcher, FEDESARROLLO, Santa Fe de Bogotá.

Ros, Jaime
Associate Professor, Department of Economics, University of Notre Dame, South Bend, Indiana.

Steiner, Roberto
Researcher, FEDESARROLLO, Santa Fe de Bogotá.

FOREWORD

Foreign Capital in Latin America is the seventh book in the series published under the Centers for Research in Applied Economics Project sponsored by the Inter-American Development Bank. In keeping with the centers' objective of addressing the major economic and social problems affecting Latin America and the Caribbean, this volume examines the recent trend of direct foreign investment in the region. The case studies of Argentina, Chile, Colombia, and Mexico were chosen specifically for the extraordinary amount of investment activity they have generated from abroad over the last few years. The book does more than simply trace the growth in the size of capital flows into the region; instead, the authors face the unique task of looking beyond the numbers and examining the true nature and effects of this capital.

The questions raised are many. For example, where is all this capital coming from? Did certain conditions or policies attract foreign investors to these countries? By what means does this money make its way into these Latin American economies? Then, once it is there, what is being done with all this funding and what overall macroeconomic impact will it have? Finally, and most importantly, is this just a temporary trend, some sort of fashionable investment opportunity brought about by exogenous factors in the global investment climate, or is it the beginning of a long-term investment process that will require constant and special attention from policy makers?

Obviously, foreign funds provide a welcome complement to national savings in Latin American efforts to boost investment. There are, however, some concerns about the potentially destabilizing impact these foreign capital flows may have on domestic economies, and those concerns sometimes result in policies which can discourage capital formation, at least in the short term. Attempts to sterilize the monetary effect of foreign capital flows tend to push interest rates up in many cases, thus impacting negatively on investment. Also, sterilization can have the troublesome effect of reducing the appreciation of the exchange rate, making imported capital goods more costly. Some countries, then, find their foreign exchange earnings buying them less than perhaps they expected, while at the same time finding it increasingly difficult to price their exports attractively.

Generalized answers to the questions raised above are easy to provide, but the more specific answers contained in each chapter merit very close attention. In Argentina and Chile, for example, much of the capital from abroad came as a result of their privatization and debt-conversion processes. In Colombia, however, where privatization has been slow in taking shape and there is considerably less foreign debt to reckon with, most of the new capital has been attracted by expectations of high returns on financial assets because of higher interest rates and a perception that Colombia's currency is still undervalued. Of all the countries in the region, Mexico attracts more foreign capital than any other. However, while its levels of investment have been rising, the recent decline in national savings could compromise the country's ability to support current rates of investment.

Of course, Latin America's recent success at achieving greater macroeconomic and political stability has attracted investors, and capital repatriation has played an important part in the flows for all the countries studied. Also interesting, though, are some of the less familiar aspects of these foreign capital flows: the innovative means used to attract capital; the effect the flows have on domestic securities markets; the growing investment in service sectors; and the exchange rate effects resulting from the governments' sterilization measures. In the final analysis, this book provides policy makers with a useful compass for guiding themselves through the macroeconomic management challenges that are bound to accompany economic success in the future.

Nohra Rey de Marulanda
Manager, Economic and Social
Development Department

CONTENTS

CHAPTER ONE

FOREIGN CAPITAL
IN LATIN AMERICA:
AN OVERVIEW

José Antonio Ocampo and Roberto Steiner

In 1990 and 1991 foreign capital flowed into some Latin American countries in quantities not witnessed for over a decade. Table 1.1 shows that the flow of capital into the developing countries of the Western Hemisphere rose from an annual average of $8 billion between 1985 and 1989 to levels near $20 billion in 1990, $40 billion in 1991 and $60 billion in 1992. It should be noted, however, that this phenomenon was largely restricted to a few countries such as Argentina, Chile, Colombia, Mexico, and Venezuela (ECLAC, 1992).

Table 1.1. Balance of Payments for Developing Countries of the Western Hemisphere, 1980-91
(Billions of dollars)

	Current account	Capital account[1]	Overall balance
1980	-30.3	34.0	3.7
1981	-43.5	41.9	-1.6
1982	-42.2	23.0	-19.2
1983	-11.6	13.6	2.0
1984	-2.0	11.7	9.7
1985	-3.2	4.8	1.6
1986	-17.7	10.7	-7.0
1987	-10.8	14.1	3.3
1988	-11.1	3.7	-7.4
1989	-7.7	9.6	1.9
1990	-5.9	20.5	14.6
1991	-19.8	39.9	20.1
1992	-36.8	60.8	24.0

[1] Includes errors and omissions.
Sources: For 1980-91, Calvo, *et al.* (1992); for 1992, IMF, *World Economic Outlook.*

These increasing inflows of capital made it possible not only to finance larger current account deficits but also to effect a significant increase in the level of international reserves. Table 1.1 shows that the current account deficit financed in 1991, although smaller than those observed prior to the onset of the debt crisis, far exceeded the deficits recorded every year from 1983 on. While the capital flows have reached quantities similar to those of that period, a much higher proportion (40 percent of income in 1991 and 1992) has been devoted to increasing the international reserves of the region's countries (see Calvo, *et al.*, 1992).

According to the literature on economic development, the return to a positive transfer of financial resources is a return to normalcy. It follows, then, that developing countries need to receive a positive flow of external resources to supplement domestic savings in the financing of investment, to reduce or eliminate the external gap, and to slow the transfer of resources from the private to the public sector.

Factors of both "attraction" and "expulsion" were involved in the recent flow of capital into Latin America. Among the most important of the former were the implementation of structural reforms designed to emphasize the interplay of market forces and the increased macroeconomic stability of various countries in the region. However, regarding the role of these factors in the current economic situation, it must be emphasized that capital flowed more readily to some countries where reforms were in the beginning stages (e.g., Brazil) and only slowly to countries where structural changes were well-established (e.g., Chile). The recession and the low interest rates in several developed countries (the "general external shock" referred to by Calvo, *et al.*, 1992) were among the principal reasons why capital flowed out of those countries and into Latin America.

This reversal in the trend of capital flows included a substantial repatriation of capital, innovative ways of gaining access to the international market (including, most significantly, the floating of bonds and shares in the markets of developed countries and the initiation of "country funds" operations), and the inflow of capital associated with privatization processes. It also coincided with a stock market boom in various countries of the region.

It is widely recognized that the easing of external constraints resulting from the inflow of capital permits either higher levels of expenditure than would be possible with domestic income alone (in which case the capital inflows are counterbalanced by a current account deficit) or an increase in the country's international liquidity. If investment is the spending component that is financed by the greater availability of external resources, then the trade deficit will be associated with increases in capital goods imports. Conversely, if external savings are used to restore levels of consumption depressed by previous financing deficiencies, it is possible that the current account deficit is, in essence, signaling a decline in exports and increased consumer goods imports. The implications for economic growth are entirely different for both alternatives.

Latin America's experience in handling positive transfers has not been very successful in recent decades and in fact led to a crisis that several countries have yet to overcome entirely. The inflow of capital in the late 1970s and early 1980s into the Southern Cone countries, which were then in the process of deregulating their economies, led some analysts to conclude that financial deregulation should come after trade liberalization, since the former tends to appreciate the exchange rate by attracting foreign capital, thereby hampering the process of adjusting the domestic productive apparatus, a prerequisite for trade liberalization (Edwards, 1984).

The link between capital inflows and real exchange rate appreciation was again demonstrated in Latin America over recent years. The real exchange rate in Mexico and Argentina returned in 1991 to levels similar to the averages of the 1970s and continued falling in 1992. In Chile and Colombia, efforts to prevent substantial appreciation of the real exchange rate made macroeconomic management even more difficult.

In their eagerness to alleviate the pressure on the exchange rate, some central banks intervened actively in the foreign exchange markets. To counteract the monetary effect of that intervention, they were forced to execute costly sterilization operations, which not only adversely affected the "quasi-fiscal" balance but, even more seriously, may have increased the yield spread between Latin America and the rest of the world, which is surely one of the reasons for the flows in the first place. This problem was recently discussed from a theoretical perspective by Calvo (1991).

In these circumstances, a great many interesting opinions were expressed in Latin America concerning the objectives of monetary and exchange policies in more open economies and whether there were any tools that could be used to directly control the inflow of capital, other than those traditionally used to control trade. The argument against the capital inflow is that real appreciation such as that experienced in the Southern Cone in the late 1970s and early 1980s is detrimental to the processes of trade liberalization currently underway in nearly all the countries of the region.

Nevertheless, the assumption that this process of capital inflows, real exchange rate appreciation, and potential balance of trade deterioration is detrimental to growth is true only if the terms of trade deterioration is not accompanied by an upturn in capital goods imports and, more generally, in the level of investment. If capital formation increases, long-term structural adjustment may not be adversely affected because the new capital can contribute to the success of the liberalization process to the extent that the new investments are made in sectors that produce internationally marketable goods and services. However, adjustment can be achieved through a different route: increased productivity. This being the case, the trade-liberalization/capital-flows relationship is characterized by a trade-off between the negative effects of the capital flows on exports (and the import-substitution sectors) and their favorable impact on investment.

The presumption that capital flows are incapable of stimulating investment and, conversely, that they negatively affect savings, is supported by the experience of the Southern Cone in the late 1970s and early 1980s. There are, moreover, various theoretical approximations of this same phenomenon. Thus, for example, in a context of volatile domestic expectations,[1] inflows of capital make domestic interest rates more erratic, which negatively affects investment decisions. In these circumstances, there is some justification for taxes on or greater reserve requirements for capital transactions (Tornell, 1990) or adopting capital transaction controls or a dual exchange system, which partially insulates the economy from the speculative pressures of international capital flows (Guidotti, 1988).

There are, however, some examples of successful liberalization processes in which there were abundant capital inflows and economic growth was "propped up" by investment. In Spain, the current account of the balance of payments changed from a surplus position to a huge deficit in the latter half of the 1980s. This process coincided with a substantial revaluation of the peseta and an increase in foreign investment, both direct and portfolio, which provided the financing for the current account deficit and facilitated an unprecedented surge in the rate of investment (Banco de España, 1992).

Similarly, there is empirical evidence of the favorable effects that greater access to capital markets had on investment in developing countries in the 1970s (Zaidi, 1985) as well as the subsequent unfavorable effect of the debt crisis and capital flight (Pastor, 1990). This upward and subsequently downward trend of investment suggests that the beneficial effects of capital flows are closely related to their duration.

The link between external financing and investment depends on the type of foreign resources obtained, a subject that has been discussed by Dunley and Seiver (1987), among others. The volatility of such resources becomes a crucial factor not only because it affects the expectations of various economic agents but also because the perception regarding the permanence of the resources will greatly influence macroeconomic policy. Of course, such volatility is largely endogenous, and the stability of the resources depends in large measure on the response of macroeconomic authorities to the greater abundance of external capital.

In particular, the authorities' estimation of the permanence of the resources will be a determining factor in their decision either to allow the capital inflows to have a significant impact on the exchange rate or to prevent them from doing so. As discussed below, the relationship between these flows and the exchange rate is complex, and the causality can work in both directions. The tendency of these

---

[1] These are generally linked to the perception that the inflow of capital will be followed by a flow in the opposite direction.

flows to cause exchange rate appreciation has been amply discussed; no less important is the fact that they might well be the answer to exchange imbalances.

In summary, a precise analysis of the economic impact of the capital inflows will encompass three interdependent aspects. First, the size and nature of these flows must be determined. Second, a detailed analysis of the economic policy adopted to manage the inflows is necessary to assess the efficacy of the various stabilization measures. Finally, an in-depth study is needed regarding the flows' effect on the amount and composition of domestic investment, since the latter variable is a key element in determining whether the capital inflows serve the basic purpose of contributing to economic growth.

The subject of this study is the recent experiences of Argentina, Chile, Colombia, and Mexico with large capital inflows. The three aspects mentioned above have been analyzed for these countries. In each case, the aim of the respective authors was to identify the most important policy recommendations.

This chapter provides an overview of the case studies. In the first section the size of the capital inflows is approximated and the determinants of these flows are analyzed. Common elements such as the implementation of more market-oriented financial and exchange policies are highlighted. It is also shown that some factors—such as the direct foreign investment (DFI) involved in the privatization process—are not significant in all cases.

Next, a comparative analysis is presented regarding the macroeconomic management alternatives employed by the authorities of the four countries. Particular emphasis is given to the role of the real exchange rate in these experiences and to sterilization efforts or the use of direct controls on the capital flows. Elements common to the experiences of Chile and Colombia are illustrated, chief among which are the attempts to prevent substantial appreciation of the real exchange rate. Several similarities between the Argentine and Mexican experiences are also pointed out.

The next section contains evidence concerning the effects that the expanded capital resources have on investment. As will be seen, the experiences in this respect are fairly dissimilar. Finally, the main conclusions of the study are summarized. It is shown that there is, of course, no single formula for managing the increasing capital flows and that the best policy a country can follow is one which is specific to the type of resources involved and which provides for their efficient absorption, without becoming an additional source of macroeconomic instability.

Volume and Types of Flows

Volume of Flows

Table 1.2 was prepared as an initial approximation of the volume of flows, based on balance of payments data from the International Monetary Fund. It also serves as a basis for comparison with Table 1.1. The reader should realize, however, that problems of a methodological and computational order suggest the need for caution in analyzing the figures in Table 1.2, which, while having the advantage of coming from a single source, cannot substitute for the information provided for each country in the case studies.

The overall balance indicated in Table 1.2 is the sum of the current account and the capital account. When the free movement of capital is restricted, the current account usually conceals what are in fact capital transactions. This problem is especially acute in the case of Colombia, as we will later see. The capital account figures for Argentina and Chile do not include debt service arrears; consequently, they show what the result would have been had all obligations been promptly satisfied.[2]

The figures for the capital account suggest that the improvement in Mexico was spectacular. Its capital account has already topped the levels reached at the start of the last decade; in fact, Mexico has received nearly half of all the flows into the region in recent years. Although a sizable percentage of these expanded inflows was used to augment the country's international reserves, especially in 1991, most of the capital was used to finance an equally rapid rise in the current account deficit. Mexico's net current account balances are also larger than they were in the early 1980s.

Although not as rapid, the turnaround was equally dramatic in Argentina, which used the additional resources to finance a significant current account deficit and a substantial rise in international reserves. In 1991 an enormous amount of exceptional financing was needed to cover both the current account deficit and the accumulation of reserves. Even so, as a percentage of GDP, Argentina's current account deficits in recent years have been smaller than they were in the early 1980s.

In Chile, the resources obtained through the capital account were used primarily to build up central bank reserves. Moreover, recent current account deficits are extremely small compared to those observed prior to the debt crisis.[3]

Because of substantial inconsistencies in the way its current account is measured, Colombia is more difficult to analyze on the basis of the figures in Table 1.2. Still, the fact remains that in recent years no significant levels of external financing were added to Colombia's capital account. The current account surplus

---

[2] The difference between the obligations incurred and those actually paid appears in the "exceptional financing" column. The sum of the latter and the overall balance is not necessarily the same as the accrued reserves because some of the exceptional financing consists of liabilities which, being short-term, are not part of the international reserves held by the monetary authority.

[3] According to the figures indicated in the case study, capital inflows represented between 11 and 14 percent of GDP in 1977-81; in the most recent business cycle they represented between 2 and 8 percent.

Table 1.2. Balance of Payments, 1980-92
(Billions of dollars)

	Current account				Capital account[1]				Balance				Exceptional financing				Change in reserves			
	Arg.	Chi.	Col.	Mex.	Arg.	Chi.	Col.	Mex.	Arg.	Chi.	Col.	Mex.	Arg.	Chi.	Col.	Mex.	Arg.	Chi.	Col.	Mex.
1980	-4.8	-2.0	-0.2	-10.8	1.9	3.2	1.1	11.6	-2.9	1.2	0.9	0.8	0.2	0.0	0.0	0.0	-2.7	1.3	1.2	0.9
1981	-4.7	-4.7	-2.0	-16.1	1.1	4.8	1.9	17.4	-3.6	0.1	-0.1	1.3	0.4	0.0	0.0	0.0	-3.4	0.0	0.2	1.3
1982	-2.4	-2.3	-3.1	-6.3	-2.3	0.9	2.2	-5.3	-4.7	-1.4	-0.9	-11.6	4.1	0.2	0.0	6.8	-0.8	-1.4	-0.7	-3.3
1983	-2.4	-1.1	-3.0	5.4	-2.7	-3.2	1.2	-9.7	-5.1	-4.3	-1.8	-4.3	2.8	3.7	0.0	7.6	-1.3	0.1	-1.8	3.2
1984	-2.5	-2.1	-1.4	4.2	0.0	0.0	1.0	-4.9	-2.5	-2.1	-0.4	-0.7	2.5	2.1	0.0	2.8	-0.1	0.4	-1.2	3.4
1985	-1.0	-1.4	-1.8	1.1	0.4	-1.2	2.0	-4.8	-0.6	-2.6	0.2	-3.7	1.9	2.5	0.0	1.0	2.0	0.1	0.3	-2.4
1986	-2.9	-1.2	0.4	-1.7	0.8	-1.6	0.9	1.2	-2.1	-2.8	1.3	-0.5	1.3	2.6	0.0	0.4	-0.6	0.0	1.4	0.9
1987	-4.2	-0.8	0.3	4.0	-0.2	-1.1	0.1	0.1	-4.4	-1.9	0.4	4.1	2.3	2.0	0.0	1.5	-1.1	0.2	-0.1	6.8
1988	-1.6	-0.2	-0.2	-2.4	0.3	1.0	0.4	-8.8	-1.3	0.8	0.2	-11.2	3.2	-0.1	0.0	4.5	1.7	0.7	0.3	-7.1
1989	-1.3	-0.8	-0.2	-4.0	-8.3	1.2	0.6	3.8	-9.6	0.4	0.4	-0.2	8.3	0.0	0.0	0.4	-1.9	0.5	0.2	0.4
1990	1.9	-0.6	0.5	-7.1	-2.5	2.9	0.1	9.4	-0.6	2.3	0.6	2.2	4.0	0.0	0.0	0.1	3.1	2.2	0.7	3.5
1991	-2.8	0.1	2.3	-13.8	2.0	1.1	-0.5	21.8	-0.8	1.2	1.8	8.0	3.4	0.0	0.0	0.0	1.4	1.1	1.9	7.8
1992	-8.4	-0.6	0.9	-22.8	10.8	3.1	0.3	24.6	2.4	2.5	1.2	1.7	2.2	0.0	0.0	0.0	4.1	1.7	1.2	1.1

[1] Includes errors and omissions.

Sources: IMF, *International Financial Statistics*. The 1992 figures for Colombia are from the Banco de la República. Those for Chile are from chapter three of this publication.

has thus been used to finance the substantial accumulation of reserves in the last few years. Nevertheless, some current account transactions, especially transfers, have recently concealed sizable capital flows.

Consequently, and as an initial approximation, it can be concluded that regardless of the precise amount, the recent surfeit of capital has had somewhat different consequences. In Argentina and Mexico, the inflow financed fairly large current account deficits and, to a certain extent, the accumulation of international reserves. In Chile and Colombia, the capital was used primarily to build up international reserves. Of course, this was the result of differences in macroeconomic policy between these two groups of countries, as will be seen in the following section.

Types and Determinants of Flows

As Goldstein, *et al.* (1991) point out, a distinction must be made between gross and net capital movements. A high level of the former, which can reflect, among other things, on portfolio diversification decisions, does not necessarily lead to a high level of the latter; gross movements between countries can be completely neutralized. For net capital movements to reach significant levels, there must be imbalances between savings and investment within the countries.

The inadequacy of domestic savings to finance acceptable levels of investment has been amply documented in Latin America. Understanding why the international market has financed such deficits in some countries and not in others is complex. At least three factors concerning the origin or cause of the capital inflow must be analyzed. First, as has already been mentioned, there may be a "common external shock," which draws capital away from the developed countries. Another important factor may be domestic macroeconomic policy, which determines combinations of interest rates, exchange rates, and other variables that make domestic investments profitable or unprofitable. Finally, the implementation of structural reforms can play a vital role in creating a more favorable climate for investment (particularly foreign investment), be it direct or portfolio. As will be seen below, the four case studies suggest—in one way or another, and some more forcibly than others—the existence of these elements as determinants of the recent inflow of capital.

For the purposes of this study, it does not seem necessary to explain "common external shock," a concept discussed at length by Calvo, *et al.* (1992). Their work concludes that, regardless of the existence of attractive investment opportunities in certain Latin American countries, the real rate of return in a number of developed countries has fallen significantly. Nevertheless, the case study on Mexico makes the noteworthy conclusion that internal factors played a much more decisive role in attracting large capital inflows to Mexico, the main recipient country of the region. Similarly, and because there are some very thorough studies on the subject (IMF, 1992), we will not describe in detail any of the various financial instruments that have been developed recently, which have surely facilitated a greater flow of capital into the region.[4]

Therefore, we will concentrate our efforts on explaining the impact that structural reforms and macroeconomic policy have had on capital flows. Because of this, one way of coherently summarizing the major findings of the studies is by separately analyzing the inflows that have taken the form of DFI and those that have been categorized as speculative.

In our opinion, this method of presentation has the additional advantage of throwing light on the potential stability of the inflows. It is reasonable to suppose that flows received in the form of DFI are more stable than resources attracted by the temporary yield spreads of financial assets. As noted in the preceding section, macroeconomic policy is influenced by how stable the resources are thought to be. Nevertheless, the volatility of capital cannot be determined empirically; in reality, any resource, whether in the form of direct investment or not, is potentially stable, provided that the appropriate macroeconomic conditions exist.

Foreign Investment

The case studies served as the basis for the preparation of Table 1.3, which, for classification purposes, is not necessarily comparable with the balance of payment information provided in Table 1.2. Given the size of the respective economies, the largest net foreign investment consistently received was in Chile and the smallest, by far, was in Colombia.

It is interesting to note that in Argentina in 1990 a significant upturn was observed in the flow of foreign investment; indeed, in dollar terms it rose by almost 100 percent that year. Foreign investment accounted for more than half of the $12.8 billion Argentina received between 1990 and the third quarter of 1992, either through the capital account or through special financing. This suggests that it recovered more rapidly and more steadily than the other components of the capital account, which showed no signs of substantial improvement until 1992. It is not unreasonable, then, to conclude that these developments were the result of various structural reforms implemented in 1989.[5]

---

[4] The publication mentioned contains an excellent analysis of the use that various Latin American countries have made of the new products available in the international financial markets. In the region as a whole, Mexico has taken the lead. To a lesser extent, Argentina and Chile have also participated. As of 1992, the publication makes no mention of Colombia.

[5] In particular, these include the State Reform Law, which promoted the privatization of public enterprises with foreign debt capitalization, and the Economic Emergency Law, which established equal treatment for national and foreign capital.

Table 1.3. Net Foreign Investment, 1980-92
(Millions of dollars)

	Argentina[1]	Chile[2]	Colombia	Mexico
1980	739	331	48	2,156
1981	927	533	228	2,835
1982	257	646	330	1,655
1983	183	258	512	461
1984	269	127	558	390
1985	919	185	1,015	491
1986	574	437	592	1,160
1987	-19	1,177	335	1,796
1988	1,147	1,576	186	635
1989	1,028	2,252	547	2,648
1990	2,036	2,297	471	2,548
1991	2,439	1,122	419	4,742
1992[3]	2,446	1,036	610	5,366

[1] Includes privatizations.
[2] Includes portfolio investments.
[3] For Argentina, figures until September.
Sources: For Argentina, Chile, and Colombia, see their respective chapters in this publication; for Mexico: IMF, *International Financial Statistics.*

Of the total foreign investment in Argentina between 1990 and the third quarter of 1992, 28 percent was associated with the privatization process, i.e., the purchase of existing assets. That percentage rises to 90 percent if only the first three quarters of 1992 are considered. The Menem administration's view of DFI's role in the Argentine development process represents a significant break with the past: while it was formerly regarded as a means of supporting the domestic investment process, DFI is now seen as a useful tool for increasing the availability of external savings.

Of the four countries considered in this study, Chile has received the most foreign investment. The figures in Table 1.2 show that between 1988 and 1992 there was a surplus in the Chilean capital account of approximately $9.3 billion. The figures in Table 1.3 suggest that nearly 90 percent of this amount can be explained by the performance of net foreign investment. It should be noted that although most of the foreign investment in Chile has been direct investment, portfolio investment has also acquired some importance in recent years, whether through investment funds or through the sale of Chilean stocks on the New York Stock Exchange (i.e., through American Depositary Receipts, or ADRs). These mechanisms reached a record high in 1990, when they combined to represent 19 percent of all foreign investment.

Some of the structural reforms carried out in Chile, which have undoubtedly created a more favorable environment for foreign investment, date to 1974. In that year, Decree Law 600 established equal treatment for foreign investors and Chilean citizens. Then, in 1985, the central bank authorized direct investment through this mechanism to convert debt to capital.[6] Until 1989, most of the DFI that Chile received was through this mechanism. As discussed in detail in the case study on Chile, it is difficult to tell whether the investment received through this channel replaced investment that had previously flowed through traditional channels, or whether these were additional resources to which access would not have been possible without the debt-for-equity process. What is clear is that as the secondary price of Chilean foreign debt rose dramatically and debt-for-equity swaps consequently became less attractive, foreign investment—although it declined—continued arriving in large amounts, at least until 1990. In 1991 all of the DFI was through conventional mechanisms other than debt-for-equity swaps, a change which, among other things, makes it more practicable to use the resources recently received to finance new investments rather than to purchase existing companies.[7] Reference to the sectoral utilization of DFI will be made later in this chapter.

The case study on Mexico indicates that while trade liberalization and, in particular, the relaxing of investor rules in 1984 had a positive impact on DFI, these effects were negated by the country's sluggish economic growth as compared to pre-debt crisis trends, which has discouraged such flows. On the other hand, the deregulation of portfolio investment helped accelerate capital inflows to such an extent that by 1992 it had become the most important item of the capital account.

In Mexico, privatization directly stimulated portfolio investment, but it was above all part of a policy of reorganizing public finances which, together with the Brady Agreement of July 1989 and the expectations generated by the negotiation of the North American Free Trade Agreement, significantly lowered its risk premium. According to the case study, this reduction, as well as the widening gap between investment and *private* savings (which is discussed below), played a much more decisive role in the recent capital boom than the merely exogenous factors (of "expulsion").

In Colombia, foreign investment has been sluggish, not only historically but also in the most recent business cycle, when large amounts were flowing into other parts of the region. Most of the resources were associated with large projects

---

[6] In the case study it is suggested that some financial facilities such as foreign bank accounts create a situation wherein "the legislation and regulations in force give preferential treatment to foreign investors."

[7] The case study cites the estimates of Ffrench-Davis, which indicate that between 25 and 56 percent of the resources involved in debt-for-equity swaps between 1985 and 1989 were used to purchase existing companies.

in the mining and hydrocarbons sector. Excluding petroleum, 43 percent of the foreign investment received prior to 1991 was in the mining sector and 54 percent was in the manufacturing sector (Steiner, 1992). This relatively poor showing may be explained in part by the fact that Colombia, unlike Argentina, has made little progress in the field of privatization. It could also be argued that Colombia, unlike Chile, has not had any major external debt problems, which has made the promotion of debt-for-equity swaps impracticable.

In summary, the four case studies show that the trend of foreign investment has been closely related to the economic reform process. In Chile, this process is of relatively long standing and, consequently, foreign investment has been an important source of financing for quite some time. In Argentina and Mexico, the reforms have been recent and have at the same time generated important capital inflows. As a result, the inflow has been slower in coming, but also more significant. Finally, in Colombia, the reforms have not only been rather late but also more limited. As evidence of this, the flow of foreign investment has not yet reached significant levels.

Speculative Capital

As the case studies suggest, the perception exists that a large percentage of recent capital flows has been speculative in nature. In other words, regardless of the final use of the resources received, their very existence is explained in large part by the possibility of exploiting the differences between domestic and foreign interest rates.

Generally speaking, little is known about the size of these flows, not only because in many cases they are, by nature, not registered but also because it is difficult to differentiate them from other headings in the capital accounts. In the final analysis, it is unclear what is meant by speculation. Direct foreign investment also exploits yield spreads; the same is true of income from drug trafficking, which is significant in Colombia. The case studies take different approaches, but they all have in common the fact that DFI and medium- and long-term debt are not considered speculative. In some cases the short-term financing of foreign trade is included, which might not be considered a speculative activity by the person using the resources but would be by the person providing them. On the other hand, portfolio investment can be stable and, to a certain extent, considered a form of DFI; nevertheless, it has some of the characteristics of capital movements that exploit the yield spreads of financial assets.

In keeping with the general points summarized in the preceding section, which suggest that DFI has been important for Argentina, Mexico, and Chile but of little significance for Colombia, the subject of speculative flows has attracted a great deal more attention with respect to the latter country.

Since speculative flows cannot be precisely measured, there is little point in attempting comparisons of their relative size in the various countries. A more interesting exercise would be to try to determine in which cases they can be satisfactorily explained by yield spreads.

In the case study on Argentina, Fanelli and Damill liken this type of flow to the external indebtedness of companies quoted on the stock exchange, because they are a representative group of large companies with access to the international capital market. It is their belief that these flows must stand in a positive relationship to capital goods imports and in a negative relationship to the country risk premium. The latter is defined as the difference between the interest rate on government bonds denominated in dollars (Bonex) and the external interest rate (LIBOR).

In developing the model for the 1982-92 period, Fanelli and Damill found that external indebtedness does in fact correlate positively and significantly with capital goods imports and negatively, and also significantly, with the risk premium. Because of this, they conclude that under the Convertibility Plan, both factors had the effect of promoting the inflow of capital, because there was a substantial appreciation of the real exchange rate (which spurred capital goods imports), and devaluation expectations subsided since the public considered the exchange pattern sustainable.[8]

In Chile's case, the speculative flows are associated with the inflows of private, short-term capital. In the chapter on Chile, Agosin defines the flows as the sum of short-term movements affected by the private and banking sectors and direct commercial credit transactions. That this definition still holds after a fairly reasonable length of time is demonstrated by the fact that these flows were extremely positive both in 1980-81 and in 1988-90. Nevertheless, the small number of observations rules out the use of the corresponding series in a careful econometric analysis. Because of this, a most detailed study must be limited to analyzing the determinants of external financial credits of less than one year on the books of the central bank. According to the model developed, these flows correlate positively with the interest rate differential (corrected for devaluation expectations)[9] and negatively with both the country risk (approximated by a "dummy" variable referring to problems associated with the handling of external debt) and exchange regulations recently established to discourage the entry of such resources.

---

[8] As discussed later in this study, the authors warn that if the current account deficit continues to grow, a reversal in the direction of the capital flows will become a possibility as economic agents begin to doubt the sustainability of the nominal exchange rate.

[9] Because of the exchange management rule, devaluation expectations are estimated on the basis of the spread between domestic and external inflation.

The results are quite interesting. They indicate that the speculative flows respond positively to the yield spread and negatively to the country risk. Furthermore, there is evidence that the exchange regulations recently established to curb these flows, which are discussed in detail later in this study, have proven effective. More interestingly, the coefficient of the interactive variable consisting of the country risk and the interest differential suggests that when the former is large enough, the inflow of capital is discouraged, regardless of the yield spread.

The chapter on Colombia summarizes a number of studies that attempt to explain the dynamics of speculative flows and also provide new evidence. Because it was only recently that steps were taken to deregulate the capital account of the balance of payments, all the studies assume that most of the capital flows in Colombia occur through changes in current account items. Naturally, there is disagreement about how to estimate the size of these flows. By now, virtually all the possibilities have been explored, and various specifications for the determinants thereof have also been examined.

The work of Correa (1984) was the first to address this topic. In it, as well as in a later study by Herrera (1991), evidence was found to suggest that speculative flows are explained by the interest rate differential. The first attempt to analyze the recent episode is that of Steiner, *et al.* (1992), which shows that the behavior of speculative flows—defined as the temporary component of current account items more likely to conceal capital transactions—can be very satisfactorily explained by the (de/re)valuation expectations that arise when comparing the observed real exchange rate with the equilibrium real exchange rate, where the latter is the permanent component of the former.

An estimate of (exogenous) drug trafficking income is a key element of the study by O'byrne and Reina (1993), which utilizes a model wherein the flows are exogenous and the yield spreads endogenous, reflecting the fact that the central bank adjusts the interest rate in order to sterilize such income. In addition, Correa (1992) has developed a means of testing the cointegration between domestic and external interest rates, corrected for devaluation; the results seem to suggest a significant degree of integration between Colombian and international money markets.

In their chapter here on Colombia, Cárdenas and Barrera suggest that the explicative value of the interest differential and the exchange premium[10] is not great for a definition of capital flows which, although extensive, does not take into account the possibility of flows resulting from the overinvoicing of exports and the underinvoicing of imports.

---

[10] The exchange premium refers to the difference between the official exchange rate and the parallel exchange rate, a concept that was highly relevant in the period preceding 1991, when, because of the exchange controls in force, the parallel market was significant.

Although Ros' chapter on Mexico does not specifically address the subject of speculative flows, it constructs an aggregate model of the asset markets, in which the domestic interest rate is estimated as a function of the rates of return of alternative assets and the external liabilities of the private sector as a function of the wealth of that sector and the rates of return of various assets. The results indicate the existence of active interest rate arbitrage (although with clear evidence of imperfect capital mobility as well), which has increased significantly since the opening of the money market to foreign investors in early 1991.

Another of the author's exercises provided evidence of an "overadjustment" of the financial market to the structural reforms in progress, which was reflected by very heavy capital inflows and an overvalued exchange rate, as compared with the long-term equilibrium levels of these variables. Although the complement of this result is a domestic interest rate higher than its equilibrium level, the author interprets it more as the enthusiastic response of business owners to the results of economic reform than as a reaction to opportunities for interest rate speculation.

In short, it can be affirmed that for all of the countries studied there is empirical evidence that speculative flows (which are defined differently in the case studies) respond to yield spreads, among other variables. Chile's experience also suggests the effectiveness of administrative measures aimed at minimizing capital inflows. The possible impact of yield spreads on the flows is enormously important in terms of the handling of economic policy. In particular, and as discussed in the following section, the advisability of sterilizing the flows is questionable if the sterilization backfires, which is what occurs if raising the domestic interest rate to check the monetary growth effect of capital inflows leads instead to even larger flows.

Moreover, the case studies as well as the studies cited herein tend to agree that the speculative flows have been substantial. This suggests that, regardless of what causes them, a considerable percentage of the recent capital inflows may be only temporary, which has important policy implications. If the capital inflows are viewed as a permanent phenomenon, it could lead to a consensus that the macroeconomic adjustment should be based to a large extent on appreciation of the real exchange rate. Conversely, the fact that speculative flows are usually temporary suggests extreme caution regarding the handling of the exchange rate.

Macroeconomic Management and Capital Inflows

As mentioned earlier in this chapter, a substantial inflow of capital resources usually poses a major macroeconomic policy challenge. The benefit of being able to supplement domestic savings with external savings in order to increase investment ratios must be weighed against the potentially adverse effects of these flows on the handling of exchange rate, monetary, and fiscal policies.

To a greater or lesser extent, the economic authorities of all the countries have the objective of achieving high, sustained growth rates in an environment of relative price stability. With a view to overcoming structural limitations, it is usually considered desirable that economic growth be tied to sectors involved with international trade. The growth of these sectors is in turn linked to the maintenance of competitive real exchange rates. The dilemma confronting Latin American economies that have recently received significant capital resources has to do, then, with their ability to absorb the inflow of resources while attempting to minimize the degree of real exchange rate appreciation, which can occur either because the authorities decide to maintain a low rate of devaluation or even to permit a nominal appreciation of the currency, or because even with a higher rate of devaluation, inflation accelerates. Because controlling inflation is also a key objective of economic policy, especially in countries where prices have soared, the authorities may prefer to keep the rate of devaluation fairly low or even to openly fix the exchange rate, with the expectation that such a policy will also help slow inflation.

Notwithstanding the difficulties of macroeconomic management created by massive capital inflows, it is incorrect to assume that the latter affect the viability of reforms and macroeconomic stabilization the same way in different countries. Moreover, as explained in the following section, capital inflows in Argentina, as in Mexico, have been an essential complement to a macroeconomic policy that is fundamentally oriented toward reducing the rate of inflation (although they make macroeconomic management more difficult), because the reforms themselves provide the external financing necessary to offset the trade deficit that usually results when a fixed (or virtually fixed) exchange rate is established in an inflationary environment. Therefore, the handling of capital inflows will depend to a large extent on what is perceived as essential for growth: promoting exports or promoting investment, two concepts that are potentially complementary in the long term but which may be mutually exclusive in the short term, given a massive inflow of external financing.

Perhaps the best way of approaching the topic of macroeconomic policy is by describing and analyzing the experiences of the countries in question with respect to four basic aspects: the handling of the exchange rate, monetary policy, fiscal policy, and the establishment of controls on capital mobility.

Exchange Rate Policy

It can be safely concluded that the main differences between the macroeconomic management of Argentina and Mexico on the one hand, and Chile and Colombia on the other, rests for the most part on different conceptions of the role that the exchange rate ought to play. While in Argentina and Mexico the nominal exchange rate played an active role in the fight against inflation, in Chile and Co-

Table 1.4. Real Exchange Rate Indices, 1980-92
(1985=100)

	Argentina	Chile[1]	Colombia	Mexico
1980	31.7	66.5	79.1	83.4
1981	54.7	49.6	76.5	74.0
1982	117.5	56.7	71.0	109.9
1983	104.9	75.0	72.9	124.2
1984	96.8	76.7	77.8	100.3
1985	93.7	100.0	100.0	100.0
1986	75.0	121.2	108.3	139.1
1987	87.3	132.2	108.0	145.0
1988	83.8	130.5	105.8	117.9
1989	116.6	121.2	113.7	110.3
1990	64.4	124.6	126.6	108.0
1991	44.1	117.9	115.0	98.9
1992	38.9	114.4	112.5	90.3

[1] Exchange rate for exports deflated by wages. Figures for 1992 adjusted for the variation of the real exchange rate deflated by the wholesale price index.
Sources: Argentina: chapter two, this publication; Chile: ECLAC; Colombia: Banco de la República, *Monthly Review*, various issues; Mexico: 1980-91, authors' estimates; 1992, ECLAC.

lombia priority was given to protecting the real exchange rate, despite the inflationary bias generally imputed to this type of strategy.

Table 1.4 presents real exchange rate indices for the four countries. What stands out with regard to Argentina is the very high level attained in 1989, when hyperinflation had become critical.[11] Its decline since 1990 preceded the establishment of the fixed exchange rate system and in fact occurred to a great extent in 1990 in an environment of exchange flotation in which the annual rate of inflation remained above 1,300 percent. In early 1991 the new economic team announced fiscal austerity measures and took advantage of a comfortable reserve position to guarantee the stability of the exchange rate, establishing a managed floating system. Once the exchange rate had stabilized in the first half of 1991, the Convertibility Law was passed fixing the exchange rate and providing full foreign exchange backing of the monetary base.

Although it is evident that the authorities have been successful at fighting inflation with this decision, efforts to bring the trend of consumer prices into line with the norms in the developed countries have failed. As the Argentine study

---

[11] As described at length in the case study, the level of the real exchange rate in 1989 would eventually prove beneficial by permitting the accumulation of reserves, which was to become essential for the continued viability of the Convertibility Plan.

points out, despite the stability of the exchange rate and of public service rates, the "residual" inflation of the convertibility program can be estimated at 15 to 20 percent. This has led to further real appreciation of the exchange rate, with the usual effects on the pattern of spending and the trade balance.

The cumulative real appreciation between 1989 and 1992 is truly astonishing—67 percent, according to Table 1.4. It should be noted, however, that two-thirds of this deterioration occurred in 1990, before the Convertibility Plan went into effect. The appreciation in 1992 was only 11 percent. Considering that during this process the annual rate of inflation (measured by the CPI) fell from 1,344 percent in 1990 to 18 percent in 1992, the inevitable conclusion is that exchange management was successful because it accomplished its main task. The prospect of continued exchange appreciation is troubling indeed, since it could prove to be disastrous for the sectors that produce internationally marketable goods.

In Mexico, the prior announcement of moderate devaluations of the peso was a major element of macroeconomic management, starting with the stabilization program announced in late 1987—what was called the Economic Solidarity Pact. This program and those that followed on a regular basis also included "unorthodox" mechanisms for reaching agreement on wage and income policy between the government, workers, and employers, as well as more conventional components: an austere fiscal policy, sweeping trade liberalization, and other structural reform measures referred to in previous sections of this chapter.

As in Argentina, the use of the exchange rate as an anti-inflationary tool caused substantial real appreciation of the Mexican peso in 1988. Appreciation was fairly rapid in the early phases of the stabilization process; it has continued, although at a slower pace, in recent years. Its results in terms of inflation have also been very encouraging: while in 1987 the annual growth rate of prices was 159 percent, in 1992 it fell to only 12 percent.

The above-described aspects are somewhat similar to those observed in Spain. This country's experience is quite interesting. It joined the European Economic Community (EEC) in January 1986 and became part of the "wide band" of the European monetary system in June 1989. Even so, it did not avoid a real appreciation of the currency, as indicated by the much faster rise in the prices of nontradable goods (construction and services) than of tradable goods. This process was therefore accompanied by a growing current account deficit, financed with capital inflows (Galy, et al., 1993). The real appreciation of the peseta could not be tolerated in the long term, as indicated by the various par value adjustments that occurred in the EEC in 1992 and 1993.

The trend of the real exchange rate has been much the same in Chile and Colombia since 1980 (see Table 1.4), and their handling of the nominal exchange rate in the recent period of massive capital inflows has been quite similar. Even so, there are different reasons why both countries had high real exchange rates at the close of the last decade. In Chile, it was the result of efforts to strengthen the balance of trade in order to offset the heavy external debt burden. In Colombia, it was due to the adjustments made in the mid-1980s to improve the balance of payments and to the belief that the success of the trade liberalization program introduced in 1990 would require a prior devaluation effort.

In the recent business cycle, exchange policy was adjusted in both countries from a position of resolutely defending the real exchange rate (because it was believed that the flows were only temporary) to a position of greater exchange flexibility as the realization grew that some of the capital inflows might not be speculative and could, therefore, be more permanent in nature. An excellent description of how the central bank of Chile altered its exchange policy as capital continued to flow into the country is found in Bianchi (1992).

The method of introducing greater exchange rate flexibility has differed substantially in the two countries. In Chile the central bank utilizes a "nonintervention" band. Recently, the band was widened, and the exchange rate is now based on a basket of currencies around which the bands of flotation are fixed. Still, intervention has occasionally occurred when currency values fall within that band. In Colombia the relaxation has been more recent, as a result of structural reforms adopted since 1990. In essence, it consists of a publicly divulged "nonintérventionist" band with a range of 12.5 percent. Nevertheless, the Bank of the Republic has intervened in a discretional, behind-the-scenes manner, specifically to establish a band with a range of no more than 6 percent. Both countries have had to make some nominal currency revaluations (of the band of flotation) over the course of the process.

Although in both Chile and Colombia it is possible to speak of a successful absorption of capital, since in both countries significant appreciation of the real exchange rate was avoided, it should be noted that only in Chile was there a substantial decline in the rate of inflation. In fact, while in Chile the annual rate of CPI increases fell from 27 percent in 1990 to 13 percent in 1992, during the same period in Colombia the rate went from 32 percent to 26 percent, which is higher than the average for the previous decade. As explained below, these differences are due in part to the fact that a more restrictive fiscal policy was adopted in Chile,[12] although other factors such as the greater openness of the Chilean economy may also have played an important role by increasing the effectiveness of the exchange policy in combating inflation.

In summary, for the four case studies, a clear relationship is observed between lower inflation and appreciation of the real exchange rate. While in Argentina and Mexico currency appreciation was considerable and the reduction in inflation substantial, in Chile and Colombia less importance was attached to fighting inflation because of the authorities' efforts to maintain competitive real exchange

---

[12] Not necessarily as a result of the inflow of foreign resources.

rates. Naturally, and as Fanelli and Damill point out in their chapter, whether the Argentine process is sustainable is not entirely clear, given the considerable balance of trade deterioration. Ros also argues that the relationship between the current account deficit and economic growth deteriorated in Mexico and that the real exchange rate is below its long-term equilibrium level. Even so, he suggests that the current situation might be tolerable and, in fact, that the authorities have much more latitude than they did in the 1980s for managing a possible exchange crisis.

Monetary Policy

It is well known that in an environment of capital mobility, monetary policy is largely ineffective in a fixed exchange rate system. In this case, equilibrium in the money market is determined by what happens to the demand for money. Given this situation, it is not surprising that Argentina has taken a passive approach to monetary policy. In accordance with the Convertibility Law, the central bank of Argentina can only issue pesos for the purpose of acquiring reserves; in fact, the money stock is fully backed by the central bank's foreign assets. Because of the massive inflow of capital, the monetary aggregates have grown to very high levels, even in real terms.

As demonstrated in the case study, the trend of the monetary aggregates in Argentina appears not to have caused much concern and, consequently, has not prompted any efforts to neutralize the monetary effect of the capital inflow. Certainly, since much of the inflow of foreign exchange consists of the repatriation of capital, the apparently high level of the monetary aggregates reflects the reorganization of the financial portfolios of Argentine citizens in favor of financial assets in domestic currency. Without fear of increasing inflationary pressures, the central bank increases the money stock to meet the higher levels of demand.

Both in Chile and in Colombia a different concept has prevailed, although in the latter country a radical policy change occurred in late 1991. Despite the fact that in both countries significant structural reforms have made the holding of domestic financial assets more attractive, the recent changes have been far less dramatic in Colombia than in Argentina. In Chile, on the one hand, the major reforms occurred some time ago; in Colombia, on the other, the reforms have not been so ambitious. Consequently, a marked increase in the demand for money is considered unlikely, which is why there is great fear that a sharp rise in monetary aggregates will generate undesirable inflationary pressures. The above, together with the policy of maintaining the real exchange rate, made sterilization of the inflow an essential part of the macroeconomic program. In both countries it was achieved through the issuance of securities by the central bank.

The case studies (as well as others of a more specific nature) suggest that sterilization, while generally possible, is certainly limited and costly (Bianchi, 1992, concerning Chile; and Junguito, 1992, concerning Colombia). The limits have to do with the fact that such a strategy requires the central bank to raise interest rates, which can represent an additional incentive for speculative capital. The costs are related to the fact that the securities issued by the central bank pay higher interest than the international reserves it has acquired. In both countries, the "quasi-fiscal" deficit generated by sterilization has climbed to significant levels: 0.5 percent of GDP in Chile and nearly 1 percent of GDP in Colombia. Moreover, sterilization represents a disincentive to capital deepening because it involves higher interest rates.

Apparently, the limits of sterilization were reached more quickly in Colombia than in Chile. The Central Bank of Chile, although it was forced to raise its interest rates, only offered real annual yields of 6 percent. Today, it is widely recognized that sterilization, although debilitating and expensive, proved to be very effective. As soon as it was observed that it was losing its effectiveness, it was supplemented with more interventionist measures, which are discussed below.

In Colombia, the real interest that the Bank of the Republic accepted on the securities it floated for sterilization purposes was over 15 percent. Because of this, there was a growing consensus that the continuing flow of capital was largely the result of the sterilization policy itself; therefore, a radical change was made. In the final quarter of 1991, the recently installed Board of Directors of the Bank of the Republic decided that the central bank would no longer lead market interest rates and that the Bank's securities would, until further notice, bear negative real interest.[13] Nevertheless, the sterilization policy was not jettisoned; instead, it concentrated on an instrument specific to the Colombian institutional context: exchange certificates.

These certificates are issued to anyone who sells foreign exchange to the Bank of the Republic, but they can be used to make foreign payments. In June 1991 it was decided that they could only be redeemed for pesos three months after issuance, which gave them the character of a forced investment. The redemption period was extended to 12 months in October of that year. The unusual characteristic of this mechanism, when the certificates are not immediately redeemable, is that the tasks of exchange intervention and monetary sterilization are accomplished via a single instrument. The yield of such securities has been significantly lower than pre-1991 interest rates. Moreover, since they were negotiable in the market, they led to a revaluation of the nominal exchange rate; this more or less eliminated undervaluation of the exchange rate, which had been fostering revaluation expectations. These expectations, for their own part, were encouraging the speculative inflow of capital, as seen in the study of Steiner, *et al.* (1992). The model presented in that study provides a fairly satisfactory expla-

---

[13] As in Chile, the structural reforms in Colombia included a constitutional amendment whereby the Central Bank became an autonomous entity, separate from the government.

nation of the capital inflow, not as a function of the interest rate differential but rather of the degree of exchange rate undervaluation.

In summary, it cannot be categorically stated that Colombia discontinued its sterilization policy. The most significant change was that the Bank of the Republic stopped exerting upward pressure on interest rates. It continued sterilizing the inflow of foreign exchange, but this was probably not something that the Bank itself promoted. The policy of interest rate reduction had other consequences, some of which are described below. Not only did it represent an important stimulus for investment, it also significantly increased the demand for money, which is why substantial increases in the monetary aggregates were permitted, although to a lesser extent than in Argentina.

Fiscal Policy

The role of fiscal policy in the four countries under study has varied considerably. As will be seen below, to speak of a fiscal adjustment strategy prompted almost entirely by the need to compensate for the expansive effect of capital inflows on overall demand is probably relevant only with respect to Colombia. In the other three countries, the move toward a policy of true fiscal austerity preceded the capital boom.

Table 1.5 presents information about the consolidated public sector deficit in the four countries. The improvement in Mexico's fiscal position is the most spectacular: from a deficit of 15.5 percent of GDP in 1987 to a surplus of 3.4 percent in 1992. Its fiscal reform policy is, in fact, the most outstanding element of the Mexican government's macroeconomic policy in recent years. Privatization and the reduction of the current account deficit led to a dramatic lowering of the risk premium inherent in the differentials between domestic and external interest rates, adjusted for devaluation expectations. As seen in a previous section, this in turn attracted capital and permitted the reduction of domestic interest rates. According to Ros, a continuing reversal of the positive trend of domestic interest rates, which began in the second quarter of 1992 as a result of increased devaluation expectations, would jeopardize the most important result of the entire macroeconomic adjustment process in recent years.

The improvement in Argentina's fiscal position was also remarkable: the deficit shrank from 8.6 percent of GDP in 1988 to 2.2 percent in 1991. Still, the adjustment was not enough to attain the goals set with the IMF. Fiscal policy also plays a vital role in this country's macroeconomic policy, although it is secondary to exchange management. The sustainability of the fixed exchange rate by definition requires that destabilizing pressures from the money market be eliminated; the Convertibility Law bars financing the government through the central bank; external financing is largely conditional upon the attainment of strict fiscal goals; and recovery of the rate of investment is tied to the possibility of private

Table 1.5. Fiscal Balance, 1987-92
(Percentage of GDP)[1]

	Argentina	Chile	Colombia	Mexico
1987	-6.7	2.6	n.a.	-15.5
1988	-8.6	3.9	-2.1	-12.5
1989	-4.8	5.5	-1.9	-5.7
1990	-5.1	1.5	-0.4	-4.0
1991	-2.2	1.7	0.1	1.8
1992[2]	n.a.	1.8	-0.4	3.4

[1] Of the nonfinancial public sector; deficit (-).
[2] Preliminary.
n.a. Not available.
Source: ECLAC, 1992.

sector access to abundant financial resources, which are only available if the state does not pressure the financial market.

For all of the above reasons, in the case of Argentina it is improper to speak of a macroeconomic adjustment to deal with capital flows. On the contrary, the adjustment preceded the flows; in fact, it was largely responsible for them, either indirectly by fostering a macroeconomic environment favorable to the repatriation of capital, or directly through the aggressive privatization program. In any case, as Fanelli and Damill point out, the inflow of capital is an essential complement of the entire program. On the one hand, because of the Convertibility Law, external credit is the government's basic source of financing. On the other, given the predictable real appreciation of the exchange rate at the inception of a fixed exchange rate system, the capital inflow finances the current account deficit.

In Chile, as in Argentina and Mexico, the reorganization of public finances is an integral part of the macroeconomic program. In particular, the increase in public sector savings has been essential for dealing with the heavy burden of external debt. In fact, much of the strategy for reducing external liabilities was related to debt rescheduling programs, the ultimate goal of which, in many cases, was the privatization of public enterprises. As the chapter on Chile points out, the persistent efforts to counteract recent tendencies toward exchange appreciation were linked primarily to the monetary sterilization policy, which, because inadequate, was supplemented with exchange measures aimed at discouraging capital inflows. Apparently, fiscal policy has not been used as a compensating mechanism to reduce the flows, given the fact that the posture since 1991 has been fairly neutral.

Colombia has a tradition of fiscal discipline that is probably without equal among the major Latin American economies. It also has a relatively small government and, unlike Argentina and Chile, does not have a very large external debt burden. Consequently, fiscal policy was not an integral part of the structural reforms introduced in 1989. These reforms focused on trade, labor, and finance.[14]

In 1991 the substantial inflow of capital was viewed as a destabilizing element that could derail the structural reforms in progress. As seen in the preceding section, the initial reaction of the authorities was a rigorous sterilization strategy. When the limitations of this approach became apparent, the Bank of the Republic concluded that the stabilization policy would have to be based on one of two alternatives: either a drastic appreciation of the exchange rate or a significant fiscal adjustment. While the first of these alternatives had unfavorable effects on the trade liberalization process, the second was questionable from the viewpoint of distributing the costs of the adjustment. Very much in the Colombian tradition, and as explained in detail in Junguito (1992), a mix of the two was chosen: some appreciation of the real exchange rate was permitted and a substantial fiscal adjustment was made, although not in keeping with the central bank's recommendations. It must be emphasized that the entire fiscal adjustment was based on expanded revenue, given that public spending increased significantly in real terms between 1990 and 1992.

Control of Capital Mobility

As we have seen, the inflow of capital was welcomed in Argentina and Mexico, but was received more cautiously in Chile and Colombia, at least insofar as the speculative component of those flows was concerned. In the latter two countries, once the limited effectiveness and high fiscal cost of monetary sterilization was recognized, other methods were used both to counteract the expansive effect of the inflow and to reduce the volume thereof.[15]

In Chile, high reserve requirements were established for the external indebtedness of the financial system. As shown in the chapter on Chile, these requirements appear to have been fairly effective. Restrictions on the outflow of capital were also eased, in particular by authorizing pension funds to hold a certain percentage of overseas investments and by relaxing the time allotted for capital repatriation and the remittance of profits from foreign investments included in the debt conversion process. An interesting discussion about whether Chile should accelerate the liberalization of its capital account is found in Williamson (1991). He suggests doing so only if it is certain that other tools are available to control

---

[14] Interestingly, like fiscal policy, trade policy also came to depend on the trend of capital flows. To relieve the upward pressure of these flows, a decision was made in August of 1991 to speed up the tariff reduction process by three years.

[15] An interesting case that partakes of both situations is that of Spain. Although the inflow of capital was fundamental to the credibility of Spain's participation in the European Monetary System, Spain still had some controls on the mobility of capital as late as 1992 in order to preserve some of its monetary autonomy.

aggregate demand, which is linked to the possibility of allowing a more freely floating exchange rate.

In Colombia, taxes were levied in 1991 on certain income derived from personal services, which, presumably, were the conduit for a large portion of the flows. This measure was apparently not very effective, for although the inflow of personal income was reduced, income from tourism increased significantly. Furthermore, the commercial banks were required to hold more assets than liabilities denominated in foreign currency. The goal—apparently successful—was to encourage the financial agents to utilize some of their resources in domestic currency to acquire central bank reserves. Finally, a deadline was set for remittances on imports, which sought to limit external commercial debt. In contradictory fashion, at the beginning of 1992 they chose to relax the restrictions on external private debt, with the object of forcing financial intermediaries to lower their lending rates.

In Mexico, several steps were taken to reduce the speculative flows, but their scope was extremely limited. In August 1991, a 50 percent liquidity requirement was imposed on the foreign currency liabilities of banks, which was replaced in April 1992 with a ceiling of 10 percent on local and foreign currency deposits that could give rise to foreign exchange liabilities. This ceiling was raised to 20 percent in November 1992. Furthermore, all exchange controls were eliminated with the final consolidation in November 1991 of the auction and managed rates in effect in the country since the debt crisis.

In summary, it can be affirmed that the fixed exchange system is the core of Argentina's macroeconomic policy. There has been no effort to regulate the flows or to sterilize their macroeconomic impact. Fiscal policy has played a key role, since the convertibility of the currency eliminates the possibility of the central bank providing financing for the government. The main question concerning the program is whether fiscal discipline can be maintained, given that it has been based largely on the privatization process, which obviously has temporal limitations.

In Mexico, fiscal reform and the preannounced slowing of devaluation are also the center of economic policy, but the macroeconomic rules are not as inflexible as they are in Argentina: the exchange rate is not fixed and no regulations directly affecting capital inflows have been imposed. "Unorthodox" mechanisms for reaching agreement on wage and income policy have, moreover, been used in a complementary manner. Additionally, fiscal reform has progressed much farther than in Argentina and, therefore, is not so dependent on the privatization process. In both countries inflation has been reduced substantially, but the real appreciation that has occurred throughout the disinflation process and the deterioration of the current account of the balance of payments have reached levels that may well be intolerable.

In Chile, an all-out effort was made to maintain the real exchange rate, including intense monetary sterilization and, to a lesser extent, measures aimed specifically at discouraging the inflow of capital and encouraging its outflow. In

Colombia, the defense of the real exchange rate has also been an emphasized element of the macroeconomic program, but, last year at least, less importance was attached to the sterilization effort, and the compensating effect was achieved largely through fiscal policy. Both countries were successful in limiting the degree of real exchange rate appreciation. The dissimilar results of the two countries in combating inflation may be due in part to the fact that the fiscal adjustment in Colombia did not include reduction of public spending. Likewise, the greater openness of the Chilean economy very probably increased the anti-inflationary impact of its exchange rate policy.

The Impact on Investment

The real effects of capital flows have to do essentially with their impact on exports and investment. The link between capital flows and exports is the real exchange rate; the DFI in sectors that produce exportable goods establishes an additional connection between these two variables. We have fully discussed the efforts that the various countries have made to minimize appreciation of the exchange rate, efforts which are justified by the premise that every attempt must be made to prevent the inflow of capital from adversely affecting the growth of the export sector. In this section we will focus on the effects that capital inflows have had on investment.

There are three kinds of connections between these variables. The first, obviously, is the one created by direct foreign investment, insofar as it is not oriented exclusively toward the purchase of existing productive assets. Second, the flows ease the savings and financing constraints that affect investment. According to all of the existing analyses, these constraints were the root cause of the decline in the rate of investment in the region over the last decade. Finally, the real exchange rate appreciation caused by the greater availability of foreign exchange lowers the cost of imported capital goods, which are essential for boosting the rate of investment. Although there are other effects that weaken this relationship, most of the empirical studies suggest that, in the short term at least, real appreciation has favorable effects on investment.[16]

The severe economic crisis in Argentina in the 1980s was clearly reflected in the level of investment. As a percentage of GDP, this level dropped from a low of 14 percent in the mid-1980s to 12 percent in 1991 (Table 1.6).[17] Such levels are

---

[16] Strictly speaking, a real appreciation lowers the cost of imported capital goods in terms of domestic goods, but the opposite occurs in the productive sector of tradable goods: the real cost of new capital increases, and investment decreases (Serven and Solimano, 1991).

[17] The figures in Table 1.6 are not necessarily from official sources. An individually consistent series was used for each country. Therefore, the table is useful not as a means of comparison between countries but rather as an illustration of the trends in each country.

Table 1.6. Gross Investment, 1981-92
(Percentage of GDP)

	Argentina	Chile	Colombia	Mexico
1981	17.7	19.5	17.4	26.5
1982	14.8	15.0	17.7	22.2
1983	14.5	12.9	17.7	16.6
1984	14.1	13.2	17.3	17.0
1985	13.9	14.8	15.9	17.9
1986	12.8	15.0	16.2	16.4
1987	14.4	16.4	15.5	16.0
1988	13.7	17.0	16.5	16.8
1989	11.7	18.6	15.1	17.8
1990	10.7	19.5	14.0	18.9
1991	11.6	18.2	12.5	19.5
1992	n.a.	19.8	14.0	20.4

Sources: For Argentina, Chile and Mexico, see their respective chapters in this publication; for Colombia: National accounts and GNP for 1992.
n.a. Not available.

incompatible with acceptable economic growth rates. This situation was caused by low savings levels, high net outlays for the servicing of factors, and an insufficient complement of external savings.

Lacking specific data on the composition of spending, Fanelli and Damill utilize other indicators that suggest a remarkable upsurge in investment in 1992, although they also indicate that this variable remains at a historically low level. The authors suggest that the impact of DFI on the recovery of investment has been modest since most of the resources have gone toward the privatization process, i.e., the purchase of existing assets. Furthermore, on the basis of information from the balance sheets of the major companies quoted on the stock exchange, the authors conclude that external financial assets have been replaced both by domestic financial assets and by real assets, which has led to a marked improvement in the financial structure of the companies.

The case study's interesting analysis of the sectors that attract foreign investment suggests that the nontradable goods sector heads the list, which is logical since most of the privatized companies do not produce internationally tradable goods. This is troubling as far as the outlook for the export sector is concerned, especially in view of the substantial appreciation of the real exchange rate in Argentina. Moreover, since the external debt burden remains heavy and there are no signs that domestic savings will recover, it is unclear whether the upward trend of investment will continue; this obviously depends on a sustained inflow of capital, which is uncertain, among other things, because of the natural winding down of the privatization process.

In Chile, the rate of investment began to recover in the middle of the last decade; in 1992 it represented nearly 20 percent of GDP. The case study suggests that although there is empirical evidence that investment in Chile correlates positively with the real exchange rate, this effect seems to have been more than offset in recent years by the negative impact of real appreciation on aggregate demand. Moreover, it is argued that it is scarcely likely that the capital inflow positively affected investment by easing the constraints either on foreign exchange or on credit: the former because the authorities discouraged the external indebtedness of Chilean companies and the latter because of monetary sterilization. Based on the foregoing, the fundamental channel through which the capital flows have had a positive impact on investment is DFI. The figures provided by the case study suggest that the latter accounted for more than 40 percent of the rise in aggregate investment between 1981 and 1991. Clearly, a very large percentage of such investments were in sectors concerned with exports, primarily the mining sector.[18] Finally, there appears to have been a relationship—marginal at best—between the inflow of capital and the stock market boom.

The figures in Table 1.6 concerning Colombia indicate that the trend of its rate of investment was distinctly different from that of the other countries analyzed. In fact, unlike the regional trend, investment in Colombia declined in the second half of the last decade. This decline coincided with the fall in net external financing, because national savings did not deteriorate over these two years (Ocampo, 1988). Nevertheless, this reduction was entirely concentrated in public investment, which has a markedly anticyclical behavior in Colombia, as noted in the case study. In fact, during these years there was a sharp increase in private investment.

On the other hand, despite the inflow of capital, aggregate investment declined in 1991 due to the comprehensive sterilization policy adopted in that year by the authorities, which caused a sudden rise in interest rates and a domestic recession. Although completely reliable data are not available, various indicators suggest a reversal of this process in 1992 and 1993, normalizing the pattern in relation to the other countries studied.

The case study estimates a demand for investment based on its profitability, the utilization of installed capacity, the financing constraints, and several measures of uncertainty. According to this line of reasoning, capital flows affect capital formation because, by exerting pressure on the securities market, they presum-

---

[18] In the case study it is estimated that, between 1985 and 1991, two-thirds of the DFI received as a result of Decree Law 600 was absorbed by the export sectors, and half of that amount went to mining. Much the same occurred with the investment received through debt conversion, which was concentrated in sectors involved in the extraction and processing of raw materials.

ably increase its profitability and, in addition, help to ease the credit squeeze. Note that nothing is said about the possibility of the flows affecting investment via the real exchange rate; nor is any direct assessment made of the effect of interest rates. The results suggest that investment is sensitive to the flows primarily because they ease the credit squeeze.

In Mexico, investment has also recovered significantly in recent years. This recovery has been limited exclusively to private investment, which, as a percentage of GDP, rose three points between 1989 and 1992. According to the case study, two of these three points can be attributed to DFI. The recovery of investment was accompanied, however, by a dramatic decline in private savings, which fell from 13.6 percent to 5 percent of GDP in these years. The cumulative effect of these two trends is that the net position of the private sector went from a small surplus in 1989 to a large deficit in 1992—a little more than 10 percent of GDP.

According to the case study, the decline of private savings is one of the chief weaknesses of the Mexican economy today (see Ros, 1993). In fact, the author's econometric estimates show that the consequent decline of Mexican private sector wealth is the most significant determinant of the recent capital inflows. It also contrasts sharply with the reorganization of public finances which, because of the steep decline in the risk margin, also encouraged such inflows, although in a far healthier way. Continuation of the recent savings trends would compromise the country's ability to maintain current investment levels, not to mention recovery of the historic rates of capital accumulation that enabled the Mexican economy to achieve high rates of economic growth in the years prior to the debt crisis.

The experiences of the four countries regarding the impact of capital inflows on investment differ substantially, although it is worth noting that the lack of current data prevents a very detailed empirical analysis. In Argentina, Chile, and Mexico the main connection between the capital flows and investment was through DFI. While in Chile and Mexico the inflow of capital seems to be related to well-established structural reforms, in Argentina the link is to privatization processes that are obviously limited in time. Moreover, in the latter country the rate of investment remains extremely low, and DFI has been directed more toward acquiring existing assets than toward increasing the productive capacity.

In all cases, appreciation of the real exchange rate has prompted a significant upturn in capital goods imports, but this could eventually act as a restraint on investment, insofar as it negatively affects the growth of the tradable goods sectors. The deterioration of private savings has, for its part, been an extremely vulnerable element that could adversely affect investment, particularly in the case of Mexico, where this variable has experienced a marked decline.

Finally, in both Chile and Colombia, monetary sterilization has decreased the possibility of the capital flows easing the credit squeeze, which in the past has constituted a restraint on investment. In Colombia, it is interesting to note the coincidence between the apparent recovery of investment in 1992 and the dwindling of sterilization efforts in late 1991, which could denote a very close relationship between the trend of investment and interest rate policy.

Conclusions

Although with a different emphasis and at different rates, all of the countries covered under this study have moved or are moving toward economic structures in which the dominant role is played by the private sector. These structural reforms have contributed to the recent recovery of investment, as revealed by analyses of the effects of the privatization process or the reduction of the risk premium inherent in interest rate differentials. The capital inflow has in turn facilitated implementation of the current reforms.

The macroeconomic advantages of expanded capital inflows have had to be weighed against the possible macroeconomic disturbances they can cause. In particular, there was great concern in some countries about minimizing the potential impact on the real exchange rate. In others, however, exchange policy has been subordinated to the objective of combating inflation.

The latter has in fact been the top priority in Argentina and Mexico. While inflation only slowly converges toward international levels, the real exchange rate necessarily appreciates when the nominal rate is used to anchor the price system, which is what occurred in both countries. Argentina's Convertibility Law and Mexico's tripartite mechanisms for reaching agreement on wage and income policy, along with the plentiful international reserves accumulated in both countries as a result of capital inflows, have mitigated the harmful effects that appreciation can have on the expectations of economic agents. Continued appreciation, however, may be intolerable; it is therefore illogical to assume that growing trade deficits can be financed indefinitely with extraordinary capital inflows.

Although in both countries there was considerable real exchange rate appreciation, it was greater in Argentina; it should be noted, however, that substantial real appreciation preceded the decision to fix the exchange rate in that country. In both countries, the slowdown in the rate of inflation was remarkable. Nevertheless, because monetary policy is relatively ineffective in a fixed exchange system with unrestricted capital mobility, and because it is not easy to deepen the fiscal adjustment—which in both cases was remarkable, although much more so in Mexico—it is clearly advisable to have an additional anti-inflationary tool: wage and income policy. Furthermore, it hardly seems logical to try to alleviate inflationary pressures by restricting capital inflows when in fact these flows are essential for financing the current account deficit and ensuring the permanence of the exchange system.

In Chile and Colombia, the authorities have assigned greater priority to protecting the exchange rate as an essential variable of an economy much more open to international trade. Controlling inflation has not, however, been stricken from their agenda. In these circumstances, partial sterilization of the capital flows has been a significant component of macroeconomic policy; its increasing loss of effectiveness was offset by controls on capital mobility in both countries and by fiscal adjustment in Colombia.

In both countries, the authorities have had great success in preventing real exchange rate appreciation. Moreover, inflation in Chile has been lowered substantially, with a resultant surge in productive activity. In Colombia, inflation has slowed only slightly and growth has not recovered. The greater openness of the Chilean economy may have been responsible for its comparative success in combating inflation. The trend of productive activity can be linked, at least in part, to the type of capital flows in the two countries: DFI in Chile and speculative capital in Colombia.

The reaction of investment to the recent capital boom was not the same in all cases. The most healthy responses were in Chile and Mexico, which in both cases were largely associated with DFI. The precipitous decline of private savings in Mexico could nevertheless become a serious impediment to the reinforcement of this trend. There was a recovery in Argentina, but investment remains at very low levels and DFI has been limited mostly to the purchase of existing assets. In Colombia, however, following an initial decline caused by massive sterilization efforts, investment recovered when these efforts waned.

Bibliography

Banco de España. 1992. Financiación del déficit público y balanza de pagos: el caso de España, 1975-92. *Boletín CEMLA* 38 (6).

Bianchi, A. 1992. Overabundance of Foreign Exchange, Inflation and Exchange Rate Policy: The Chilean Experience. International Forum on Latin American Perspectives. Paris.

Calvo, G.A. 1991. *The Perils of Sterilization*. IMF Staff Papers, 38 (4). International Monetary Fund, Washington, D.C.

————, L. Leiderman, and C. Reinhart. 1992. Capital Inflows and Real Exchange Rate Appreciation in Latin America: The Role of External Factors. International Monetary Fund, Washington, D.C. Mimeo.

Correa, P. 1984. Determinantes de la cuenta de servicios de la balanza cambiaria. In *Ensayos sobre política económica* (6).

————. 1992. Paridad entre la tasa de interés real interna y externa: Notas sobre el caso colombiano. *Coyuntura económica* 22 (1).

Dunley, J., and D. Seiver. 1987. Foreign Finance, Wealth Effects and Economic Development. *Applied Economics* 19: 4.

Economic Commission for Latin American and the Caribbean (ECLAC). 1992. *Balance preliminar de la economía de América Latina y el Caribe 1992.*

Edwards, S. 1984. The Order of Liberalization of the External Sector in Developing Countries. *Princeton Essays in International Finance* 156.

————, R. Frenkel, and G. Rozenwurcel. 1993. Transformación estructural, estabilización y reforma del Estado en la Argentina. In *Estabilización y reforma estructural en América Latina*, ed. E.J. Amadeo.

Galy, M., G. Pastor, and T. Pujol. 1993. *Spain: Converging with the European Community*. Occasional Paper 101. International Monetary Fund, Washington, D.C.

Goldstein, M., D.J. Mathieson, and T. Lane. 1991. *Determinants and Systemic Consequences of International Capital Flows*. Occasional Paper 77. International Monetary Fund, Washington, D.C.

Guidotti, P.E. 1988. Insulating Properties Under Dual Exchange Rates. *Canadian Journal of Economics* 21: 4.

Herrera, S. 1989. Determinantes de la trayectoria del tipo de cambio real en Colombia. In *Ensayos sobre política económica. Banca y Finanzas* (15) .

————. 1991. Movilidad de capitales y la economía colombiana. *Banca y Finanzas* (21).

International Monetary Fund. 1992. *Private Market Financing for Developing Countries*. International Monetary Fund, Washington, D.C.

Junguito, R. 1992. Reflexiones sobre el manejo macroeconómico en Colombia. In *Apertura: Dos años después*, ed. A. Martínez.

Loser, C., and E. Kalter. 1992. *Mexico: The Strategy to Achieve Sustained Economic Growth*. Occasional Paper 99. International Monetary Fund, Washington, D.C.

O'byrne, A., and M. Reina. 1993. Flujos de capitales y diferenciales de interés en Colombia: ¿Cuál es la causalidad? In *Movimiento internacional de capitales en los años noventa: La experiencia colombiana bajo análisis,* eds. L.J. Garay and M. Cárdenas.

Ocampo, J.A. 1988. Una nota sobre la relación entre financiamiento externo, ahorro e inversión. In *Ensayos sobre política económica* (13).

Pastor, M. 1990. Capital Flight from Latin America. *World Development* 18 (1).

Ros, J. 1993. Ajuste macroeconómico, reformas estructurales y crecimiento en México. In *Estabilización y reforma estructural en América Latina,* ed. E.J. Amadeo.

Serven, L., and A. Solimano. 1991. *Adjustment Policies and Investment Performance in Developing Countries*. Working Papers. World Bank, Washington, D.C.

Steiner, R. 1992. Los flujos internacionales de capitales: Deuda externa, inversión extranjera, especulación cambiaria. In *Gran Enciclopedia de Colombia*.

————, R. Suescún, and F. Melo. 1992. Flujos de capital y expectativas de devaluación. *Coyuntura económica* 22 (2).

Tornell, A. 1990. Real vs. Financial Investment: Can Tobin Taxes Eliminate the Irreversibility Condition? *Journal of Development Economics* 32: 2.

Warner, A. 1992. Did the Debt Crisis Cause the Investment Crisis? *Quarterly Journal of Economics* 107 (4).

Williamson, J. 1991. Costs and Benefits of Liberalizing the Chilean Capital Account. Institute for International Economics, Washington, D.C. Mimeo.

Zaidi, I.M. 1985. Savings, Investment, Fiscal Deficits and the External Indebtedness of Developing Countries. *World Development* 13: 5.

CHAPTER TWO

EXTERNAL CAPITAL FLOWS TO ARGENTINA

José María Fanelli and Mario Damill[1]

In the last two years a significant change occurred in the trend of external capital flows to Argentina. Following two episodes of runaway inflation—in mid-1989 and in early 1990—the process of capital flight slowed perceptibly and then changed direction, while at the same time increasing access was gained to voluntary sources of financing that were unavailable in the previous period. In 1992, however, the economy generated a trade balance deficit for the first time in 10 years, and all projections indicate that this situation will continue in 1993. In a surprisingly brief period of time, Argentina's macroeconomic position changed drastically, again demonstrating the crucial role that the flow of capital plays in the country's economic growth, since this flow determines to a large extent the severity of the external constraint.

The most relevant factors in the reversal of the flow of capital concern domestic institutional and macroeconomic aspects and the trend of international financial markets. In this study, the international factors are accepted as fact. The main objective is to analyze the role of the internal determinants of the capital flows.

The study is divided into three sections. The first contains an analysis of the external nature and size of the flows and their relationship to the structural reform initiated in mid-1989, the basic objectives of which included regulating capital flows from abroad. In the second section, the macroeconomic management of external flows is discussed and, in the third, the relationship between capital flows, investment, and growth is examined.

[1] The authors wish to thank Gustavo González and Ernesto Schargrodsky for their assistance with the research and José Antonio Ocampo, Jorge Sapoznikow, Willy Van Ryckeghem, Manuel Agosin, and Mauricio Cárdenas for their helpful comments on the preliminary version. They also wish to express their gratitude for the dedicated work of the Secretary of the Economic Area, Delia Cabral.

Structural Reform and Capital Flows

A key objective of the structural reforms introduced by the Menem administration was to create a "climate of investment" that would make sustained growth viable. The tools selected were market liberalization and deregulation, economic integration with the rest of the world, and reform of the public sector, all of which revolved around an ambitious privatization program. In this context, it could be concluded that the reforms aimed at regulating the flow of external capital were just another component of a set of more far-reaching policies. Such a conclusion would be erroneous, however. Because of the way the economy is structured, the success of the reform was closely linked to the possibility of changing the direction of the flows observed in the previous decade; hence the importance ascribed by the authorities to measures aimed at attracting direct foreign investment, generating a stronger flow of external financing, and promoting the repatriation of capital. In a similar manner, the policies aimed at expanding the domestic financial market also gained relevance, not only because a larger market would be more attractive to foreign investors but also because the market should be capable of efficiently converting external savings into domestic capital deepening.

Structural Reform

A brief review of the structural factors that contributed to promoting external capital flows within the framework of the reform process will be useful in defining its context and understanding its direction and structure.

The first significant factor is the low rate of national savings. After the severe fiscal and external shocks that followed the debt crisis, and in an environment of macroeconomic instability and stagnation, public and private savings both suffered a serious decline. Because of this, it was inevitable that the process of structural transformation would rely heavily on external savings, at least in the early stages.

A second essential structural characteristic is that when the reform was being planned, the economy was suffering from a serious and chronic external constraint caused by the heavy burden placed on the current account by the interest on external debt. This necessitated curbing domestic consumption. Investment was at levels incompatible with an acceptable growth rate. The recovery of growth required not only greater savings but also a more fluid supply of foreign exchange. It was essential, therefore, that the reform help to promote the investment of foreign funds in the domestic financial market. This was also important because the investment decisions of the economic agents, by giving preference to foreign investments, not only exacerbated the shortage of foreign exchange but also caused a portion of national savings to be used for the purchase of foreign assets rather than the financing of domestic capital deepening.

These structural characteristics—insufficient savings and severe external constraints—also helped to change the perception of direct foreign investment. In the period before the crisis, direct foreign investment was seen primarily as a means of supporting the industrial investment process, improving the level of business management, and gaining access to advanced technologies. The emphasis was on promoting investment through new capital deepening projects. This view was radically changed by the time the current policy was developed. The first priority in promoting direct investment was to increase the level of external savings and the supply of foreign exchange. Particular emphasis was given to the purchase of existing productive assets, even in old technology sectors. Privatization programs were the instrument par excellence of this strategy because they facilitated the orientation of direct investment toward the purchase of this type of asset. The sale of an existing physical asset, in this sense, is no different from obtaining an external credit.

A third structural characteristic was the advanced dollarization process the economy had been experiencing for years. Not only was a sizable percentage of agents' portfolios in dollars, in many contracts between residents the dollar was specified as the currency of denomination and the one to be used in transactions. This increased the transactions demand for dollars, which had the effect of "crowding out" the national currency and further eroding domestic financial brokering, as evidenced both by the constant decline of the coefficients of monetization and the systematic trend of financial investments toward the very short term. Obviously, the contraction of supply and terms of domestic credit played a part in this process. To finance the recovery of investment, therefore, it was necessary to obtain long-term credit in the international market, at least until significant progress was made in developing the domestic financial market.

A fourth structural characteristic influencing the reform was the very high degree of financial fragility in the public sector following a decade of continuing fiscal crisis. The strategy chosen to overcome this situation was to initiate a thorough restructuring of the public sector balance sheet by privatizing a large number of real assets. This strategy required a policy shift toward external capital flows because the domestic financial market was extremely tight and was not in a position to handle the supply of new assets associated with the privatization of state property. Plans to swap external debt for profitable state assets became the basic tool of this strategy.

Specific reforms concerning financial flows from abroad, the exchange market, and the domestic financial market were implemented in a surprisingly short period of time and effected a drastic change in the institutional characteristics of these markets, significantly increasing the sources of external financing. The most important tools were the following:

- The State Reform Law (Law No. 23,696 of August 1989) provided the legal bases for the process of privatizing public enterprises through the restructuring of external debt.

- The Economic Emergency Law (Law No. 23,697 of August 1989) established equal treatment for national and foreign capital invested in productive activities in the country and eliminated the requirement of obtaining prior approval for direct foreign investment.
- The Convertibility Law (Law No. 23,928 of March 1991) established a fixed exchange rate between the peso and the dollar, recognized the validity of contracts executed in any currency, and imposed the requirement that the money stock be backed 100 percent by exchange reserves held by the Central Bank of the Republic of Argentina (BCRA).
- The Deregulation Decree (No. 2,284 of November 1991) repealed an entire series of regulations affecting a wide range of economic activities. Regarding the financial market, it included various provisions aimed at reducing intermediation costs through transactions in the securities market. In particular, the tax on the sale of securities was eliminated, the tax stamp on stock market transactions was abolished, and the commissions of brokers in this market were decontrolled.
- The National Securities Commission was authorized to introduce a series of new regulations aimed specifically at expanding the stock market and creating new financial instruments to be traded in the securities markets, as a means of mobilizing domestic savings and attracting external capital. Thus, access to the stock market was facilitated for new companies, and innovative financial instruments such as Negotiable Bonds (Law No. 23,962 of July 1991) and Commercial Papers (short-term negotiable bonds) were established.
- To remove tax barriers to the repatriation of capital, the Tax "Amnesty" Law (No. 24,073 of April 1992) was enacted, establishing a special system for the reporting of goods and assets held abroad and for the regularization of assets in foreign currency held within the country.[2]
- The Central Bank Law (Law No. 24,144 of September 1992) abolished the official deposit guarantee, prohibited monetary financing of the deficit, and established strict limits on both the placement of government bonds in the Central Bank and the granting of discounts to commercial banks. It also established the BCRA as an independent institution.

---

[2] In the case of goods or assets held abroad, the taxpayer protects himself against an audit that would detect such assets–until such time as regularization within a period of not more than four years is decided on–by paying a monthly rate and using a blank deposit slip. In the case of assets in foreign currency held within the country, up to $500,000 can be sheltered, with the requirement that these assets be deposited in the financial system for 180 days to allow for the granting of "soft" credits based on these deposits. In addition, the principle of world income was adopted as the basis for income tax to avoid encouraging the transfer of capital abroad.

- Through various Central Bank Communications, regulations were established to promote development of the segment of deposits and credits in dollars carried out through banks in the domestic financial system (Communications "A" 1493 of July 1989 and "A" 1820 of March 1991). In addition to specific financial measures, the development of this segment, known as "Argendollars," received a substantial boost from the full deregulation of the exchange market (Communications "A" 1589 of December 1989 and "A" 1822 of April 1991) and the establishment of a fixed exchange rate by the above-cited Convertibility Law.

Nature and Trend of the Capital Flows

Within the framework of the debt crisis and macroeconomic disorder caused by the debacle involving the liberalization model implemented in the late 1970s, the first five years of the 1980s were characterized by a process of "chaotic adjustment," the principal features of which were massive capital flight of private funds, severe rationing, and in the case of the public sector, difficulties in gaining access to multilateral credit mechanisms.

The chaotic adjustment period ended with the implementation of the Austral Plan. This plan marked the end of that period since it was the first comprehensive, post-crisis stabilization policy. In other words, it was the first to apply a coherent policy to internal stabilization measures and to specifically target flows of external capital. The most obvious result of this new strategy was complete renegotiation of the external agreements concluded in 1987 and an incipient reversal of the phenomenon of private capital flight. Many of the dynamic mechanisms behind the capital flows, both in the past and at present, began to take shape in this period, regarding not only the relationship between capital inflows and macroeconomic stabilization but also the relationship with international organizations and the plans involving debt-equity swaps. However, this new system failed to take root, and as a result the economy entered another period of unusual macroeconomic turbulence.

The considerably improved conditions in the international financial market in the 1990s, along with the replenishment of international reserves in the post-hyperinflationary period (made possible by a record trade balance of $8 billion in 1990, which was a byproduct of macroeconomic imbalances), enabled Argentina to reestablish a much more fluid relationship with the international financial market in late 1990 and early 1991.

Our purpose here is to provide an analytical description of the current process of reversal in the flows of external capital. In order to define the context of this analysis, we will begin by studying what has happened since 1985 with the various components of the capital account.

The Period Prior to the Reform

A simple method of analyzing the balance of payments information is to compare the sources of supply and demand of loanable foreign funds. The first two columns of Table 2.1 indicate the funds needed. These consist of the requirements for financing the current account deficit, on the one hand, and the accumulation of reserves, on the other. The next two columns group the financing sources under two headings: those originating in autonomous capital flows and those due to compensatory foreign credit flows. Since the balance of payments data are *ex post facto*, obviously, the sum of the first two columns equals the sum of the last two.

As the table shows, the country's aggregate net demand for foreign funds was $12.507 billion between 1985 and 1990. Of this amount, $9.125 billion was needed to cover the current account deficit and $3.382 billion to finance the accumulation of reserves. In theory, the demand for loanable funds had to be covered by the supply of autonomous or market capital and the supply of compensatory capital.

The financial contribution of autonomous capital, however, was negative: when the flows observed throughout the period are added together, the autonomous capital account shows a net outflow of funds totalling $5.193 billion. This means either that debt was amortized or assets were acquired abroad. Therefore, to the financing requirements associated with the current account deficit and the accumulation of reserves must be added those generated either by the amortization of commercial debt or by the purchase of foreign assets. Taking this into account, between 1985 and 1990 the aggregate demand for funds in the rest of the world was $17.7 billion.

The first significant conclusion to be drawn from the above is that Argentina generated, on average, a net annual demand for financing from the rest of the world of $2.95 billion, which was covered only by making use of compensatory capital flows. What type of compensatory financial flows were used to satisfy this demand? Table 2.2 shows the most important items in the compensatory capital account.

The most surprising observation is the smallness of the contribution by the International Monetary Fund (IMF), given the influence that negotiations with that organization had in determining the economic policy of the period. In net terms, the IMF only contributed an average of $186 million annually. Moreover, given that the organization is dedicated to wiping out the cycles caused by external liquidity problems, the temporal trend of disbursements vis-à-vis amortizations is also surprising. The IMF made a significant contribution with the Austral Plan in 1985-87 and, subsequently, dedicated itself to collecting the payments regardless of the country's external liquidity status. Thus, for example, the peaks in the amortization of IMF debt occurred in completely different years: in 1989, "the year of runaway inflation," and in 1991, "the year of stability."

Table 2.1. Argentina: Balance of Payments Summary, 1977-92
(Millions of current dollars)

Period	Current account deficit (1)	Reserve variation (2)	(1)+(2) = (3)+(4)	Compens. capital mov. (3)	Autonomous capital mov. (4)
1977	-1,290	2,226	936	-253	1,189
1978	-1,833	1,998	165	-1,201	1,366
1979	537	4,442	4,980	65	4,915
1980	4,768	-2,796	1,972	-281	2,253
1981	4,714	-3,521	1,193	38	1,155
1982	2,358	715	1,643	5,451	-3,808
1983	2,461	1,684	4,145	4,256	111
1984	2,391	99	2,490	1,843	647
1985	953	2,017	2,970	2,573	397
1986	2,859	514	2,345	1,561	784
1987	4,238	-1,274	2,964	2,826	138
1988	1,572	1,961	3,533	3,342	191
1989	1,292	-1,559	267	5,326	-5,593
1990	-1,789	2,751	962	2,072	-1,110
1991	2,803	1,880	4,683	6,566	-1,883
1992*	5,719	2,281	8,000	319	7,681
Sum1985-90	9,125	3,382	12,507	17,700	-5,193
Sum1991-92	8,522	4,161	12,683	6,885	5,798

* First nine months.
Source: Author's calculations based on Central Bank data.

Contrasting sharply with the IMF's role, in terms of both the size and the temporal distribution of net disbursements, is the contribution of the Paris Club members. Not only did the Club grant average net credit of $804 million annually, but the largest contributions were made with the launching of the Austral Plan and during the periods of runaway inflation.

A second source of great importance in the provision of compensatory financing is the placement of External Bonds (Bonex). The total resources obtained through this instrument represent a little more than half the Paris Club amount: an average of $436 million annually. To a large extent, this significant contribution is related to domestic factors. The high point in the series was in 1989, when this financing was used to convert domestic debt into external debt through the issuance of Bonex securities within the framework of the so-called "Bonex Plan."[3]

---

[3] The balancing entry for this operation appears in the "others" item of the autonomous capital account as an outflow of funds. This is so because, from an economic point of view, the conversion of

Table 2.2. Argentina: Balance of Payments Summary, 1977-92: Compensatory Capital Movements

(Millions of current dollars)

Period	Compens. capital mov. (1)=2+3+4+5+6	Net IMF loans (2)	Net BONEX placement (3)	Net Paris Club loans (4)	Increase in arrears (5)	Others (6)
1977	-253	-42	9	0	0	-220
1978	-1,201	-414	-94	0	0	-693
1979	65	0	-140	0	0	205
1980	-281	0	-142	0	0	-139
1981	38	0	-79	0	0	117
1982	5,451	0	1,583	0	2,540	1,328
1983	4,256	1,178	492	0	682	1,904
1984	1,843	-33	387	0	940	549
1985	2,573	1,007	-217	1,617	-2,445	2,611
1986	1,561	145	-132	897	-1,174	1,825
1987	2,826	614	99	384	39	1,690
1988	3,342	18	-300	151	2,344	1,129
1989	5,326	-485	3,276	1,402	2,927	-1,794
1990	2,072	-185	-113	372	1,912	86
1991	6,566	-516	60	697	1,788	4,537
1992*	319	28	-209	229	618	-347
Sum1985-90	17,700	1,114	2,613	4,823	3,603	5,547
Sum1991-92	6,885	-488	-149	926	2,406	4,190

* First nine months.
Source: Author's calculations based on Central Bank data.

Even if we were to continue listing other items of lesser significance in the compensatory financing account, we would not come close to the figure of $2.95 billion per year. This is due to the fact that Argentina had exhausted every source of financing in this period and still did not manage to close its external accounts. Because of this, a new "financing" item appeared in the 1980s: the arrears in payments to creditors. A distinguishing characteristic of this period, however, is

---

domestic debt into external debt is similar in its results to what would happen if private agents voluntarily got rid of their domestic debt in order to purchase assets abroad. Had they acted in such a manner, the country's reserves would have fallen and the government would have been forced to obtain compensatory financing to replenish them. The total for this operation was $3.389 billion.

that these arrears represented a basic source of balance of payments financing. In terms of size, only the amount contributed by the Paris Club was larger: between 1985 and 1991, Argentina almost systematically incurred arrears in its payments abroad, which, on average, totaled $601 million annually. Only in 1987 was this amount smaller, due to the fact that across-the-board rescheduling that year permitted rectification of the situation. Nevertheless, new unpaid bills began to accumulate the very next year because a steep decline in the trade balance made it impossible to continue fulfilling the terms of the 1987 refinancing.

This "last resort" means of satisfying financing requirements was not only significant quantitatively, but it also had an impact on macroeconomic stability, primarily because the private sector views the amount of arrears as an indicator of how difficult it will be to close the external gap. This is why the recent comprehensive refinancing obtained by Argentina under the Brady Plan has had very beneficial effects in this regard. Converting existing arrears into Eurobonds rectified its debt position, which helped to reduce domestic interest rates because as macroeconomic uncertainty decreased, so did the differential due to the "country risk."

As mentioned above, the autonomous capital account balance was negative throughout the period. Nevertheless, by reducing the level of aggregation, it is seen that this results from the contrasting behavior of the various items it comprises. This is illustrated clearly in Table 2.3.

One of the most negative items is the financing of foreign trade. A total of $4.313 billion was spent on this category in the six years under consideration. Of particular note is the trend of import financing, the figures for which are consistently negative, with the notable exception of the last two years. Because the financing of foreign purchases is defined as the difference between the value of the inflows of goods and the payments made, it is to be hoped that the corresponding capital flows will be positive when imports are on the rise and negative when they contract. Nevertheless, even in periods of increasing foreign purchases (e.g., 1986-87), financing decreased. This was probably due to capital flight, which occurred through operations apparently related to commercial transactions or the financing thereof.

The item "loans to companies" indicates a deficit of $2.241 billion. This result was strongly influenced, however, by programs promoting the early retirement of corporate debt on concessional terms. In this sense, the capital flow through this account was hardly "autonomous." Finally, the item "others" shows a deficit of $5.615 billion. It should be kept in mind, however, that this amount includes some bookkeeping adjustments such as the one for the Bonex Plan and other debt consolidation operations, as explained below.

The two sectors with totally different results, in the sense that they have a positive balance, are the loans to government account, with a balance of capital inflows totaling $428 million, and the direct foreign investment account, which

Table 2.3. Argentina: Balance of Payments Summary, 1977-92: Autonomous Capital Movements
(Millions of current dollars)

Period	Autonomous capital mov. (1)=(2)+(7)	Private capital mov. (2)=3+4+5+6	Privatizat. and direct investment (3)	Loans to private comps. (4)	Export & import financing (5)	Others (6)	Govt. capital mov. (7)=(8)+(9)	Govt. securities and loans (8)	Loans to public comps. (9)
1977	1,189	216	52	393	-81	-149	973	5	968
1978	1,366	-83	295	514	-398	-494	1,449	624	825
1979	4,915	3,639	235	3,543	772	-912	1,276	585	691
1980	2,253	-743	739	3,886	-86	-5,283	2,997	1,016	1,981
1981	1,155	-3,469	927	3,112	-3,386	-4,122	4,624	2,695	1,929
1982	-3,808	-4,017	257	-521	-2,720	-1,032	209	481	-272
1983	-111	-2,514	183	-1,831	-411	-456	2,403	2,249	154
1984	647	-1,558	269	-2,674	500	347	2,205	2,210	-5
1985	455	-894	919	-1,733	-812	732	1,349	1,156	193
1986	987	420	574	-459	-539	844	567	521	46
1987	255	-695	-19	-24	-492	-160	950	538	412
1988	526	393	1,147	-228	-693	167	133	30	103
1989*	-5,474	-5,242	1,028	111	-2,228	-4,153	-232	-272	40
1990	-1,079	-466	2,036	92	451	-3,045	-613	-609	-4
1991**	-1,884	-2,636	2,439	345	1,758	-7,178	752	647	105
1992***	7,681	8,506	2,446	461	2,426	3,173	-825	-678	-147
Sum 1985-90	-4,330	-6,484	5,685	-2,241	-4,313	-5,615	2,154	1,364	790
Sum 1991-92	5,797	5,870	4,885	806	4,184	-4,005	-73	-31	-42

* In 1989, because of the BONEX plan, which converted some private domestic financial assets into foreign debt, column (6) is explained as follows: -4,153 = -764 -3,389, where the last figure reflects the "flight" of funds associated with the BONEX issue. Consequently, the overall private capital balance was arrived at as follows: -5,242 = -1,853 -3,389. Similarly, the overall balance of the autonomous capital account, without said transaction, would be -2,204 million dollars.

** In 1991, an operation to consolidate public debt by issuing securities worth $5,457 million affects the figures in much the same way as that referred to in the preceding note. Without said operation, the balance of private capital movements would be +2,821, and the overall balance would be +3,574.

*** First nine months.

Source: Author's calculations based on Central Bank data.

had a positive balance of $5.685 billion. These figures clearly demonstrate the importance of direct foreign investment in satisfying the economy's foreign exchange requirements. In the seven years under consideration, this account had a positive average balance of $948 million. Note, however, that the balance increased, reflecting the acceleration of the privatization program since 1990. Starting in 1984, debt restructuring programs were also very important in terms of augmenting the balance of this account.

Capital Flow after the Reform

Can any significant change in the trend of external capital be identified by separately analyzing the 1991-92 period, which was characterized simultaneously by a sharp decline in international interest rates and the implementation of structural reforms at home?

Important changes have indeed occurred since late 1990. First, the use of net external funds in the economy increased dramatically. In the 1985-90 period, the average requirement for financing the current account deficit, together with the amounts accumulated as reserves, was $2.085 billion annually. Between 1991 and the third quarter of 1992, that average increased more than three times, to $7.247 billion. It is actually rather surprising that the total external funds used between 1991 and the third quarter of 1992, as Table 2.1 shows, is practically the same as the amount accumulated between 1985 and 1990 (approximately $12.5 billion). This was the result of both an increase in the current account deficit (the annual average of which went from $1.521 billion to $4.869 billion) and a quickening in the pace of reserves accumulation. Between 1985 and 1990, an average of $564 million in reserves was accumulated each year, while in the period from 1991 until the third quarter of 1992, the annual average was $2.378 billion.

Clearly, these phenomena are associated with the effects of the Convertibility Plan of April 1991: the lag in the real exchange rate caused a sharp increase in the trade deficit, and greater confidence in the exchange rule led to a substantial remonetization, which, in a context of convertibility, was counterbalanced by a rise in Central Bank reserves.

What was the role of autonomous and compensatory funds in the financing? In answering this question, it was concluded that a great change occurred in this respect as well. Unlike the period between the Austral Plan and the episodes of runaway inflation, the autonomous capital account played a preferential role in the financing starting in late 1990. This was especially true in 1992, when, over the course of three quarters, autonomous capital totaling $7.681 billion was received, given that the autonomous capital balance in 1991 was still negative. Nevertheless, this situation is due primarily to the accounting effect of that year's public debt consolidation operations, which totaled $5.457 billion. If the accounts are "cleared" of these operations, the balance of the autonomous capital account for 1991 becomes a positive $3.574 billion.[4]

Deduction of the consolidation operations makes the change in the dynamics of the capital flows clear: Between the 1985-90 period and the 1991-92 period, the roles of the autonomous and compensatory capital accounts were reversed. At present, it is the autonomous capital account that leads the financing process, while the role of the compensatory capital account has dwindled considerably. Between 1991 and the third quarter of 1992, the amount of compensatory capital received was only $1.428 billion.[5] In these circumstances, the trend of IMF debt is worth noting: since the Convertibility Plan went into effect, $488 million of the amount owed that organization has been paid off. This means that the plan was carried out with negative financial support from the IMF. Another item that was negative, unlike previous periods, was the placement of external bonds (Bonex), while there were no major changes in the contribution of the Paris Club and the arrears.

As Table 2.3 shows, the reversal of the role of autonomous capital was mostly private in origin. During the years in which runaway inflation occurred, the balance of the private capital flow was extremely negative: $1.853 billion in 1989 and $466 million in 1990.[6] This phenomenon was completely reversed in 1991, when the inflow of private investment was $2.821 billion. Moreover, it tended to intensify over time: in the first three quarters of 1992, a total of $8.506 billion was received.

Regarding the role of the various flows of private financing, the trend of every item in this account, as Table 2.3 shows, is positive. Two facts should be stressed, however. First, both the "financing of foreign trade" item and "others" that have been the traditional vehicles of capital flight have very large positive balances, which is an indication of the scope of the capital repatriation process. Second, the inflows of capital as a function of privatization have the largest balances, which is a reflection of the public sector reform policy. Given the importance of this policy, a brief review of its most important features is presented below.

---

[4] In the same way, the balance of the compensatory capital account must be lowered from $6.566 billion to $1.109 billion. This is so because the government's debt consolidation operations are recorded in the balance of payments as an outflow of capital in the "others" item of the autonomous capital account and as new financing in the compensatory capital account.

[5] The preceding note explains the calculation of the compensatory capital account balance.

[6] As in the case of the private capital account balance for 1991, the amount of debt consolidation under the Bonex Plan—$3.389 billion—must be deducted from the private capital balance. The compensatory capital balance must also be adjusted by the same amount.

Table 2.4. Argentina: Summary of Privatizations, 1990-92

	1990	1991	1992	Total
Companies sold	6	2	25	33
Services/companies given in concession	3	7	9	19
Oil				
Concessions	37	22	27	86
Partnership agreements		5	4	9
Sale of shares of privatized companies	0	1	1	2
Receipts (in millions of US$)				
Cash	790.5	1,892.5	2,658.9	5,341.9
Debt paper	6,740.2	12.0*	41.8*	6,794.0*
		2,633.8**	2,633.8**	

*   Par value.
** Equivalent cash value.
Source: Author's calculations based on data from the Subsecretariat of Privatization of the Ministry of Economy.

Debt Conversion Programs and Privatization

The first truly important privatization efforts occurred in November 1990. After that, the policy of selling off public sector enterprises continued without pause and, in fact, because of its scope and the speed with which it was implemented, it is almost unique. As can be inferred from Table 2.4, the public sector has so far collected $5.342 billion in cash and, in addition, through debt conversion programs has managed to retire external debt instruments totaling $6.794 billion dollars.

To get an idea of the importance of this figure, it must be remembered that at the start of the privatization process, the total external debt of the public sector was $58.4 billion. The retirement of debt instruments therefore represents nearly 12 percent of this amount.[7]

The role of external capital in the purchase of public sector assets was substantial. This explains the sizable increase in the direct investment item of the private capital account. Of the $11.327 billion positive balance shown in the pri-

---

[7] It is estimated that the state could receive as much as $20 billion in revenue when the process of selling public enterprises and granting concessions ends. Of the total cash receipts from the sale of assets, the largest amount came from the sale of the telephone company, ENTEL, and the second largest from the sale of primary and secondary oil-producing areas. Significant revenue was also generated in the privatization of enterprises in the electricity, gas, aviation, and defense sectors.

vate capital account between 1990 and the third quarter of 1992, $3.267 billion is accounted for by privatization. If to this is added the amount of direct foreign investment, which, because of the method of accounting, also includes a large number of the retired instruments, the total is $4.885 billion.[8] These amounts suggest that the quarterly flow of foreign investment in this period averaged $698 million. This trend signified a qualitative gain in the performance of this balance of payments item. For example, it is three times larger than the quarterly average between 1985 and 1989, during which period several debt conversion programs had already been implemented that were obviously far less ambitious in their objectives.

External Flows and the Domestic Financial Market

The inflow of private capital had profound repercussions on the domestic financial market, affecting the trend of both the existing financial instruments and those created as a part of the reform. Similarly, institutional changes in the exchange and financial markets—which were clearly oriented toward deregulation and the reduction of transaction costs—facilitated the relationship between the external flows and domestic financial transactions. Moreover, greater financial integration and the increase in the quantity and diversity of financial instruments, together with growing macroeconomic stability, led to a sizable decrease in the country risk, which in turn encouraged the inflow of capital. A large part of these private flows, which we identified by analyzing the balance of payments, were channeled through the financial system.

The changes made in the regulations to attract deposits in dollars spurred the growth of the dollarized segment of the domestic financial system (Argendollars). Through the repatriation of capital and the dishoarding of resident holdings, private banks accumulated dollar reserves of more than $1.2 billion. On this basis, and through secondary expansion, they generated new credit in Argendollars of approximately $10 billion, or more than a third of the total credit granted by the domestic financial system to private individuals and public entities. Likewise, the establishment of a system for the convertibility of the peso encouraged the accumulation of Central Bank reserves. Between April 1991 and December 1992, Central Bank reserve assets rose from $5.543 billion to $12.948 billion. The secondary expansion of the basic increase brought about by this jump in reserves led to a sharp rise in assets denominated in pesos. In reaction to the increase in deposits in pesos and Argendollars, the credit supply expanded dramatically. Between April 1991 and December 1992, the aggregate loanable capacity of the financial system

---

[8] The accounting rule followed is that of including all cash payments in the privatization item of the balance of payments, while debt instruments are included in the direct foreign investment item.

grew by more than $15 billion. This increase contributed greatly to the growth of effective demand observed after the introduction of the convertibility plan and, consequently, to the rise in domestic consumption associated with the growing trade deficit then being observed. Although these figures concerning the growth of demand for assets originating in the Argentine financial system are impressive, it must be kept in mind that the coefficients of financial deepening are still very small, because that growth occurred as a result of the unusually low level of post-hyperinflationary monetization. In late 1992 the ratio of total deposits in dollars and pesos to GDP was approximately 23 percent.

The institutional changes that spurred the development of a negotiable bonds market and expansion of the stock market in conjunction with the inflow of private capital led to appreciable increases in the use of these instruments. Similarly, improved access to the international voluntary credit market made participation in the Eurobonds market possible for both the public and the private sector. Eurobonds were the single most important factor in terms of directly attracting external savings, with private companies placing a total of $1.14 billion, with maturities varying from one and a half to five years. The government, on the other hand, placed two Eurobond issues: "República Argentina" ($300 million) and "República 2" ($250 million). Nevertheless, negotiable bonds also had a hand in attracting external capital. Issues of negotiable bonds—denominated in both pesos and dollars—have totaled $462.7 million in the period since their creation. The maturity dates varied from two to 12 years.

The expansion of the stock market was evidenced by a sharp increase in the overall capitalization level of the market, which rose from $5.272 billion in the first quarter of 1991 to $18.435 billion in the final quarter of 1992. The increase in capitalization was due both to the boom in the prices of existing securities and to the listing of new companies. Of particular importance was the sale in 1991 and 1992 of part of the block of telephone company shares, which represented a total of $2.056 billion. Despite this positive trend, there are some aspects that indicate that complete recovery of the domestic financial market is still far off. In the first place, a characteristic common to all the sales of negotiable bonds and Eurobonds was that only the largest national companies had access to that market and, moreover, a certain saturation point was ultimately reached in the sales. Secondly, the current market prices of the securities fluctuated wildly, indicating that the level of uncertainty remains high. Finally, the increase in the sale of securities did not signal a turnaround in the dollarization process. Most of the new financial assets are still being denominated in dollars. As discussed below, this process is potentially unstable due to the fact that although the credits are denominated in dollars, the payment capacity of the debtors is closely linked to the trend in the level and stability of domestic business activity.

Figure 2.1. Argentina: Risk Premium Trend Annualized Rates
(July 1981-December 1992)

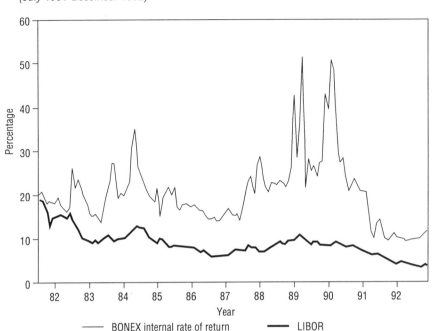

Note: The risk premium is the difference between the BONEX internal rate of return and LIBOR.

The Country Risk Premium and Capital Movements

The reduced country risk observed over the last two years is one of the factors which probably weighed most heavily in the generation of a positive capital flow into Argentina. This reduction of risk can be seen in Figure 2.1 as the differential between the BONEX internal rate of return and the LIBOR.

In general, variations in the country risk are closely related to the trend of macroeconomic stability. Both the variance and the level tended to increase in the turbulent first half of the 1980s and between the moratorium on external debt payments in the first quarter of 1988—when the arrears began to accumulate—and the runaway inflation of 1989-90. Under the Austral Plan and the Convertibility Plan, the opposite occurred.

For the holder of physical or financial assets in the domestic market, the country risk is a systematic or market risk and it is, therefore, nondiversifiable. The only way to avoid it is by "abandoning" the economy through investment in external

Figure 2.2. Argentina: Predicted Devaluation
(Projected less actual rate)

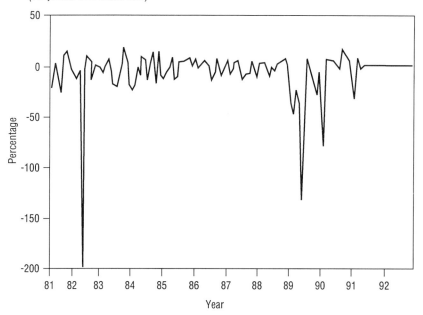

assets. Thus, capital flight and the rationing of credit by foreign banks are merely defensive actions in response to a risk against which there is no "insurance."

From the viewpoint of financial investments, one of the most direct ways that macroeconomic instability affects holdings is through unexpected devaluations. There are two reasons for this: first, it diminishes the real value of assets denominated in pesos (by accelerating inflation) and, second, it increases the delinquency of portfolios, whether in dollars or in pesos, by causing drastic changes in relative prices in the contractive phase that usually follows devaluations. Figure 2.2 is an attempt to illustrate the relationship between macroeconomic and devaluation shocks, on the one hand, and expectation errors, on the other, the latter being calculated on the basis of interest rate parity equations.[9]

---

[9] Arbitrage would tend to iron out the rates using a formula such as the following:

(1) $i = r + s + E$,

where i is the domestic nominal interest rate (for deposits), which must equal the sum of the international nominal interest rate r, the country risk premium s, and the projected rate of devaluation E. Government securities denominated in dollars, Bonexes, which yield a return in dollars, pay a rate similar to the LIBOR, plus a premium. The internal rate of return (IRR) of these securities therefore permits an estimate of the country risk based on the market rating:

Clearly, expectation errors are much greater in periods of shock and instability than when a more or less successful stabilization plan has somehow managed to define the margin of error in forming expectations. Again, in the 1980s, the greatest gains were made while the Austral Plan and the Convertibility Plan were in effect. The latter's effectiveness was substantially greater, however, coinciding as it did with the positive trend of the financial factors and the inflow of capital. Analysis of the trend of dollar indebtedness of companies listed on the stock exchange, which are highly representative of the group of major companies with access to the international financial market, suggests that decisions concerning the amount of indebtedness is inversely proportional to the trend of the country risk. There is also evidence that the decision to borrow abroad correlates positively with capital goods imports.[10] The sharp rise in the latter under the Convertibility Plan, together with the downward trend of the country risk, must be taken into account when attempting to formulate a hypothesis concerning the factors responsible for the increasing flow of financing into the country.

Macroeconomic Policy Tools and Capital Flows

Various stabilization efforts undertaken in Argentina since the late 1970s led initially to rapid inflows of short-term capital. Like the Convertibility Plan, those efforts featured some form of fixed exchange rate (or gradual devaluation) system and more or less modified versions of the balance of payments monetary focus, although they were very different in degree and kind. In such cases, the positive flows of financial capital tended to favor remonetization of the economy, but not always at a pace consistent with the monetary objectives of the authorities. They also caused distortions in the exchange rate and in relative prices, which led to sharp rises in domestic consumption. Later, when the stabilization programs began to lose steam and the initial gains began to fade, the reversal of the short-term

---

$(2)\ s = IRR - r.$

Hence, based on (1) and (2), it is possible to estimate the devaluation forecast as:

$(3)\ E = i - IRR.$

Obviously, the value of these estimates is purely heuristic. A number of questions arise, such as the transaction costs, slow portfolio adjustments, and the serious deficiencies of the domestic financial market.

[10] The model developed provided the following results:

PAS =   1638 + 1.2 MBK - 9.2 RP + 820.5 D; R^2 = .90
        (.82)(2.17)   (-2.14)   (5.2)

The t-statistic appears in parentheses. An AR(1) was corrected using the Cochrane-Orcutt procedure. *PAS* is liabilities in dollars; *MBK,* capital goods imports; *RP,* country risk premium; and *D,* a dummy for the Falklands War period. Quarterly observations of the assets shown on the consolidated balance sheets of the 60 largest companies on the stock exchange were used. The period under consideration is from the first quarter of 1982 to the third quarter of 1992. Again, the value of this equation is purely heuristic.

capital flow often exacerbated the difficulties of both the external sector and the monetary system, leading to sudden devaluations that often ended in "overshooting" real exchange parity and excessive reductions in the levels of consumption.

As demonstrated in the previous section, after the implementation of the Convertibility Plan, a heavy inflow of private capital ensued. Some of the characteristics of this process were similar to what happened with earlier plans. It may be that the sudden change in direction of the external flows, as a result both of their brief duration and their size, causes future macroeconomic distortions that are difficult to manage. The primary objective of this section is to evaluate the problem by analyzing two key stabilization efforts, the Exchange Devaluation Plan ("tablita") and the Austral Plan.

The Exchange Liberalization and Devaluation Plan

Implemented in December 1978, this plan broke down in the first quarter of 1981 when the system of preannounced devaluation rates had to be abandoned, giving rise to a lengthy series of maxidevaluations. The main reason for implementing the plan was to combat inflation. The basic idea was that in a context of integration with the international economy, if a decreasing devaluation rate were preannounced, the law of purchasing power parity would bring domestic inflation into line with international inflation when the devaluation rate reaches zero. In these circumstances, and with unrestricted capital mobility, the quantity of money would become endogenous and no longer influenced by Central Bank interest rate policy (this would be even more true as foreign and domestic financial assets became closer substitutes).

Specifically, and with regard to exchange rate policy and capital flows, the program established a "tablita" of scheduled exchange rate adjustments and substantially eased the restrictions on capital flows: inflows of foreign funds were liberalized by eliminating all of the regulations concerning mandatory deposits; the minimum term of loans was shortened to one year; and less stringent restrictions were established for maximum individual purchases of foreign exchange, without the need for justification.[11] This study will therefore examine the interaction between capital inflows, the domestic financial market and the use of policy tools in this program.

---

[11] For readers not familiar with this topic, it will be helpful to briefly review the restrictions previously in force. The exchange market was in the process of being deregulated as early as 1976. Until then, the basic exchange controls consisted of the requirement that exporters sell foreign exchange to the Central Bank or to authorized institutions, various restrictions on both foreign purchases (prohibitions, prior approval requirements, etc.) and the payments therefor (prohibition of cash payments or repayment terms of less than 180 days, depending on the type of good imported), and restrictions on the payment of dividends and profits. With respect to capital flows, prior Central Bank approval was

Table 2.5 reveals a fairly clear pattern in private sector capital flows. In 1979, the removal of impediments to the flow of capital and growing confidence in the exchange system facilitated a $3.639 billion capital inflow, which peaked in the final quarter. The flow then slowed and became negative in the second quarter of 1980. The net balance that year was negative, and the situation deteriorated significantly in 1981, despite devaluations and a sharp rise in domestic real interest rates. In short, outflows exceeded inflows and the net balance of private capital flows in the 1978-81 period was a negative $656 million.

While capital was flowing into the country, nominal interest rates tended to decline, more or less in step with the downward trend of the devaluation rates. During this period, the real rates were negative. In this context, a sharp expansion of the demand for credit occurred, which was satisfied largely by external sources. The expansion of credit made it possible to finance a sizable increase in business activity. Together with the accelerated process of exchange appreciation associated with the gap between domestic inflation and the predetermined devaluation rates, this led to a reduction of the trade surplus in 1979 and to a record deficit in 1980. Between 1980 and 1981, the accrued deficit in the current account was more than $9.4 billion.

In mid-1979, when the external conditions became less dynamic, a gradual increase in real interest rates occurred, as did a steady rise in the differential between domestic and international interest rates. This was the result of growing doubts about the sustainability of the nominal exchange rate, given the rapid deterioration of the trade balance. Table 2.5 also shows the trend of the differential between domestic and international rates during the course of the program.[12]

---

required to obtain external credits. Such operations had to be registered and the minimum term was 180 days. The purchase of foreign exchange for other than a specific purpose was not permitted. Late that year the market was unified, putting an end to the multiple exchange system. In early 1977, more and more operations could be carried out directly through the authorized agencies. Although the requirement of prior approval for loans was abolished, the minimum term remained 180 days. Similarly, the requirement of cash payments for commodity purchases was eliminated, cash transfers for profit-taking and capital repatriation were authorized, and the purchase or transfer of up to $1,000 per person for no specific reason was permitted. Nevertheless, toward the end of 1977, in order to palliate the monetary impact of the capital flows, a minimum term of two years was established for the repayment of external loans and compulsory deposits were established for part of the financial resources obtained abroad. In theory, these deposits were 20 percent of loan operations and 10 percent of export and import financing operations. The deposit had to be in national currency, no interest was paid, and the term was the same as that of the loan. These restrictions appear to have deterred the inflow of capital, especially in the second half of 1978.

[12] This rate has been defined as the difference between the domestic interest rate and the sum of the international rate (LIBOR); the projected devaluation (which, in this case, is assumed to be the same as the devaluation rate indicated in the "tablita"); and an estimate of the differential between external and domestic financial transaction costs. This estimate is found in Frenkel and Damill (1987), where the behavior of this differential is linked to the trend of the exchange risk. In fact, as with private investments, this differential can be viewed as the "risk premium" of external indebtedness.

Table 2.5. Argentina: Summary of the "Tablita" Plan, 1978-81

| | Autonomous capital movement | | | Country risk premium (%) (Annualized rate) | Monetary base increments [*] | | |
| | Total | Private | Public | | (a) Originated in the ext. sector | (b) Originated in the domestic sector | (a)/(b) |
	(Millions of dollars)						
1978	1,366	-83	1,449				
1979:1	1,029	866	163	1.03	759	408	1.9
1979:2	1,033	773	260	1.20	1,521	467	3.3
1979:3	1,335	973	362	2.73	1,160	623	1.9
1979:4	1,517	1,027	491	2.50	1,608	-269	-6.0
Total 1979	4,915	3,639	1,276				
1980:1	1,126	398	728	1.80	176	-71	-2.5
1980:2	-793	-1,439	646	2.23	-3,702	6,545	-0.6
1980:3	1,455	1,103	352	3.57	596	1,479	0.4
1980:4	465	-805	1,270	3.00	-4,288	7,852	-0.5
Total 1980	2,253	-743	2,997				
1981:1	-1,236	-3,797	2,561	4.20	-6,035	7,358	-0.8

[*] Data in millions of australs. The monetary base at December 31, 1978, was 7.034 billion pesos.
Source: Author's calculations, based on Central Bank data.

The increase in rates negatively affected a financial system that was already fragile as a result of the liberalization program implemented in 1977, which permitted the financing of projects that were largely unprofitable and of diminishing value. As a result, late in the first quarter of 1980, a serious financial crisis erupted (which was to continue for years and would eventually result in the disappearance of many businesses). Growing uncertainty caused by the poor showing of the external and financial sectors upped the pressure on Central Bank reserves, leading to the disaster of 1981.

Table 2.5 also reveals the trend of the "offset coefficient" during this period.[13] The ratio of the expansion of reserves and of domestic credit is less than

---

[13] The "offset coefficient" is measured as the quotient of the *ex-post* variation in the reserves and the *ex-post* variation in domestic credit. The quotation marks are used because determining the trade-off ratio between the expansion of reserves and of domestic credit would require separately distinguishing the autonomous or exogenous effects of the growth of GDP, the variation in the current account, inflation, and the variation in the international interest rate on the demand for money. Obviously, if the demand for money changes (because GDP is growing) while the authorities are increasing do

one in absolute terms (-0.13), indicating that the trade-off was incomplete during this period and that monetary policy had some impact on macroeconomic
equilibrium. If the net trade-off ratio of shifts in the demand for nominal money
owing to the rise in GDP and prices is calculated, however, the reduction in
reserves due to the expansion of domestic credit would surely be greater.

The available policy tools were scarcely used to manage the heavy inflows
of external capital (or even intensified the effects of these inflows, for example,
by lowering reserve requirements) and they were ineffective later in halting the
run on the peso. In fact, when the flow of external capital changed direction,
monetary policy, through an increase in bank reserve requirements, tried to
reverse the process by further reducing the money supply, in addition to what
was already causing the capital outflow. Monetary contraction could not be
used systematically, however, since it tended to aggravate the cash flow position of banks with collection problems. In fact, the financial crisis eventually
led to loss of control over domestic monetary creation. To avoid collapse of the
payments system, the Central Bank was forced to act as a lender of last resort.
Thus, while capital flight shrank the monetary base, rediscounts were the main
source of expansion, supplying more liquid assets for the run on the peso.

Even during the most critical moments of the run on the peso, no direct
controls were ever imposed on the external flows. Actually, just the opposite
occurred; the attempt to reverse the capital outflow consisted of announcing
that there would be no retreat from the liberalization policy and, consequently,
the minimum term of one year for external loans was abolished. This approach
was unsuccessful. In fact, continuing capital flight would later necessitate the
reimposition of exchange controls.[14]

The policy of financing the fiscal deficit was used to counteract the effects
of the run, but it only made it worse. To reduce the distortions in the domestic
market, domestic public borrowing was curtailed. Since the public sector was generating a deficit, this required greater use of external credit. The foreign exchange

---

mestic credit, the effect on the reserves would be muted. To determine the "pure" ratio (instead of
calculating it after the fact, as we have done) would have required a model allowing us to distinguish
the various factors affecting the relationship between reserves and domestic credit. The brief period
during which this system was in force made econometric analysis impossible.

[14] Initially, starting in April 1982 and as a result of the Falklands War, the sale of foreign exchange,
regardless of the purpose, was subject to prior approval from the Central Bank; and external payment
arrears began to accumulate. It was established that profits, dividends, and royalties could only be
paid via the delivery of External Bonds.

Throughout 1983 and 1984, strict control over external payments was exercised by subjecting the
sale of foreign exchange (for a wide range of purposes) to the prior approval of the Central Bank. In
late 1984, meanwhile, it was established that the terms of loans in foreign currencies could not exceed 180 days without prior authorization from the Central Bank, with the possibility of paying
principal and interest directly.

Table 2.6. Argentina: Summary of the Austral Plan, 1985-88

Period	Autonomous capital movement			Country risk premium (%) (Annualized rate)	Projected devaluation (%) (Annualized rate)	Monetary base increments *		
	Total	Private	Public			(a) Originated in the ext. sector	(b) Originated in the domestic sector	(a)/(b)
	(Millions of dollars)							
1985:1	-108	-149	41	8.4	969.8	n.a.	n.a.	n.a.
1985:2	92	139	-47	11.3	1,191.5	n.a.	n.a.	n.a.
1985:3	404	311	93	9.3	65.6	741	368	2.01
1985:4	9	-1,195	1,204	9.0	46.4	-1,780	3,346	-0.53
Total 1985	397	-894	1,291					
1986:1	165	89	76	8.9	50.1	-16	12	-1.27
1986:2	437	396	41	8.4	42.6	397	277	1.43
1986:3	128	-94	222	8.0	71.9	130	328	0.39
1986:4	54	29	25	7.8	108.6	-817	1,478	-0.55
Total 1986	784	420	364					
1987:1	560	499	61	9.2	75.6	-299	550	-0.54
1987:2	-605	-950	345	7.0	95.6	-772	1,864	-0.41
1987:3	-172	-469	297	11.7	200.8	-919	2,342	-0.39
1987:4	355	225	130	14.8	141.6	-17,281	21,091	-0.82
Total 1987	138	-695	833					
1988:1	-164	-271	107	24.3	225	-695	2,783	-0.25

* Data in millions of australs. The monetary base at June 30, 1985, was 2.479 billion australs.
Source: Author's calculations based on Central Bank data.

obtained in this way compensated, at least in part, for the drain on Central Bank reserves caused by the change in the composition of private investment. This trend is clearly visible in Table 2.5. In 1980 and 1981, the autonomous capital account was positive, even though the private component of this account was extremely negative. The use of this policy tool was clearly a mistake: the foreign exchange obtained through public borrowing was acquired by individuals who speculated on the peso at an undervalued exchange rate; credibility in the "tablita" could not be restored and the long-term financial position of the public sector was seriously compromised, as would become clear in the wake of the debt crisis.

The Austral Plan

The Austral Plan was introduced in June 1985 and survived more or less intact until October 1987, when a different set of policies was implemented. It was an "unorthodox" plan since it combined fiscal and monetary adjustment mechanisms with a freeze of the nominal exchange rate and prices (for industrial goods and for services), the objective of which was to break the grip of inflation. As far as the exchange rate is concerned, nominal parity was established for a time between the national currency and the dollar, and later, together with moderation of the price freeze, periodic devaluations were carried out in an attempt to adapt the rate of devaluation to the rate of domestic inflation. In the area of exchange control, a less stringent version of the controls reimposed in 1982 was adopted. In these circumstances, the "gap" between official and parallel or "black" market prices became important in terms of the flow of capital: if the gap widened excessively, it encouraged capital flight through the overinvoicing of imports and the underinvoicing of exports.

The trend of private capital inflows and outflows over time was similar to that observed under the "tablita." Nevertheless, given the rationing of voluntary credit sources, the scale was decidedly smaller, and the flows generally consisted of short-term, speculative capital, which attempted to exploit the rate differential while confidence in the exchange policy was strong and which withdrew at the first sign of wavering. Table 2.6 shows that following implementation of the plan, between June 1985 and March 1987, there was only one quarter in which the flow of private capital was negative. It is also interesting to note that the "others" balance, which reflects speculative flows of unknown origin, is extremely positive (see also Table 2.3).[15] The opposite occurred between the second quarter of 1987 and the first quarter of 1988, when there was only one quarter in which the balance was positive. As was true when the "tablita" was in effect, the net overall balance of these flows was negative ($170 million).

One thing that differed substantially from the "tablita" period, however, was the role of the current account deficit. Although in 1978 there was a surplus and the deficit was significant only when the inflow of capital was on the wane, the Austral Plan was launched with a current account deficit, which was also sizable when the capital arrived. The burden of external interest left over from the debt crisis converted the current account deficit into a structural deficit. This revealed two basic differences. On the one hand, confidence in the exchange rule was very low since the external sector exhibited a high degree of structural imbalance,

---

15 Contrary to the statement in the text, data from the capital account balance sheet reveal an extremely high negative balance for private flows in the fourth quarter of 1985. This is the result, however, of the conversion of private external debt with exchange rate guarantees, contracted in the 1981-83 period, into public debt. Since the corresponding issues (of Promissory Notes and Bonds) are recorded in the balance of payments as public sector capital earnings, the balance of the operation is zero. These "outflows" of private capital through debt conversion totaled approximately $1.264 billion in 1985. Excluding these operations, the fourth quarter balance is a positive $69 million.

and, on the other, the monetary effect of the increase in reserves caused by the inflow of capital was more than offset by the decrease in reserves caused by the current account. In fact, the level of international reserves decreased over the entire course of the program. As the figures in Table 2.6 show, the projected devaluation was always much greater than the devaluation implicit in the program's exchange rule and, in addition, it tended to increase during periods of private capital outflow. It is interesting to note, moreover, that the country risk, although lower when the plan was launched, never fell to levels compatible with lasting macroeconomic stability. On the other hand, the temporal trend of this variable generally duplicates the trend of exchange expectations, which declined steadily throughout 1987.

Table 2.6 also shows that the trend of the external sector was contractive throughout the period, while the opposite occurred with the sources of domestic expansion. The "offset coefficient" observed in this case, however, is larger than in the "tablita" period, at minus 0.65. This indicates that the trade-off between the loss of reserves and domestic credit expansion was incomplete. It must be remembered, however, in evaluating these results, that both GDP and prices increased during the period, shifting the nominal demand for money, and that the role of the current account was contractive.

The factors that led, after 1986, to a reversal of the initial program gains are not too different from those observed during the "tablita" period: growing uncertainty over a current account situation that was becoming intolerable and loss of control over domestic monetary and fiscal factors. The causes of these imbalances were, however, quite different. The deficit in the current account worsened, not because of an explosion in domestic consumption prompted by the exchange lag, but rather because of the conjunction of negative external supply shocks. In 1986, falling agricultural prices and climatic factors led to a drop in exports of $1.544 billion, and this situation persisted in 1987. The loss of monetary control, in turn, was due not to a financial crisis but to fiscal and quasi-fiscal difficulties. The negative external shock eroded the fiscal accounts, the balancing of which depended largely on export taxes (which were lowered substantially to compensate for the impact of the shock on exports). The quasi-fiscal deficit of the Central Bank increased because of the burden of interest on the overwhelming reserves inherited from the 1980 financial crisis.

In conclusion, we have a couple of words about policy tools and capital flows. Although the flows of private capital had no monetary impact in net terms, there were brief periods when they did. When an attempt was made to use monetary policy to control liquidity, it caused serious problems. Unable to opt for the voluntary placement of bonds, forced debt was sold in the financial system (paid-in reserves). Given the high real interest rates, this form of sterilization was very costly for the Central Bank and fueled a quasi-fiscal deficit that was already close to two points of GDP. The quasi-fiscal deficit, moreover, tended to endogenize monetary growth, necessitating new bond issues. Clearly, systematic use of this sterilization mechanism would not have been viable.

Direct measures were used to discourage short-term financial flows: the minimum term of financial loans, which had been 180 days since late 1984, was extended to one year, and the periods allotted for the sale of foreign exchange obtained through foreign trade were modified. These measures enjoyed some success in impeding the inflow of very short-term investments but not in increasing the term of loans. In late 1987, when the financial flows subsided, the authorities were forced to reorganize the entire exchange system.[16]

Finally, the policy of financing the deficit was used, insofar as possible, to minimize the loss of reserves as the program unfolded. Unlike the 1978-81 period, the majority of the financing sources were international organizations. The financing obtained through these channels was needed to compensate for the flight of private capital. As Table 2.6 shows, despite private capital flight, in 1987 the balance of the autonomous capital account was positive.[17]

The Convertibility Plan

The Convertibility Plan, as explained above, was implemented in March and April 1991 and is still in force. Like the other plans discussed, its immediate objective was to combat inflation, and it combined highly orthodox fiscal and monetary measures (implicit in the Convertibility Law and the Charter of the Central Bank cited above) with other, more eclectic measures such as the legal prohibition against indexing mechanisms and pricing agreements with industrial firms. As explained in the discussion of the reforms, an exchange system was established that was even more flexible than the one in force during the period of openness in the late 1970s. Any type of differential treatment of capital based on its nature or term was abolished, and it is not even necessary to record transactions.[18] It should also be kept in mind that the exchange rate is fixed by law.

---

[16] With the launching of a new stabilization plan in October 1987, the exchange market was split into an "official" market (regulated by the BCRA) and an open market with no Central Bank intervention, liberalizing the controls previously imposed on some private sector transactions. By the end of the year, the official market handled, among others, transactions involving export earnings and payments for imports, the repayment of financial loans recorded in the External Debt Register, and the interest on amounts owed abroad in connection with the foregoing. In the open market, with a floating rate, agents were authorized to carry out any transactions not specifically reserved for the official market.

[17] In April of 1987, Argentina concluded an agreement with the creditor banks to refinance nearly $30 billion, with a more lenient repayment schedule and a lower interest rate. Also of note was the receipt of approximately $900 million in loans from international organizations, of which nearly $500 million were associated with the structural reform processes then in progress—trade policy reform and export diversification in particular.

[18] Because of this, it is difficult for the Central Bank to obtain a realistic estimate of the capital flows. This is especially true of flows not channeled through the financial system.

Table 2.7. Argentina: Summary of the Convertibility Plan, 1990-92

Period	Autonomous capital movement Total	Private (Millions of dollars)	Public	Country risk premium (%) (Annualized rate)	Projected devaluation (%) (Annualized rate)	Monetary base increments[*] (a) Originated in the ext. sector	(b) Originated in the dom. sector
1990:1	-195	-187	-8	36.25	2,263.0	n.a.	n.a.
1990:2	-68	-27	-41	18.19	163.7	n.a.	n.a.
1990:3	-1,276	-1,525	249	12.21	204.2	n.a.	n.a.
1990:4	429	1,273	-844	12.20	93.2	n.a.	n.a.
Total 1990	-1,110	-466	-644				
1991:1	-206	-163	-43	9.28	185.2		
1991:2	-25	-29	4	6.42	9.1	1,218	-402
1991:3	616	236	380	4.08	9.2	485	456
1991:4	-2,268	2,777[***]	-5,045	6.59	6.8	1,693	-428
Total 1991	-1,883	2,821	-4,704				
1992:1	2,991	3,097	-106	5.21	4.8	664	-454
1992:2	2,306	2,498	-192	5.31	6.9	856	388
1992:3	2,384	2,911	-527	6.26	5.3	-1,496	1,689
1992:4	n.a.	n.a.	n.a.	7.76	9.8		
Total 1992**	7,681	8,506	-825				

* Data in millions of pesos. The monetary base at March 21, 1991, was 4.8 billion pesos.
** First three quarters.
*** Public debt consolidation in the final quarter of 1991 not included. See note ** of Table 2.3.
n.a. Not available.
Source: Author's calculations based on Central Bank and FIEL data.

With respect to the relationship between macroeconomic stability and external flows, a number of factors are worth mentioning. Table 2.7 shows the quarterly flows of private capital.

The first conclusion to be drawn from the table is that the earliest signs of a turnaround in the outflow of capital appeared before the implementation of the Convertibility Plan. In the fourth quarter of 1990 there was a heavy inflow of private capital totaling $1.273 billion, but in the next two quarters there was an outflow due to the exchange shocks of early 1991. In the third quarter of that year, when confidence in the Convertibility Plan increased dramatically, a steady, upward trend appeared in the flow of private capital from abroad.

A second point to be kept in mind is the impressive surplus in the trade balance generated in 1990 as a result of the recession and the "overshooting" of the level of the real exchange rate during hyperinflation. This surplus was a key factor in the replenishment of international reserves, thus helping to reduce the likelihood of an external liquidity crisis in the short term. In fact, it was the replenishment of reserves in 1990 ($3.7 billion) that made implementation of the convertibility rule possible. Restoration of the level of reserves following the 1989 crisis was an essential condition for anchoring devaluation expectations and thereby achieving the significant reduction of nominal interest rates that has occurred since 1990.

The third important consideration is that in November 1990 the public sector began receiving enormous resources through privatization, which permitted greater ease in the short-term balancing of public accounts as well as strict compliance with the Convertibility Plan. Given the increase in reserves and the fact that the structural reform was providing enormous revenue for the government, the ability of the economy to resist exchange shocks was considerably strengthened.

Finally, particular emphasis should be given to the fact that during the period when private funds were flowing out of the country, the international interest rate declined steadily. The 30-day LIBOR fell from 6.7 percent in mid-1990 to less than 3 percent in late 1992. It follows, then, that because of the substitution effect, this reduction in the international rate worked in favor of the acquisition of domestic assets, especially physical assets that were being privatized since, *ceteris paribus,* a reduction in international interest rates—which are the ones used in calculating investment projects—makes capital deepening more profitable.

In these circumstances, what assessment can be made in light of past experiences? The basic lesson to be learned from the "tablita" and Austral experiences is that the "risk factors" comprise two basic elements: (1) the generation of trade deficits that render the future equilibrium of the current account untenable because they destroy confidence in the exchange rule and increase risk, causing an outflow of private capital, and (2) loss of control over the sources of monetary creation (whether as a result of financial crises or loss of fiscal control), because it gives markets both a signal of instability and the liquid resources needed to encourage a run on domestic currency.

Examined in light of these "risk factors," the current plan exhibits several weaknesses, despite the positive macroeconomic trend of the last two years. Some characteristics of the plan's continuing expansive phase are identical to difficulties encountered in our review of past experiences: increasing overvaluation of the currency, rising domestic consumption, and rapid trade deficit growth. Remember that while Argentina had a trade surplus of over $8 billion in 1990, it generated a deficit of approximately $3 billion in 1992. In other words, an $11 billion difference in two years at a time when the convergence of domestic and international inflation was as yet incomplete and, consequently, there was a risk that the domestic currency would continue appreciating. Nor can the second risk factor be entirely ignored. The sources of domestic credit expansion were eliminated for fiscal reasons, but only at a time when much of the revenue came from privatization. As far as the risk associated with financial instability is concerned, it must be remembered that the dollarization process has not been reversed and that it could cause distortions in the future. First, although some banks grant long-term credit (mortgages in particular) in dollars, the average maturity of about 80 percent of the "Argendollar" deposits backing such credit is under 90 days. In other words, there is a risk that the repayment period will be undermined. Second, of the entire loanable capacity generated by Argendollars, 77.5 percent was used to finance mortgage credit, loans to companies not involved in foreign trade and personal credits. Since this type of credit is used to purchase assets that are not marketable internationally, if there is a devaluation, it is possible that the debtors will find it difficult to honor their commitments. These credit operations, therefore, increase the vulnerability of banks to exchange risk.

It should be pointed out, finally, that the Convertibility Plan compares very favorably with earlier plans in terms of the consistency between devaluation expectations and the established exchange rule as well as in terms of the country risk (see Table 2.7). Both factors have made it possible, thus far, to achieve stabilization with surprisingly low nominal interest rates. In evaluating this phenomenon, however, it must be kept in mind that the interest rates and the external credit market are much more favorable than they were under the Austral Plan, for example, when the country risk and the domestic rates were much higher. A substantial deterioration in external conditions (affecting rates or access to credit) could lead to a higher risk premium and capital flight. In the outflow phase, the effectiveness of policy tools in deterring capital flight is greatly diminished. This, obviously, is also a third "exogenous" risk factor that must be taken into account.

Capital Flows and Investment

Aggregate Investment

The heavy inflow of private capital, the remonetization process with its accompanying expansion of domestic credit, and the new financial instruments created by the reforms of the financial market substantially eased the financing restraint that had afflicted the economy for so long. The most visible result was a rapid recovery in the level of business activity and private investment. GDP grew 8.5 percent in 1991 and, apparently, a little more slowly in 1992 (6 percent, according to official preliminary estimates).

Although current data on the composition of aggregate spending in the Argentine economy are not available,[19] the country's recent success in capital for-

---

[19] The published figures for the national accounts (in 1970 prices) only go as far as 1990. The interruption in the series is due to a revision of the accounts which, taking 1986 as a base, will reveal important changes in the prior estimates. There has been a considerable delay in publishing the new accounts, which explains the lack of data. Although the new figures for aggregate spending are unavailable at the time of this writing, double-digit aggregate data from the CIIU have been made available concerning GDP per sector and per industry for the revised accounts up to 1991.

mation can be evaluated by observing indirect indicators. Table 2.8 reveals the trend of domestic machinery and equipment output and capital goods imports, in real terms. Based on this information and on data concerning exports of the same type of goods, Aggregate I* was constructed, which is defined as the domestic output of capital goods, plus imports, minus machinery exports. This indicator is useful in evaluating the trend of capital formation in machinery and equipment since 1980. Next, the value of the construction sector output is added to this variable, giving the indicator I**.[20] Table 2.9 shows the trend of the various components of investment for the period in which information is available, according to the national accounts in 1970 pesos.

It can be seen, first of all, that the indicators I* and I**, expressed as a percentage of GDP, although at different levels, closely approximate the performance of gross fixed investment in the 1980s, according to the national accounts in 1970 prices.

Table 2.9 clearly indicates that the trend of the investment rate in the last decade was substantially affected by the debt crisis and the ensuing macroeconomic instability.[21] In the chaotic adjustment period following the collapse of the "tablita," capital goods expenditures fell off abruptly—7 percentage points of GDP between 1980 and 1982—and continued to decline, although not so precipitously, until the middle of the decade. Greater stability—in relative terms—and the expansion of business activity under the Austral Plan led to a slight recovery, which, however, did not last in the climate of growing macroeconomic uncertainty from 1987 on. The effects of hyperinflation are dramatic. Investment suddenly plummeted in the 1989-90 period, to such a level that net investment was negative. The aggregates presented in Table 2.8 duplicate the basic features of this trend, although the decline after 1982 is more moderate (I**, column 6), or nonexistent, as in the case of the machinery and equipment indicator (I*, column 4).

What do the indicators in Table 2.8 tell us about the recent trend of capital expenditures? First, between 1990 and 1991, as business activity was recovering from the years of hyperinflation and GDP returned to the 1988 level, a substantial upturn is noted in the domestic output of machinery and equipment (28 percent) and in capital goods imports, in real terms (98 percent).

Consequently, the I* variable for the machinery and equipment aggregate indicates an increase of nearly 37 percent. The gain of the indicator including construction (17 percent) was somewhat smaller, since the latter grew only 1.3 percent in 1991. It is also clear that, despite these high growth rates, the level of

---

[20] For the reasons already mentioned, information concerning the gross value of output of the various economic sectors is unavailable.

[21] Generally speaking, public and private investment share the same profile.

Table 2.8. Argentina: Investment Indicators, 1980-91
(Millions of 1986 pesos)

Period	Machinery and equipment GDP		Capital goods imports		Cap. goods exports	I* = (1) + (2) - (3)			(2)/(4) (percen-tage)	I** = I* + constr. sector GDP		
	(1)	1980=100	(2)	1980=100	(3)	(4)	1980=100	% of GDP	(5)	(6)	1980=100	% of GDP
1980	881.4	100.0	288.7	100.0	65.9	1,104.2	100.0	10.5	26.1	2,048.3	100.0	19.4
1981	711.5	80.7	225.3	78.1	47.4	889.4	80.6	8.9	25.3	1,764.1	86.1	17.7
1982	635.8	72.1	98.4	34.1	53.0	681.2	61.7	7.1	14.4	1,416.4	69.2	14.8
1983	685.2	77.7	77.5	26.8	27.5	735.2	66.6	7.4	10.5	1,432.9	70.0	14.5
1984	737.3	83.7	63.3	21.9	37.3	763.3	69.1	7.5	8.3	1,425.4	69.6	14.1
1985	666.0	75.6	62.4	21.6	48.6	679.8	61.6	7.1	9.2	1,327.5	64.8	13.9
1986	688.0	78.1	58.0	20.1	46.5	699.5	63.4	6.9	8.3	1,285.7	62.8	12.8
1987	724.6	82.2	90.2	31.2	37.5	777.3	70.4	7.5	11.6	1,498.2	73.1	14.4
1988	665.1	75.5	76.7	26.6	50.3	691.5	62.6	6.8	11.1	1,392.6	68.0	13.7
1989	520.8	59.1	62.5	21.6	53.7	529.6	48.0	5.6	11.8	1,109.2	54.2	11.7
1990	460.5	52.2	52.1	18.1	56.3	456.3	41.3	4.8	11.4	1,014.7	49.5	10.7
1991	589.5	66.9	103.4	35.8	69.0	623.9	56.5	6.1	16.6	1,189.7	58.1	11.6
Avg. 1982-88	686.0	77.8	75.2	26.1	43.0	718.3	65.0	7.2	10.5	1,396.9	68.2	14.0

Source: Author's calculations based on Central Bank data.

Table 2.9. Argentina: Gross Fixed Investment, 1975-90
(Percentage of GDP, at constant 1970 prices)

Period	GFI total	Investment in mach. & equip.	Investment in construction		
			Public	Private	Total
1975	20.24	7.62	3.54	6.60	10.14
1976	21.64	7.76	4.33	6.90	11.23
1977	24.60	10.26	5.63	6.07	11.70
1978	21.37	7.82	7.03	7.17	14.20
1979	22.01	8.97	6.20	7.44	13.64
1980	23.67	10.36	5.17	7.57	12.74
1981	19.38	7.73	4.85	7.28	12.13
1982	16.01	5.61	4.04	5.99	10.03
1983	14.25	5.57	3.54	5.07	8.61
1984	12.37	5.45	2.12	4.89	7.01
1985	10.35	4.44	1.95	4.65	6.60
1986	11.61	5.06	2.65	4.05	6.70
1987	13.25	5.81	2.99	4.44	7.43
1988	12.00	5.14	2.60	4.00	6.60
1989	8.87	3.99	1.67	3.21	4.88
1990	7.48	3.49	1.28	2.71	3.99

Source: Central Bank, National Accounts at 1970 prices.

the various indicators selected is still very low. Considering that the base for these growth rates is 1990, a year in which all the indicators (Table 2.8) reached their lowest values since 1980, this becomes obvious. In fact, the upturn in 1991 was not even sufficient for a return to the average levels of the 1982-88 period (the period following the debt crisis and preceding hyperinflation). At present, only external purchases of capital goods exceed this average. Nevertheless, although the level of capital assets imports is 37 percent above this average, such assets only represent 36 percent of the 1980 level (column 2 of Table 2.8).

The data available for 1992 do not permit reconstructing the same indicators for that year. Nevertheless, information concerning the performance of the industrial sector and the trend of imports reveal the persistence of the strong upward trend (see Table 10).

Calculations based on the figures in Table 2.8 show that if the output of machinery and equipment and imports of capital goods continue in their 1990-91 trajectory, and if construction grows at a rate similar to the one projected for GDP (approximately 6 percent), the estimated investment indicators will be slightly more than 7 percent of GDP in the case of I* and around 14 percent in the case of I**. This means that they will again reach levels comparable to their average values in the "post-crisis/pre-hyperinflation" period of 1982-88. Thus, the exter-

Table 2.10. Argentina: Imports by Types of Goods, 1977-92
(Millions of 1991 dollars)

Period	Totals	Capital goods	Consumer goods	Interm. goods	Auto- mobiles	Parts and accesor.	Fuel and lubrican.
1977	7,458	1,991	243	5,224		733	1,213
1978	6,365	1,820	352	4,193		671	783
1979	9,914	2,320	1,036	6,558		786	1,625
1980	13,663	3,101	2,407	8,155	310	1,703	1,393
1981	11,207	2,447	1,940	6,820	289	1,658	1,023
1982	6,218	1,107	460	4,651	31	1,036	750
1983	5,184	885	240	4,059	5	860	520
1984	5,151	722	281	4,148	0	910	529
1985	4,306	732	223	3,351	2	812	515
1986	5,492	714	333	4,445	13	1,070	487
1987	6,588	1,101	360	5,127	19	1,378	719
1988	5,794	922	246	4,626	13	1,146	538
1989	4,358	744	218	3,396	7	727	380
1990	4,072	619	312	3,141	12	692	317
1991	8,282	1,266	1,423	5,593	202	1,237	452
1992 *	6,458	1,222	1,677	3,558	277	1,207	155
Quarter							
1990:1	932	161	47	724			
1990:2	863	161	52	650			
1990:3	953	125	77	751			
1990:4	1,324	172	136	1,016			
1991:1	1,292	243	149	900			
1991:2	1,747	317	283	1,147			
1991:3	2,284	342	494	1,448			
1991:4	2,959	364	497	2,098			
1992:1	2,883	502	568	1,813			
1992:2	3,575	721	1109	1,745			
1992:3	4,231	n.a.	n.a.	n.a.			
1992:4	3,903	n.a.	n.a.	n.a.			

* First six months.
n.a. Not available
Source: Author's calculations, based on Central Bank and IMF data.

nal capital "boom" contributed to a return, in just a little over two years, to pre-hyperinflationary growth rates. In that period, the Argentine economy grew at an average annual rate of less than 1 percent, which was slower than the growth of the population.

What can be said about the flows of savings that financed these levels of investment? If the above estimates are correct—so that it can be assumed that these investment rates are close to the ones in the mid-1980s—and since the performance of the current account of the balance of payments indicates that the economy is financing the increase with a larger proportion of external savings, the complement must be a reduced flow of national savings. Therefore, a comparison of the pre-hyperinflationary period with the capital "boom" period reveals a definite shift in national savings, related to the inflow of capital and the resultant greater availability of savings from the rest of the world.[22]

Although the growth of consumption expenditure that would explain this apparent behavior of national savings cannot be substantiated because of the lack of national accounts data, it is nevertheless consistent with the evidence concerning the performance of industries engaged in the manufacture of consumer goods—durable goods especially—and with available information about the composition of imports.

The latter, in fact, have included external purchases of consumer goods—automobiles in particular—which increased more rapidly in the last two-year period (Table 2.10). This is due in part to the fact that this was the group most affected by quasi-tariff restrictions, which were abolished almost entirely in early 1991. Nevertheless, as a percentage of total external purchases, consumer goods purchases are currently at a level higher than the maximum reached prior to the "closing" of the economy in 1982. Purchases of capital goods, however, still have not returned to their percentage levels prior to this year.

By what means did the "boom" in external capital flows facilitate the increase in investment spending? First, it can be conjectured that the direct effect through foreign investment was initially minimal. Most of the funds invested by foreign companies were assimilated by the privatization process; i.e., purchases of existing assets. Similarly, most of the inflows recorded as "direct investment" in the balance of payments in the last two-year period actually consisted of debt conversion, which was also associated with the sale of public enterprises. Second, the financing of external purchases of capital goods seems to have played a very important role. It has already been mentioned that such purchases almost doubled, in real terms, between 1990 and 1991, and apparently they did the same in 1992. Given the fact that the percentage of financing of capital goods imports is about 60 percent (Machinea, 1992), and that the increase in such purchases accounts for more than 30 percent of the growth of the I* aggregate for investment in machinery and equipment, it can be concluded that a substantial proportion—between 15 and 20 percent—of the growth of this aggregate was financed with external commercial credit. In 1992 this

---

[22] Moreover, since public sector savings have increased, the obvious trend of national savings is explained primarily by the growth of private consumption.

proportion was larger still, due to the increased weight of capital goods imports in investments in machinery and equipment. Indications of this effect of external commercial credit on investment are also provided by the above-cited correlation between capital goods imports and the external liabilities of a large group of revenue-earning companies quoted on the stock exchange. With respect to the routing of external funds through the domestic financial market, although the capital flows obviously fueled the monetization process and the consequent rebuilding of credit, it is impossible to separate consumer credit from the credit used to finance investment.

Given the lack of information on this subject, and for the purposes of this paper, we decided to base our study directly on the analysis of corporate balance sheets. Indicators were constructed for this purpose, aggregating the balance sheets of the 59 largest companies on the stock exchange. Following are the most relevant conclusions of this analysis.

Capital Flows and Business Financing

As mentioned in the first section, following the introduction of the reforms, prices on the local stock market received a considerable boost. There was also a marked increase in the size of the market, evidenced both by a jump in the number of transactions and by a sharp rise in total market capitalization. This can be easily observed in Table 2.11.

This upward trend in the market obviously reflected the recovery of "animal spirits," produced by the surge in business activity and the reduction of credit rationing. Based on the net worth of the companies in the aggregate being considered and the trend of market capitalization, it is possible to construct a variable approximating the behavior of Tobin's Q index in the period.

As Figure 2.3 illustrates, the ratio of the "capital goods asking price" (market capitalization) to the "replacement price" (equity) increased substantially, coinciding with the reversal of capital flight.[23] This observation, moreover, is consistent with the fact that the international interest rate and the country risk declined sharply. Because both variables decreased, the discount rate applied to future profits dropped, and it therefore became more profitable to invest in domestic physical assets, which was reflected in the market by a rise in share prices. This, in principle, furnishes empirical evidence of a fact referred to above: the

---

[23] Interestingly, Figure 2.3 indicates an improvement in Tobin's Q index during the period of runaway inflation. This occurred because the replacement value fell even more rapidly than the market price of the shares. In fact, if real wages and overhead had remained as depressed as they were during the period of hyperinflation, interesting investment opportunities would have resulted. Obviously, the standard of living that would have ensued for most of the population had such investment opportunities been promoted would not seem advisable for a democratic society.

Table 2.11. Buenos Aires Stock Exchange, 1990-92:
Trend in the Volume of Transactions, Quotations, and Capitalization

Period	Total transactions of private secur. (In millions of dollars)	Quotations (MERVAL index)	Total capitalization (In millions of dollars)
1990			
I	56.6	89.7	2,592.6
II	58.0	99.0	3,240.6
III	67.2	110.1	3,360.4
IV	44.1	92.4	3,619.5
1991			
I	173.6	270.4	5,272.3
II	132.9	265.2	5,501.3
III	595.6	652.7	11,994.6
IV	660.5	800.6	18,644.0
1992			
I	1,070.8	747.8	25,745.6
II	2,146.6	660.4	25,523.5
III	1,251.8	419.8	18,210.1
IV	1,327.8	436.5	18,435.3

Source: Author's calculations.

substitution effect of the decline of international interest rates, which acted in favor of the acquisition of domestic physical assets, is just as important in explaining the repatriation of capital as the substitution effect that benefited domestic financial assets, which is demonstrated by the increase of deposits in Argendollars and other domestically negotiable instruments. Similarly, this increase in the profitability of physical investment also contributed to the government's success in selling state assets, as noted above.

In the aggregate of companies, what can be said regarding the flow of capital and the financing of activities? Table 2.12, which covers the period in which balance sheet information is available for all 59 companies, shows the trend of their indebtedness following the reversal of the capital flows.

The first obvious conclusion to be drawn from the table is that there is a causal relationship between the capital inflow, based on balance of payments information, and the substantial increase in the dollar liabilities of the top companies with direct access to the international market or to domestic sources of credit in dollars. Note that the first sizable increase in the level of foreign currency indebtedness occurs in the fourth quarter of 1990, when the private capital account of the balance of payments shows a large positive balance. Comparison

Figure 2.3. Argentina: "Q" Index
(1986=100)

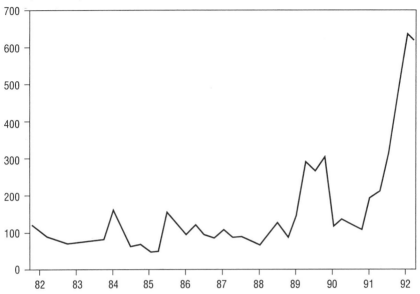

Note: The Q index is the corporations' market value divided by their total normal net worth.

of the level of dollar indebtedness at the end of the third quarter of 1990 with the level in the first quarter of 1992 reveals a jump of $888 million, or a 70 percent increase since the reversal in the flow of external funds.

Concurrently with this surge in liabilities, an increase is also observed in the holding of external assets. This increase, however, is much smaller. The differential rate of growth of assets and liabilities is such that, in the period in question, the companies' net financial exposure in dollars rose substantially (practically doubling, from $786 million to $1.466 billion). Actually, this result leads to another important finding: given the reduction of the country risk, companies that borrow in foreign currencies for productive projects had less need to "cover" the debtor positions in their portfolios. This is also demonstrated in Table 2.12 by the trend in the rate of coverage, given the devaluation risk. This rate falls from 38 percent to 32 percent between the third quarter of 1990 and the first quarter of 1992. Although for brevity's sake we did not show it in the table, for a better evaluation of these figures it should be pointed out that the sample chosen reveals similar results for the Austral period, while in the case of hyperinflation, the coverage of dollar liabilities with assets of the same denomination is over 50 percent.

Table 2.12. Argentina: Trend of Indebtedness among Companies Listed on the Stock Exchange, 1990-92

Period	Debt in dollars (1)	Assets in dollars (2)	External financing (%) (3)=(1)-(2)	Coverage index debt (4)=(2)/(1)	Total short-term debt (5)	Total long-term debt (6)	Leverage (7)
1990							
I	1,269.3	505.9	763.4	39.9	2,194.5	801.8	30.8
II	1,315.4	464.4	851.0	35.3	2,086.1	907.3	32.6
III	1,260.1	473.7	786.4	37.6	1,952.8	770.4	30.5
IV	1,703.5	583.3	1,120.2	34.2	2,176.7	668.0	32.7
1991							
I	1,733.3	618.9	1,114.4	35.7	2,253.8	695.9	33.6
II	1,766.4	653.3	1,113.1	37.0	2,525.6	743.4	38.7
III	1,880.4	621.8	1,258.6	33.1	2,641.7	765.9	40.2
IV	1,946.6	689.8	1,256.8	35.4	2,373.1	1,084.2	39.9
1992							
I	2,148.4	682.8	1,465.6	31.8	2,435.8	1,161.6	41.6

Columns (1), (2), and (3) are shown in current dollars; (5) and (6) are in constant June 1991 dollars, deflated by a mix of the wholesale and consumer price indices. For column (7), leverage is defined as the relationship between total indebtedness and equity.
Source: Author's calculations based on balance sheet information.

The trend in the level of short- and long-term debt reveals a correlation between the shift to credit in foreign currency and a prolongation in the maturity of the debt. While in the third quarter of 1990 short- and long-term debt respectively represented 65 percent and 26 percent of total liabilities, in the second quarter of 1992 short-term debt accounted for 62 percent of liabilities and long-term debt, 29 percent. A third finding, then, is that, in principle, the availability of external credit permits a better-organized balance sheet. Although the variations observed with respect to the increase in long-term debt vis-à-vis short-term debt are not pronounced, it is worth noting that this was a constant factor in other periods when the companies had easy access to the flows of external financing.[24] This was especially true in the period of scheduled exchange devaluations, from 1978 to 1981.

---

[24] See Damill and Fanelli (1988), which contains an analysis of the trend of investment decisions in the period between market deregulation and the Austral Plan. The information used is comparable because their analysis is also based on a sampling of the balance sheets of major companies, including those listed on the stock exchange.

The last finding we would like to discuss in this context is that in the period in question, the large flows of external financing seem to have given the companies more leverage. The figures in Table 2.12 bear this out. Until late 1990, the leverage ratio hovered around 30 percent. In an environment of tight credit and uncertainty, businesses did everything they could to minimize their financial exposure. Later, as credit rationing eased and the outlook for effective demand improved, the situation of financial instability that had prompted businesses to limit their financial exposure changed and the ratio began a steady climb, reaching more than 40 percent in the first quarter of 1992.

These findings lead to the conclusion that greater access to the international market and the increased availability of domestic credit in foreign currency had a positive impact on the financing structure of these companies by allowing them to lower their rates of coverage (which implies the freeing of resources for capital deepening projects) and to increase the possibilities of borrowing on longer terms, thus maintaining a higher leverage ratio without exposing themselves to excessive financial risk. Obviously, since a higher level of foreign currency indebtedness necessarily means greater vulnerability to unexpected devaluations, the above comments concerning the expansion of credit in Argendollars also apply here.

The Role of Direct Foreign Investment

The viability of the phenomena described above in connection with the sizable expansion of credit and the easing of the external restraint will require that financial market growth, remonetization, and the reversal of external flows continue. However, the reform processes are also effecting major changes in the characteristics of the investment process, many of which will most likely endure since they stem from permanent structural changes. The most significant effects in this regard will surely be seen in the sectoral distribution of investment and in the role of the various agents responsible for executing the most important revenue-producing projects. Of fundamental importance in this regard are the privatization process and the debt conversion programs, since they are bringing about profound changes in the role of the public sector and of foreign companies as investors.

To understand the current situation, it will be helpful to consider the changes that occurred in the role of foreign companies in the manufacturing sector in Argentina in the last decade. This is important because the macroeconomic framework of the 1980s,[25] characterized by the severe foreign exchange restraint and the stagnation of overall output, substantially changed the behavioral dynamics of foreign companies. Of particular relevance in explaining the reorientation of

---

[25] Our analysis of this question is based on Azpiazu (1992).

investment were the contraction of the domestic consumer market and the steep decline in investment, on the one hand, and the high level of the real exchange rate (especially in the latter half of the decade), on the other.

Although in the import substitution phase over 90 percent of all foreign investments were in manufacturing, in the 1980s only half were in that sector.[26] The sectors that benefited from this change were oil and gas, finance and, to a lesser extent, services. In industry, however, the sectors that received a large percentage of investment were those involved in the processing of natural resources and the production of foodstuffs for export.

The basic sources of funds for these investments were the plowing back of profits and participation in debt restructuring programs. As mentioned above in analyzing the balance of payments, foreign investment in the 1980s represented one of the most important sources of foreign exchange. In that period, in terms of the relationship between the repatriation of profits and the reinvestment thereof, foreign companies effected a positive net transfer: they invested $1.40 for every dollar remitted. Among the most important debt restructuring programs were the program for the conversion of debt with exchange rate guarantees, in which 183 companies restructured $183 million between 1985 and 1987, and the program for the redemption of state external bonds and notes, whereby $1.2 billion was restructured in 1987.[27] To a large extent, the funds obtained through these restructuring programs—prior to the initiation of the privatization process—were used to finance projects in sectors that produced foods and processed raw materials for export.

The new orientation of industrial strategy toward the export sectors resulted in a steady rise in industrial exports in the late 1980s. While the industrial sector in 1980 only exported between 6 and 7 percent of what it produced, in 1990 it exported 20 percent, equaling the export ratio of the agricultural sector. At first,

---

[26] The importance of foreign capital, particularly in the "second stage" of the substitution process (i.e., since the late fifties) cannot be overstated: In the mid-seventies, multinational companies produced 23 percent of the nondurable industrial goods, 30 percent of the intermediate goods, 39 percent of the durable goods, and 34 percent of the capital goods (Azpiazu, 1992). From the mid-1970s on, and especially after the debt crisis, this type of involvement became increasingly problematic since, among other things, the net effect of these industries on the balance of payments was negative and extreme.

[27] The relatively minor initial impact of the debt conversion programs was due in part to the requirement that one additional dollar be received for every dollar of restructured debt, established by the Argentine government as a means of ensuring a higher level of investment and the inflow of additional foreign exchange through this type of operation, as requested by the commercial creditor banks. No doubt, Argentina's poor international standing prior to 1987 was a decisive factor in its acceptance of the banks' requirements. In fact, the debt conversion system was liberalized that year. The additional funds requirement was reduced to a minimum of three dollars for every seven dollars of retired debt (Bouzas and Keifman, 1988).

the increase in industrial exports was dominated by the anticyclical exports of the processing industries, which exceeded local demand, but near the end of the decade the importance of industries with real or potential competitive advantages for the export of natural resources (the cellulose-paper complex, meat packing, and petrochemicals) increased dramatically. Transnational companies played an important role in this process. Between 1984 and 1988, for example, the external sales of foreign companies as a whole increased 50 percent, from $1.4 to $2.2 billion.[28]

We mention this trend among foreign companies in the late 1980s because it is possible that one of the most undesirable consequences of restructuring programs which involve the privatization of public service enterprises is precisely that of slowing the process of reorienting the economy towards exports, especially in the industrial sector.

Two effects stand out. First, most of the debt conversion programs based on privatization have targeted the nontradable goods sectors. Except for privatizations in the petroleum and petrochemical sector, all of the other enterprises already sold by the government or in the process of being privatized are basically providers of nonmarketable public services. Consequently, a very sizable percentage of the inflows of external capital in 1990 went to the service sectors. Moreover, the creation of highly attractive investment opportunities in sectors such as the telephone and transportation sectors causes some form of "crowding out" of the tradable goods sectors.[29] This effect is clearly demonstrated by analyzing the investor groups that participated in the privatization process. The largest majority by far consists of the same groups that invested in the fastest growing export sectors, such as iron and steel, in the mid-1980s.

The second effect concerns the duration of the privatization process. Because most of the privatizations have occurred within a very brief period, external capital is flowing into the country at a rate that will obviously be difficult to maintain in the future. One result of this massive and sudden inflow of capital has been a persistent lag in the real exchange rate. In addition to acting as a strong deterrent to industrial exports at present, this trend in the exchange rate is giving erroneous signals about the long term, because once the privatization process has ended, the real exchange rate will probably tend to depreciate.

---

[28] Transnationals in the iron and steel, fishing, and basic chemistry sectors were the most active. Iron and steel sales, for example, increased 2.5 times in four years. The oil and meat packing industries also played an important role. It must also be kept in mind that the contribution of transnational companies to exports is structurally important. Of the 18 companies that export more than $100 million a year, 10 are foreign-owned. Of the nine companies that export more than this amount, four are owned by nonresidents.

[29] The problem here is not the "exhaustion of investment opportunities" but of investment decisions. The agents best positioned to develop investment projects in the tradable sectors find better opportunities in the service sectors from which the government is withdrawing.

The Role of Public Investment and Privatization

One of the structural features that will no doubt characterize the future trend of capital formation will be the stagnation of public investment at the current low levels of 1 to 3 percent of GDP. Until the start of this decade, the low level of public investment was caused by the liquidity squeeze and the government's solvency problems in the wake of the debt crisis. When the privatization process comes to an end, this situation will continue, regardless of whether the public sector's liquidity position improves. Public investment will be structurally lower because the state is divesting itself of all public enterprises. Moreover, at present, a great deal of public investment is in large energy-producing enterprises that were founded years ago but which must now be sold. Once this process is completed, a further depressive effect on government investment will occur.

A 1992 FIEL study projecting infrastructure investment between 1992 and the year 2000 gives a clear picture of what will happen in the future in terms of public versus private investment in a field that has traditionally received a large share of the funds invested by the government. It is estimated that 32.932 billion pesos will be invested in infrastructure between 1992 and 2000. Adding the highway investments of the provinces, this figure rises to 35.444 billion pesos. Of this total, 26.424 billion pesos must come from the private sector and 9.02 billion pesos from the public sector. The estimated annual average, 3.66 billion pesos, is larger than the mean annual investment in the 1980s (3.385 billion pesos) but close to the average for the 1970s. In other words, no qualitative increase due to the privatization process is foreseen, and the possibility of expanding the infrastructure will depend entirely on a better return on investment.

Expressed as a percentage of GDP, the results are far from impressive. Although infrastructure investment totaled 3 percent of GDP in the 1970s and 2.6 percent in the 1980s, it is expected to fall to 2.3 percent in the 1992-2000 period. Moreover, the projected trend is downward. Investment climbs to 3.2 percent in 1993 and then falls off, mostly because the investment programs of the privatized gas, telephone, and electric companies call for a larger level of initial investment.

One final, important point concerns financing. It must be remembered that a great many public sector investment projects rely on financing from international credit organizations to which, in theory, private companies have little access. This means that in the future, market financing mechanisms, both domestic and external, must function as a relatively stable source of investment funds; otherwise, the private sector will be unable to fulfill its new role with regard to capital formation. Obviously, this also increases the importance of direct investment in the future. It should be noted, however, that since profit margins are larger for the private companies—given that the new, post-privatization rates are higher than those charged by the state companies—the ability of these companies to generate their own financing will probably be much greater.

Macroeconomic Restrictions, Capital Flows, and Investment

In view of the obligations assumed by Argentina in conjunction with the IMF Extended Facilities Loan, it is possible to predict, based on sectoral surplus and deficit projections, what the future level of domestic investment will be if the economy grows more or less in accordance with the forecasts of the authorities. It must be remembered in this regard that even after the Brady Plan and the restructuring programs, the burden of debt on both the external and the public sector is still very heavy and, as indicated above, the national savings rate does not seem to be rebounding.[30] In these circumstances, there is still a high degree of complementarity between investment and the availability of foreign savings. This adds a note of pessimism since the economy is currently absorbing enormous amounts of external credit while the rate of investment, despite its recovery, remains at historically low levels. In negotiating the Brady Plan and the IMF Extended Facilities Loan, Argentina sought to replace the unwritten rule it had been following with respect to the servicing of its debt with a more coherent organization of its external accounts.[31] Consequently, by taking a look at the agreements signed regarding the generation of deficits and surpluses by each sector, it is possible to project the country's potential level of investment.

The basic idea of the program worked out with the Fund under the Brady Plan is that the country will generate a primary public sector surplus in the next three years, large enough to make full interest and principal payments on its total debt, including all amounts owed under the Brady Plan and in connection with the international organizations, Bonexes, etc. For this reason, in the 1992-94 period, the public sector must maintain a primary surplus averaging $3.3 billion per annum. The goals have been met so far, but only by using the proceeds from privatization. What this means, theoretically, is that it will be far more difficult to achieve these goals in 1993 when the revenue from privatization will be much smaller.[32]

The second important consideration is that the growth of imports caused a serious trade deficit in 1992.[33] Because of this, and regardless of whether the

---

[30] See the appendix to this chapter for a review of the features of the agreement Argentina signed in the context of the Brady Plan.

[31] In the adjustment phase following the debt crisis, the unwritten rule that Argentina followed regarding its international obligations was that the country use all of its trade surplus to honor its external commitments. Since the latter were overwhelming, the trade surpluses generated kept domestic investment at a depressed level.

[32] It should be mentioned here that the goals for the public sector are being revised upward due to pressure from the IMF to increase the level of fiscal discipline. The goals for 1993 were raised. The required operating surplus went from $3.4 billion to $4.4 billion.

[33] According to the latest estimates, the trade deficit for the entire year will be in the neighborhood of $3 billion.

public sector generates the required surplus, dollars will be needed to pay interest. If there is no trade surplus and the international organizations have already disbursed a sizable percentage of the financing they can provide under the Brady Plan, the only possible source of dollars is the inflow of private capital. This point was taken into consideration in the program developed with the Fund. It is estimated that the country's financing needs will require a net inflow of private capital in the next three years of between $3.1 billion and $3.9 billion per year. In light of what occurred in 1992 and the projections for 1993, however, these estimates are clearly optimistic. In the first three quarters of 1992 alone the amount needed to finance the current account was $5.719 billion. Under the Convertibility Plan—according to which the only source of monetary expansion permitted is the accumulation of reserves—the amount needed to finance the current account must be increased by the additional reserves necessary to at least maintain the ratio between nominal GDP and the money supply. It is estimated that a minimum of $1 billion will be needed for this purpose.

Apart from the accuracy of the estimates, however, the central issue is that attainment of the IMF and Brady Plan goals will depend essentially on the repatriation of capital and the availability of external credit. Obviously, if no capital is repatriated and no credit is granted, the only way of obtaining the necessary foreign exchange will be to induce a deep recession which, by curbing imports, will free up the dollars needed to pay the interest on external debt. The consequences of this alternative in terms of growth require no explanation.

If the government achieves its financial objectives and the desired inflow of private capital occurs, what level of investment will be compatible with the predetermined goals? Assuming that the estimates in the government's Letter of Intent to the IMF are correct and that the projections are accurate, the rate of national savings in 1994 will be 14.8 percent of GDP (11.4 percent contributed by the private sector and 3.4 percent by the government), and external savings will be 2.6 percent. Consequently, the level of investment will be 17.4 percent, of which 13.8 percent will be made by the private sector and the rest by the government. These goals, although modest, may nevertheless be deemed ambitious, especially since the figures in the text of the agreement indicate that in 1991 public sector savings decreased one percentage point of GDP, the rate of national savings was 9.4 percent, and investment represented only 11.7 percent of GDP (2 percent in the public sector and the rest in the private sector).[34] In conclusion, these figures merely illustrate that even though a positive change occurred in the direction of the capital flows and interest rates fell substantially, the burden of external interest and the restriction of national savings remain as serious barriers to the recovery of a sustained rate of growth.

---

[34] Unfortunately, as mentioned above, the lack of national accounts data compels us to work with the "official estimates" included in the text of the agreement.

Bibliography

Arthur Anderson & Co. 1992. Mercado de capitales argentino. Relevamiento de opinión de 250 empresas. Buenos Aires. Mimeo.

Azpiazu, D. 1992. Las empresas transnacionales en una economía en transición: la experienca argentina de los años 80. ECLAC: Buenos Aires. Mimeo.

Banco Central de la República Argentina. *Memoria Anual*, various issues. Buenos Aires.

Bezchinsky, G. 1991. *Importación de bienes de capital. La experiencia argentina en la década de los 80.* Working Document No. 41. ECLAC: Buenos Aires.

Bouzas, R., and S. Keifman. 1988. Las negociaciones externas de la Argentina en el período 1982-1987. In *Entre la Heterodoxia y el Ajuste,* ed. R. Bouzas. Buenos Aires: GEL.

Chisari, O., J.M. Fanelli, R. Frenkel, *et al.* 1992. *Ahorro público y recuperación del crecimiento en la Argentina.* Working Paper No. 110. Washington, D.C.: Inter-American Development Bank.

Damill, M., J.M. Fanelli, R. Frenkel, *et al.* 1989. *Déficit fiscal, deuda externa y desequilibrio financiero.* Buenos Aires: Editorial Tesis.

————, and J.M. Fanelli. 1988. *Decisiones de cartera y transferencias de riqueza en un período de inestabilidad macroeconómica.* Documento CEDES/12. Buenos Aires.

Fanelli, J.M., and R. Frenkel. 1987a. El plan Austral un año y medio después. *El Trimestre Económico*, Special Issue. Mexico City.

FIEL. 1989. *El control de cambios en la Argentina.* Buenos Aires: Eds. Manantial.

————. 1992. *Capital de infraestructura en la Argentina. Gestión pública, privatización y productividad.* Buenos Aires.

Frenkel, R. 1983. Mercado financiero, expectativas cambiarias y movimientos de capitales. *El Trimestre Económico.* No. 100. Mexico City.

————, and M. Damill. 1987. De la apertura a la crisis financiera. Un análisis de la experiencia argentina de 1977-82. In *Ensayos Económicos,* No. 37. Buenos Aires.

Fuchs, M. 1990. Los programas de capitalización de la deuda externa argentina. Buenos Aires: ECLAC. Mimeo.

Gerchunoff, P., ed. 1992. *Las privatizaciones en la Argentina. Primera Etapa.* Buenos Aires: Instituto Torcuato Di Tella.

Machinea, J.L., and J. Sommer. 1990. *El manejo de la deuda externa en condiciones de crisis de balanza de pagos: la moratoria 1988-89.* Documento CEDES/59. Buenos Aires: CEDES.

―――. 1992. Las importaciones y el financiamiento del balance de pagos. *Nota No. 24.* Instituto para el Desarrollo Industrial. Buenos Aires: Fundación UIA.

APPENDIX

The structure of Argentina's external debt, by type of creditor as of December 31, 1991, was (in billions of dollars):

Private banks	$31.000
IMF	2.544
World Bank and IDB	5.266
Paris Club	6.866
Non-Brady banks	1.400
Bonex and other dollarized securities	9.200
Others	1.924
Total	$58.200

Of this total, only the amount owed to private banks was in arrears. An agreement had been reached with the Paris Club in September 1991; there were no arrears with official credit institutions (IDB, IMF, and World Bank); and Bonexes and other minor bonds had been amortized and serviced punctually. Since the objective of the Brady Plan is to restructure the maturity dates of the principal and to regularize arrears in interest payments to commercial banks, as soon as the agreements are signed, the country's international obligations will be completely in order. Of the $31 billion owed commercial banks, $23 billion is principal and $8 billion is arrears in interest payments. The agreement provides for different treatment of arrears and principal. The latter is fully refinanced, while the arrears are not. In every instance of a country's accession to the Brady initiative, the rule has been that the country paid approximately 15 percent of the arrears in cash as a sign of good faith in the negotiations and also that the arrears were refinanced on less favorable terms than the principal. This was generally true in Argentina's case as well: the principal (less the 35 percent forgiven) was refinanced at 30 years, part of the overdue interest was paid ($1.21 billion) and the remaining arrears ($8 billion) were refinanced at 12 years (no forgiveness) instead of 30 years (with forgiveness) like the principal. In addition, the monthly interest payment was raised from $60 million to $70 million until the agreement is signed in December, and an additional $300 million were paid in bonds. In short, the most important features of the refinancing are:

For the interest arrears of $8 billion:

Cash payments: $400 million at the conclusion of the bank-by-bank negotiations (October to December 1992). The monthly payment from April through December of this year was raised from $60 million to $70 million. The $180 million paid between December and March are counted (for a grand total of $810 million). In all, Argentina will pay $1.21 billion in cash in 1992.

Payment by special bond: Argentina subscribed a 10-year bond totally guaranteed by U.S. government zero-coupon bonds, the market value of which was calculated at $300 million at the time of issue. This bond represents a little less than 4 percent of the arrears.

Twelve-year bond: For the balance of the interest in arrears, a bond was issued by the

Argentine government, with no guarantee and a floating rate based on the LIBOR plus 13/16. The bond is for 12 years with a three-year grace period. These bonds are amortized in 19 six-month installments. For the first through the seventh payment, the amortization rate is 1 percent; for the eighth, 5 percent; and for the ninth through the nineteenth, 8 percent.

For the debt principal of $23 billion:

From late January 1992 until the ending date of the agreement (when each bank selects options for refinancing the principal in Par Bonds or Discount Bonds, estimated to be between October and December of this year), the rate applicable to the principal sum of $23 billion is 4 percent per annum.

Par Bonds: Issued for 100 percent of the principal, with an increasing rate: 4 percent in the first year, 4.25 percent in year two, 5 percent in year three, 5.25 percent in year four, 5.5 percent in year five, 5.75 percent in year six, and fixed at 6 percent per annum in years seven through 30. The Par Bonds have a maturity of 30 years with only one amortization payment at the end of the 30 years. Backed by U.S. Treasury zero-coupon bonds, with guaranteed interest payments during the first 12 months.

Discount Bonds: Subscribed for 65 percent of the principal, with 35 percent of the principal forgiven. Floating rate, based on the LIBOR plus 13/16 (now 5.25 percent per annum). Thirty years with only one amortization payment at the end of the 30 years, with the same guarantees as Par Bonds.

Statistical Annex Table 2.1. Argentina: Annual Balance of Payment Data
(In millions of dollars)

Years	1977	1978	1979	1980	1981	1982	1983	1984	1985	1986	1987	1988	1989	1990	1991	1992*
I. Current account	1290	1833	-537	-4767.8	-4714	-2357.7	-2461	-2391	-953	-2859	-4238	-1572	-1292	1789	-2803	-5719
Goods	1490	2566	1109	-2519	-287	2287	3331	3523	4582	2128	540	3810	5374	8275	3704	-1552
Exports	5652	6400	7810	8021	9143	7624	7836	8107	8396	6852	6360	9134	9573	12354	11978	9135
Imports	-4162	-3834	-6700	-10540	-9430	-5337	-4505	-4584	-3814	-4724	-5820	-5324	-4199	-4079	-8274	-10687
Real services	347	-100	-761	-740	-705	43	-400	-205	-231	-573	-285	-255	-252	-354	-902	-840
Financial services	-579	-681	-920	-1531.4	-3700	-4719	-5408	-5712	-5304	-4416	-4485	-5127	-6422	-6203	-5634	-3302
Profits and dividends	-208	-304	-416	-546	-735	-316	-425	-439	-425	-482	-558	-660	-664	-716	-805	-499
Interest paid	-499	-720	-1185	-2190	-3850	-4926	-5423	-5537	-5132	-4291	-4145	-4678	-6023	-5767	-5208	-3130
Interest collected	128	343	681	1204.6	885	533	440	264	253	357	218	211	265	280	379	327
Transfers	31	48	35	23	-22	31	16	3		2	-8		8	71	29	-25
II. Capital account	1189	1366.2	4914.5	2253.3	1155	-3808	-111	647	397	784	138	191	-5593	-1110	-1883	7681
Privatizations														1703	1974	1293
Direct investment	52.1	295	235	739.2	927	257	183	269	919	574	-19	1147	1028	333	465	1153
Export financing	222.4	8	840	-38	-1464	-504	260	511	140	-56	111	879	-717	1411	70	-1397
Import financing	-303.1	-405.8	-67.7	-48	-1922	-2216	-671	-11	-952	-483	-603	-1572	-1511	-960	1688	3823
Trade credit and deposit facility									-58	-203	-117	-335	-119	-31	1	
Loans from international organizations	28.4	99.1	59.5	82	182	114	113	123	182	394	733	386	414	489	312	-165
Government loans and securities	-23.4	525	525	934	2513	367	2136	2087	974	127	-195	-356	-686	-1098	335	-513
Loan to private companies	392.8	513.9	3543.3	3886.3	3112.3	-521.3	-1830.6	-2674.3	-1733	-459	-24	-228	111	92	345	461
Loan to public companies	968.4	824.9	691.2	1980.7	1928.7	-272.3	154.3	-5.1	193	46	412	103	40	-4	105	-147
Foreign currency deposit amortization									-219	-43	-71	-80				

(continues)

83

Statistical Annex Table 2.1. Argentina: Annual Balance of Payment Data (Cont.)

(In millions of dollars)

Arrears written off without offsetting entry									590							
Others [1,2]	-148.6	-493.9	-911.8	-5282.9	-4122	-1032.4	-455.7	347.4	361	887	-89	247	-4153	-3045	-7178	3173
III. Net international reserves variance	2479	3199.8	4377	-2515	-3559	-6166	-2572	-1744	-556	-2075	-4100	-1381	-6885	679	-4686	1962
IV. Balance of payments financing	-2479	-3199.8	-4377	2515	3559	6166	2572	1744	556	2075	4100	1381	6885	-679	4686	-1962
Reserve assets (increase-)[3]	-2226	-1998.4	-4442	2796	3458	755	-1445	-207	-1871	563	1111	-1785	1559	-2751	-2261	-3135
Net LAIA					63	-40	-239	108	-146	-49	163	-176			381	854
Government securities															-848	98
BONEX placement [4]	8.7				1583	492	387		108	178	476	62	3688	403	594	216
BONEX amortization		-94.4	-140	-142.2	-79				-325	-310	-377	-362	-412	-516	-534	-425
IMF loans						1178			1007	547	1253	541	233	510	471	1029
IMF amortization	-41.8	-414.2						-33		-402	-639	-523	-718	-695	-987	-1001
Paris Club refinancing									1714	1046	571	278	1646	908	1122	832
Paris Club amortization									-97	-149	-187	-127	-244	-536	-425	-603
Others BCRA	-226.4	-856.8							-706	71	157	488	-1734	-799	5484	-420
Swap rate variation adjustments	9.3	166	131.9	-212.9	-363	-80	1254	27	401	367	-142		-5	-97	167	68
Swaps					484	896	-152		-208	-91	-68	-94	-19	-17	-115	-68
Bank financing							1230	600	3096	1207	1244	454		-114		
Arrears					2540	512	682	940	-2445	-1174	39	2344	2927	1912	1788	618
Others[2]	-2.8	-2	73.1	74.1			-428	-78	28	271	499	281	-36	1113	-151	-25

* Figures for the first three quarters.

[1] Includes errors and omissions.

[2] In 1991 this item includes operations to consolidate public debt with the issue of Treasury Bonds, Consolidation Bonds, and Supplier Bonds. In the fourth quarter of 1991 the total issued was $5.457 billion. In the first three quarters of 1992, $325 million were withdrawn.

[3] In 1989 and 1990 includes net LAIA.

[4] The high level of Foreign Bond placement in 1989 is due to the implementation of the BONEX plan.

Source: Author's calculations based on Central Bank data.

Statistical Annex Table 2.2. Argentina: Quarterly Balance of Payments Data, 1985-92

(In millions of dollars)

	1985 I	1985 II	1985 III	1985 IV	1985 TOTAL	1986 I	1986 II	1986 III	1986 IV	1986 TOTAL	1987 I	1987 II	1987 III	1987 IV	1987 TOTAL
I. Current account	-780	187	110	-470	-953	-803	-456	-508	-1092	-2859	-1021	-798	-1098	-1321	-4238
Goods	826	1643	1331	782	4582	592	814	541	181	2128	241	362	-15	-48	540
Exports	1803	2570	2310	1713	8396	1513	1968	1897	1474	6852	1441	1741	1618	1560	6360
Imports	-977	-927	-979	-931	-3814	-921	-1154	-1356	-1293	-4724	-1200	-1379	-1633	-1608	-5820
Real services	-163	-29	-39	-231	-248	-73	-118	-134	-573	-217	-37	-31	-285	-169	32
Financial services	-1441	-1428	-1221	-1214	-5304	-1147	-1196	-934	-1139	-4416	-1042	-1157	-1044	-1242	-4485
Profits and dividends	-115	-150	-80	-80	-425	-125	-159	-100	-98	-482	-145	-180	-115	-118	-558
Interest paid	-1400	-1317	-1215	-1200	-5132	-1122	-1116	-940	-1113	-4291	-976	-1036	-977	-1156	-4145
Interest collected	74	39	74	66	253	100	79	106	72	357	79	59	48	32	218
Transfers	-2	1	1	2	3	2	-3	-3	-2	-8	-1	2	2	2	3
II. Capital account	-108	92	404	9	397	165	437	128	54	784	560	-605	-172	355	138
Privatizations	169	1534	1703	127	333	906	608	1974	963	197	133	1293			
Direct investment	153	172	305	289	919	153	184	108	129	574	160	-416	122	115	-19
Export financing	-32	403	-255	24	140	54	256	-442	76	-56	539	-281	-456	309	111
Import financing	-304	-339	-83	-226	-952	-198	-61	31	-255	-483	-283	-220	150	-250	-603
Trade credit and deposit facility	-58	-58	-99	-26	-35	-43	-203	-24	-62	-9	-22	-117	-22	-126	-130
Loans from international organizations	33	23	43	83	182	44	35	213	102	394	95	37	329	272	733
Government loans and securities	-40	-118	1	1131	974	150	-22	54	-55	127	-17	-26	-49	-103	-195
Loan to private companies	-54	-33	-224	-1422	-1733	-214	-116	-98	-31	-459	-32	19	-16	5	-24
Loan to public companies	48	48	49	48	193	-19	54	-10	21	46	7	396	26	-17	412
Foreign currency dep. amortization	-80	-139	-219	-35	-3	-2	-3	-43	-56	-11	7	-11	-71	-26	7
Arrears written off without offsetting entry	581	9	590												
Others[1,2]	88	-64	67	270	361	329	136	309	113	887	171	-41	-276	57	-89
III. Net international reserves variance	-888	279	514	-461	-556	-638	-19	-380	-1038	-2075	-461	-1403	-1270	-966	-4100
IV. Balance of payments financing	888	-279	-514	461	556	638	19	380	1038	2075	461	1403	1270	966	4100
Reserve assets (increase)[3]	421	-876	-1205	-211	-1871	565	-1505	388	1115	563	84	1155	432	-560	1111
Net LAIA	-85	120	-125	-56	-146	-27	70	-5	-87	-49	50	17	24	72	163
Government securities	-621	-109	-167	49	-848	-49	150	-3	98						
BONEX placement[4]	44	42	7	15	108	31	11	31	105	178	382	36	50	8	476
BONEX amortization	-293	-32	-325	-271	-39	-310	-283	-22	-72	-377	-286	-16	-1	-59	-362
IMF loans	513	494	1007	270	277	547	1027	226	1253	541	541	233	233	0	243
IMF amortization	-104	-144	-154	-402	-151	-167	-152	-169	-639	-303	-83	-50	-87	-523	-160
Paris Club refinancing	1228	162	162	162	1714	135	135	135	641	1046	120	174	120	157	571
Paris Club amortization	-85	-12	-97	-43	-78	-28	-149	-52	-29	-58	-48	-187	-30	-79	-18
Others BCRA	-549	442	-1211	612	-706	-25	-19	76	39	71	593	66	-530	28	157
Swap rate variation adjustments	251	150	401	467	-100	367	-142	-142	-15	-10	-68	19	-5	-6	3
Swaps	-49	-159	-208	-37	-8	-45	-1	-91	-67	-1	454	-39	-55	-94	-13
Bank financing	2295	801	3096	1207	1207	1244	1244	542	-40	-48	-216	-23	-55	-36	-114
Arrears	-621	-204	-928	-692	-2445	-3	-529	13	-655	-1174	143	121	22	112	39
Others[2]	-21	67	-19	1	28	43	56	109	63	271	-32	52	336	-32	499

(continues)

Statistical Annex Table 2.2. Argentina: Quarterly Balance of Payment Data (Cont.)
(In millions of dollars)

	1988 I	1988 II	1988 III	1988 IV	1988 TOTAL	1989 I	1989 II	1989 III	1989 IV	1989 TOTAL	1990 I	1990 II	1990 III	1990 IV	1990 TOTAL
I. Current account	-838	-415	24	-343	-1572	-843	-64	266	-651	-1292	252	564	926	47	1789
Goods	548	897	1215	1150	3810	949	1512	1788	1125	5374	1855	2351	2479	1590	8275
Exports	1713	2304	2673	2444	9134	2117	2546	2813	2097	9573	2771	3197	3431	2955	12354
Imports	-1165	-1407	-1458	-1294	-5324	-1168	-1034	-1025	-972	-4199	-916	-846	-952	-1365	-4079
Real services	-20	-98	-255	-413	103	72	-14	-252	-159	20	-43	-172	-354	-493	-80
Financial services	-1216	-1344	-1172	-1395	-5127	-1381	-1681	-1597	-1763	-6422	-1451	-1824	-1526	-1402	-6203
Profits and dividends	-170	-216	-137	-137	-660	-169	-211	-139	-145	-664	-134	-294	-120	-168	-716
Interest paid	-1084	-1180	-1097	-1317	-4678	-1305	-1519	-1510	-1689	-6023	-1380	-1579	-1505	-1303	-5767
Interest collected	38	52	62	59	211	93	49	52	71	265	63	49	99	69	280
Transfers	1	8	7	17	16	31	71	20	3	6	29	-9	-7	-9	-25
II. Capital account	-164	-22	560	-183	191	-715	-1525	471	-3824	-5593	-195	-68	-1276	429	-1110
Privatizations															
Direct investment	252	285	284	326	1147	324	327	192	185	1028	69	126	48	90	333
Export financing	-12	294	469	128	879	68	-823	42	-4	-717	854	589	-266	234	1411
Import financing	-725	-333	-75	-439	-1572	-406	-397	-176	-532	-1511	-237	-375	-338	-10	-960
Trade credit and deposit facility	-57	-335	-56	-25	-28	-10	-119	-12	-5	-9	-5	-31	2	4	-5
Loans from international organizations	85	125	34	142	386	165	157	15	77	414	44	62	293	90	489
Government loans and securities	-28	-95	-79	-154	-356	-185	-226	-103	-172	-686	-43	-82	-83	-890	-1098
Loan to private companies	-92	-30	-57	-49	-228	-10	-9	120	10	111	37	10	16	29	92
Loan to public companies	72	13	2	16	103	84	-18	16	-42	40	3	-16	48	-39	-4
Foreign currency dep. amortization															
Arrears written off without offsetting entry															
Others[1][2]	-26	-35	-80	16	103										
III. Net international reserves variance	332	-162	138	-61	247	-699	-1558	737	-4475	-6885	-910	-377	-1154	-604	-3045
IV. Balance of payments financing	-1002	-437	584	-526	-1381	1558	1589	-737	4475	6885	57	496	-350	476	679
Reserve assets (increase-)[3]	1002	437	-584	526	1381	1669	591	-1357	656	1559	88	-1351	-228	-1260	-2751
Net LAIA	149	-418	-1250	-266	-1785	n.a.	n.a.	n.a.	n.a.	n.a.	-57	-496	350	-476	-679
Government securities	-146	59	-52	-37	-176						n.a.	n.a.	n.a.	n.a.	n.a.
BONEX placement[4]	7	23	30	2	62	52	231	16	3389	3688	28	49	326	403	585
BONEX amortization	-323	-24	-4	-61	-412	-335	-17	-80	-84	-516	-354	-16	-64	-100	-534
IMF loans	0	267	510	-516	261	277	471	496	533	1029	-218	-269	-223	-987	-284
IMF amortization	-165	-209	-184	-718	-1276	-124	-162	-173	-695	-277	908	261	181	379	301
Paris Club refinancing	120	158		278		1646	279	198	232	199	-193	-193	-39	-425	-261
Paris Club amortization	-127	-108	-108	-28	-244	-188	-85	-172	-91	-536	-301	-172	-62	-264	
Others BCRA	223	-155	174	246	488	-210	-763	-140	-621	-1734	68			-799	-799
Swap rate variation adjustments	-58	-36	-97	-24	-215	112	-29	167	4	60					
Swaps	-6	-19	-17	-17	-59	-12	-81	-115	-68	-68					
Bank financing															
Arrears	40	824	626	854	2344	653	1742	924	-392	2927	843	847	867	-645	1912
Others[2]	115	114	58	-6	281	140	-176	-36	-178	-11	1302	1113	26	-144	-33

	1991					1992			
	I	II	III	IV	TOTAL	I	II	III	TOTAL*
I. Current account	-811	-30	-132	-1830	-2803	-2142	-1487	-2090	-5719
Goods	1047	1630	1179	-152	3704	-325	-240	-987	-1552
Exports	2348	3372	3455	2803	11978	2562	3329	3244	9135
Imports	-1301	-1742	-2276	-2955	-8274	-2887	-3569	-4231	-10687
Real services	-157	-172	-902	-639	-53	-148	-840		
Financial services	-1385	-1583	-1160	-1506	-5634	-1169	-1187	-946	-3302
Profits and dividends	-118	-251	-105	-331	-805	-124	-264	-111	-499
Interest paid	-1372	-1433	-1150	-1253	-5208	-1146	-1026	-958	-3130
Interest collected	105	101	95	78	379	101	103	123	327
Transfers									
II. Capital account	-206	-25	616	-2268	-1883	2991	2306	2384	7681
Privatizations									
Direct investment	53	107	76	229	465	71	148	934	1153
Export financing	1100	213	-641	-602	70	-72	-409	-916	-1397
Import financing	-48	157	656	923	1688	919	1227	1677	3823
Trade credit and deposit facility	1								
Loans from international organizations	-43	90	30	235	312	-95	-100	30	-165
Government loans and securities	-46	-100	297	184	335	-23	-13	-477	-513
Loan to private companies	32	52	-10	271	345	317	56	88	461
Loan to public companies	44	10	58	-7	105	12	-79	-80	-147
Foreign currency dep. amortization									
Arrears written off without offsetting entry									
Others[1,2]	-1427	-891	-751	-4109	-7178	899	1279	995	3173
III. Net international reserves variance	-1017	-55	484	-4098	-4686	849	819	294	1962
IV. Balance of payments financing	1017	55	-484	4098	4686	-849	-819	-294	-1962
Reserve assets (increase-)[3]	974	-588	-849	-1798	-2261	-672	-1472	-991	-3135
Net LAIA	332	29	24	-4	381	183	359	312	854
Government securities									
BONEX placement[4]	9	594	14	202	216				
BONEX amortization	-330	-31	-64	-425					
IMF loans	-426	-291	-1001		832				
IMF amortization									
Paris Club refinancing	1122	376	167	289					
Paris Club amortization	-50	-292	-603						
Others BCRA	-65	-18	5567	5484		-159	-230	-420	
Swap rate variation adjustments									
Swaps									
Bank financing									
Arrears	440	825	312	211	1788	215	222	181	618
Others[2]	-151	-25	-25		-31				

* Figures for the first three quarters.
[1] Includes errors and omissions.
[2] In 1991 this item includes operations to consolidate public debt with the issue of Treasury Bonds, Consolidation Bonds and Supplier Bonds. In the fourth quarter of 1991 the total issued was $5.457 billion. In the first three quarters of 1992, $325 million were withdrawn.
[3] In 1989 and 1990 includes net LAIA.
[4] The high level of foreign bond placement in 1989 is due to the implementation of the BONEX plan.
n.a. Not available.
Source: Author's calculations based on Central Bank data.

Statistical Annex Table 2.3a. Argentina: Central Bank Reserve Assets
(End-of-period balances in millions of dollars)

Period	Reserves total	Gold	Net LAIA*	Foreign exchange & conversion	SDRs	Others**
1977	3,862.4	176.7	533.4	3,063.4	88.9	0.0
1978	5,828.9	180.6	693.0	4,573.3	209.0	173.0
1979	10,163.7	183.6	556.9	8,878.7	342.0	202.5
1980	7,288.3	184.6	384.9	6,054.6	325.3	338.9
1981	3,222.4	184.6	-224.0	2,584.0	401.3	276.5
1982	2,507.5	184.6	-184.0	2,407.3	0.0	99.6
1983	2,662.8	1,421.2	55.0	1,164.0	22.6	0.0
1984	2,631.7	1,421.2	-53.0	1,238.0	25.5	0.0
1985	4,801.1	1,421.1	94.0	3,273.0	13.0	0.0
1986	4,287.1	1,421.1	143.0	2,717.0	6.0	0.0
1987	3,018.1	1,421.1	-20.0	1,617.0	0.0	0.0
1988	4,979.1	1,421.1	157.0	3,363.0	38.0	0.0
1989	3,419.4	1,421.2	297.8	1,404.7	237.0	58.7
1990	6,010.1	1,613.4	913.2	3,242.2	0.0	241.3
1991	8,974.4	1,430.2	509.70	5,945.6	0.0	1,088.9
1992	12,948.8	1,445.8	-409.20	10,027.4	0.0	1,884.8

* Until 1980, figures are for payment agreements and other claims on foreign entities.
** Includes IMF ending balance, public securities in foreign currency, and others.
Source: Central Bank, Annual Reports and Economic Indicators.

Statistical Annex Table 2.3b. Argentina: Central Bank Reserve Assets
(End-of-month balances in millions of dollars)

Period	Total reserves	Gold	Net LAIA*	Foreign exchange	SDRs	Securities Bonex 82	Bonex 84	Bonex 87	Bonex 89	Bonex 92	Total
January 1990	2,369.3	1,421.2	256.9	1,280.4	302.8	0.3	0.5	387.6	0.0	0.0	388.4
February	2,464.7	1,421.2	312.6	953.0	342.5	0.3	0.5	387.6	0.0	0.0	388.4
March	2,508.1	1,421.2	360.5	1,185.5	338.2	0.1	0.5	387.6	0.0	0.0	388.2
April	4,143.6	1,421.2	376.8	1,592.8	364.6	0.1	0.5	387.6	0.0	0.0	388.2
May	4,470.0	1,421.2	294.3	2,321.1	45.2	0.1	0.5	387.6	0.0	0.0	388.2
June	5,044.3	1,421.2	314.4	2,865.0	55.5	0.1	0.5	387.6	0.0	0.0	388.2
July	4,950.4	1,421.2	350.4	2,706.5	84.1	0.1	0.5	387.6	0.0	0.0	388.2
August	4,874.6	1,421.2	359.1	2,698.3	7.8	0.1	0.5	387.6	0.0	0.0	388.2
September	5,270.9	1,375.7	278.0	3,082.0	147.0	0.1	0.5	387.6	0.0	0.0	388.2
October	5,377.6	1,375.7	349.8	3,111.9	152.0	0.1	0.5	387.6	0.0	0.0	388.2
November	5,989.9	1,375.7	359.5	3,714.3	152.2	0.1	0.5	387.6	0.0	0.0	388.2
December	6,588.4	1,375.7	392.0	4,325.4	107.1	0.1	0.5	387.6	0.0	0.0	388.2
January 1991	6,072.3	1,375.7	286.9	3,887.2	307.4	0.0	0.2	214.9	0.0	0.0	215.1
February	5,585.8	1,375.7	318.4	3,372.5	304.1	0.0	0.2	214.9	0.0	0.0	215.1
March	5,482.0	1,546.8	609.4	2,463.5		0.0	0.2	215.4	646.7	0.0	862.3
April	5,543.9	1,546.6	665.8	2,412.2		0.0	0.2	228.9	690.2	0.0	919.3
May	6,101.4	1,563.0	473.2	3,013.3		0.0	0.2	227.4	824.3	0.0	1,051.9
June	6,386.8	1,597.5	538.3	3,279.9		0.0	0.2	231.2	739.7	0.0	971.1
July	6,619.5	1,481.6	637.6	3,529.9		0.0	0.2	231.6	738.6	0.0	970.4

(continues)

Statistical Annex Table 2.3b. Argentina: Central Bank Reserve Assets (Cont.)
(End-of-month balances in millions of dollars)

Period	Total reserves	Gold	Net LAIA*	Foreign exchange	SDRs	Bonex 82	Bonex 84	Bonex 87	Bonex 89	Bonex 92	Total
								Securities			
August	5,698.1	1,418.4	650.4	3,419.5		0.0	0.2	236.6	873.0	0.0	1,109.8
September	7,299.1	1,431.4	507.8	4,221.9		0.0	0.2	237.6	900.2	0.0	1,138.0
October	7,292.0	1,460.0	474.9	4,217.7		0.0	0.2	237.6	903.4	0.0	1,139.4
November	7,882.5	1,493.9	489.6	4,807.9		0.0	0.2	232.0	858.9	0.0	1,091.1
December	8,974.4	1,430.2	509.7	5,945.6		0.0	0.2	227.7	861.0	0.0	1,088.9
January 92	9,157.5	1,535.9	426.8	6,087.9		0.0	0.2	236.6	870.1	0.0	1,106.9
February	8,966.4	1,529.2	399.7	5,935.6		0.0	0.2	231.4	870.3	0.0	1,101.9
March	9,503.5	1,489.1	322.7	6,553.3		0.0	0.2	236.6	901.6	0.0	1,138.4
April	10,091.9	1,456.7	234.7	7,252.8		0.0	0.1	243.4	904.2	0.0	1,147.7
May	10,518.5	1,459.3	81.5	7,851.9		0.0	0.1	243.2	882.5	0.0	1,125.8
June	10,381.2	1,485.2	-40.6	7,948.7		0.0	0.2	242.2	745.5	0.0	987.9
July	10,882.0	1,548.4	-167.7	8,602.3		0.0	0.2	240.0	658.8	0.0	899.0
August	10,853.0	1,474.0	-270.2	8,765.0		0.0	0.2	226.2	657.8	0.0	884.2
September	12,320.6	1,507.3	-81.7	9,904.1		0.0	0.2	231.4	759.3	0.0	990.9
October	13,212.4	1,468.4	-15.1	10,199.8		0.0	0.2	231.3	759.8	568.0	1,559.3
November	11,616.9	1,445.8	-420.9	8,682.9		0.0	0.5	219.7	891.2	797.7	1,909.1
December	12,948.4	1,445.8	-409.2	10,194.8		0.0	0.5	219.6	699.2	797.7	1,717.0

* Until 1980, figures are for payment agreements and other claims on foreign entities.
Source: Central Bank, Annual Reports and Economic Indicators.

Statistical Annex Table 2.4. Argentina: Public and Private Foreign Indebtedness
(End-of-period debt balance in billions of dollars)

Period	Total	Public	Private
1975	7.9	4.0	3.9
1976	8.3	5.2	3.1
1977	9.7	6.0	3.7
1978	12.5	8.4	4.1
1979	19.0	10.0	9.0
1980	27.2	14.5	12.7
1981	35.7	20.0	15.7
1982	43.6	28.6	15.0
1983	45.1	31.7	13.4
1984	46.2	35.5	10.7
1985	49.3	40.9	8.4
1986	51.4	44.7	6.7
1987	58.3	51.8	6.5
1988	58.5	53.5	5.0
1989	63.3	58.4	4.9
1990	61.0	n.a.	n.a.
1991	60.0	n.a.	n.a.
1992*	58.0	n.a.	n.a.

* Estimate.
Source: ECLAC.
n.a. Not available.

Statistical Annex Table 2.5. Argentina: Privatizations Concluded as of December 31, 1992

			Millions of dollars	
Year	Sector/Enterprise	Type of transfer	Cash	Debt paper
1990	TV channels	15-year concession	13.9	
1990	Roads	Concession of 10,000 km of national highways	100 per year	
1990	Petrochemicals	Sale of 30%	45.7	130.2
1990	Petroleum	Concession of 37 marginal areas	256.9	
1990	ENTEL (telephones)	Sale of 60%	214.0	5000.0
1990	Aerolíneas Argentinas	Sale of 85%	260.0	1610.0
1991	Broadcast transmitters	Concession of 6 radio stations		
1991	Petroleum	Partnership in 5 central areas, 50%	858.5	
1991	Petroleum	Concession of 22 marginal areas	140.5	
1991	Tourism	Sale of a hotel	3.7	12.0
1991	Railroads	Concession of a Rosario-Bahía Blanca branch line		
1991	ENTEL Telefónica	Sale of shares, 30%	830.0	
1991	Tandanor	Sale of shipyard	59.8	
1992	Petroleum	Partnership in 7 central areas	464.8	
1992	Petroleum	Sale of a refinery	64.1	
1992	Petroleum	Concession of 27 marginal areas	67.1	
1992	ENTEL Telecom	Sale of shares, 30%	1,226.9	
1992	Electricity	Sale of 7 plants, 60%	252.9	80.00*
1992	Electricity	Sale of 51% of the distribution	65.0	1012.9*
1992	Petrochemicals	Sale of 39% of a plant	7.3	
1992	Railroads	Concession of 3 lines and one branch line, 12,849.5 km		
1992	Ports	Concession of two and sale of one lift		
1992	Gas	Transport, sale of 70%	128.0	447.4 *
1992	Gas	Distribution, sale of between 60 and 90%	172.0	1102.7 *
1992	Racetrack	Concession	61.5	
1992	Livestock market	10-year concession	12% of income	
1992	Steel	Sale of one steel plant and one blast furnace	143.3	41.8 *
1992	Sanitation	20-year concession		

*Equivalent cash value at the time of transfer, all others are nominal values.
Source: Subsecretariat of Privatization, Ministry of Economy.

Statistical Annex Table 2.6. Argentina: Financial System Credit, 1991-92
(End-of-quarter balances in millions of current dollars)

Period	Credit in national currency			Credit in foreign currency			Total Credit
	Pub. sect.	Priv. sect.	Total	Pub. sect.	Priv. sect.	Total	
1991							
I	1,293	5,030	6,323	1,639	5,921	7,560	13,883
II	1,551	6,979	8,530	1,793	6,957	8,750	17,280
III	1,567	7,761	9,328	2,324	8,021	10,345	19,673
IV	1,753	8,967	10,720	2,393	9,192	11,585	22,305
1992							
I	1,920	9,175	11,095	2,412	9,620	12,032	23,127
II	2,170	10,130	12,300	2,520	10,309	12,829	25,129
III	n.a.	n.a.	12,628	n.a.	n.a.	14,488	27,116
IV	n.a.	n.a.	13,440	n.a.	n.a.	15,799	29,239

n.a. Not available.
Source: Carta Económica

Statistical Annex Table 2.7. Argentina: Deposits in Foreign Currency in the Financial System, 1989-92

(Monthly averages of daily balances, in millions of dollars)

Period	Total	Percent change[1]	Demand deposits	Savings bank	Fixed term	BCRA account
1989						
I	1,567.58		17.26			1,550.32
II	870.29	-44.48	16.04			854.25
III	859.26	-1.27	18.41		334.19	506.67
IV	1,605.40	86.84	34.39		1,028.71	542.32
1990						
I	1,132.25	-29.47	42.98		662.33	426.94
II	1,197.25	5.74	90.20		676.27	430.78
III	1,870.79	56.26	267.30		1,113.40	490.10
IV	2,641.93	41.22	523.85		1,896.02	222.06
1991						
I	3,270.76	23.80	779.29		2,366.76	124.71
II	4,208.08	28.66	664.96	376.72	3,141.13	25.28
III	5,258.68	24.97	653.35	746.55	3,856.33	2.45
IV	6,344.43	20.65	743.35	1,035.08	4,565.65	0.36
1992						
I	7,438.60	17.25	803.23	1,345.04	5,290.33	
II	8,533.59	14.72	853.47	1,511.05	6,169.07	
III	10,453.00	22.49	833.10	1,699.40	7,959.20	
IV*	10,986.00	5.10	898.90	1,870.20	8,216.90	

[1] Percentage of change with respect to the preceding quarter.
* Provisional figures.
Source: Central Bank, Economic Indicators.

Statistical Annex Table 2.8. Argentina: Reserve Ratio
(Percentage of GDP)

Period	M1/GDP	M3/GDP	Public securities/GDP[1]	Domestic assets/GDP
1980	7.5	28.4	3.4	31.8
1981	6.3	28.2	2.6	30.8
1982	4.9	20.0	3.6	23.6
1983	3.8	13.6	1.1	14.7
1984	3.8	12.8	0.9	13.7
1985	3.6	12.4	0.7	13.1
1986	5.7	17.2	0.5	17.7
1987	5.2	18.2	2.6	20.8
1988	3.3	15.4	2.4	17.8
1989	2.8	13.2	1.5	14.7
1990	2.5	5.5	1.5	7.0
I	2.0	4.0		
II	2.3	4.7		
III	2.5	5.9		
IV	3.0	7.2		
1991	4.4	8.5	1.7	10.2
I	3.3	7.3		
II	4.3	7.9		
III	4.5	8.8		
IV	5.4	9.8		
1992	7.6	0.0	1.2[3]	16.0
I	7.4	12.3		
II	7.5	13.7		
III	7.6	16.1		
IV[2]	7.8	17.0		

[1] Includes the circulation of securities issued by the government in national currency at cash value, net of Central Bank holdings.
[2] Provisional data.
[3] Average for the first and second quarters.
Source: Author's calculations based on data from the Secretariat of Finance, the Central Bank, and ECLAC.

Statistical Annex Table 2.9. Argentina: Estimated Rate of Country Risk
(Annual rates, percentages)

Period	BONEX IRR*	LIBOR**	Estimated rate of country risk
1981			
III	20.30	18.71	1.47
IV	18.38	14.66	2.97
1982			
I	18.41	15.33	1.57
II	16.62	15.14	0.98
III	23.88	12.85	10.31
IV	20.15	9.96	8.48
1983			
I	15.48	9.50	5.30
II	5.04	9.67	5.57
III	23.27	10.44	15.74
IV	22.22	9.79	9.49
1984			
I	21.34	10.52	10.86
II	30.76	12.44	12.02
III	23.01	12.12	9.14
IV	19.11	9.73	8.31
1985			
I	18.70	9.52	8.98
II	20.73	8.46	10.89
III	18.43	8.37	7.65
IV	17.78	8.10	8.77
1986			
I	17.46	7.81	9.15
II	15.91	6.96	7.58
III	14.67	6.08	8.38
IV	14.34	6.10	8.19
1987			
I	16.19	6.42	8.49
II	15.01	7.46	6.25
III	20.25	7.69	13.70
IV	23.73	7.73	18.01
1988			
I	24.76	7.04	13.82
II	22.04	7.84	13.47
III	22.81	8.79	12.98
IV	23.69	9.15	15.5

(continues)

Statistical Annex Table 2.9. Argentina: Estimated Rate of Country Risk (Cont.)
(Annual rates, percentages)

Period	BONEX IRR*	LIBOR**	Estimated rate of country risk
1989			
I	36.12	10.23	24.09
II	33.27	9.58	17.79
III	25.36	8.79	13.77
IV	32.35	8.29	31.91
1990			
I	45.98	8.48	36.25
II	28.78	8.65	18.19
III	21.86	8.21	12.21
IV	22.15	7.87	12.20
1991			
I	19.36	6.81	9.28
II	11.61	6.37	6.42
III	12.01	5.96	4.08
IV	10.31	4.90	6.59
1992			
I	10.11	4.40	5.21
II	9.46	4.17	5.31
III	9.89	3.50	6.26
IV	11.15	3.73	7.76

* Average of BONEX internal rates of return.
** 180-day LIBOR rate.
Sources: FIEL and Macroeconómica.

Statistical Annex Table 2.10. Argentina: Real Exchange Rates
(Base: July 1985=100)

Period	XRAGRXP[1] Qtr.	XRAGRXP[1] Yr.	XRINDXP[2] Qtr.	XRINDXP[2] Yr.	XRFT[3] Qtr.	XRFT[3] Yr.
1978		56.02		57.44		55.27
1979		47.56		49.79		39.15
1980		38.47		40.28		31.67
1981		44.32		46.40		54.72
1982		87.24		91.34		117.53
1983		90.37		94.62		104.86
1984		85.05		89.05		96.80
1985		95.70		100.20		93.70
1986		88.20		88.60		75.50
1987		99.90		96.90		87.30
1988		101.00		94.90		83.80
1989		107.70		103.20		116.60
1990		76.90		76.30		64.40
I	111.33		103.00		90.47	
II	78.57		80.97		67.63	
III	66.20		68.87		56.40	
IV	51.67		52.57		43.00	
1991		63.40		57.60		44.10
I	63.37		57.80		47.30	
II	65.03		58.87		44.50	
III	62.40		56.80		42.67	
IV	62.80		57.03		42.03	
1992		59.20		53.70		38.90
I	60.73		55.10		40.17	
II	59.13		53.60		39.13	
III	57.80		52.43		38.27	
IV	59.30		53.30		38.13	

[1] Agricultural exports exchange rate.
[2] Industrial exports exchange rate.
[3] Free exchange rate.
Source: Carta Económica.

Statistical Annex Table 2.11. Argentina: Composition of Imports
(Percentages)

Period	Total	Capital goods	Consumer goods	Intermed. goods	Automobiles	Parts and accesories	Fuel and lubricants
1977	100	27	3	70		10	16
1978	100	29	6	66		11	12
1979	100	23	10	66		8	16
1980	100	23	18	60	2	12	10
1981	100	22	17	61	3	15	9
1982	100	18	7	75	0	17	12
1983	100	17	5	78	0	17	10
1984	100	14	5	81	0	18	10
1985	100	17	5	78	0	19	12
1986	100	13	6	81	0	19	9
1987	100	17	5	78	0	21	11
1988	100	16	4	80	0	20	9
1989	100	17	5	78	0	17	9
1990	100	15	8	77	0	17	8
1991	100	15	17	68	2	15	5
1992*	100	19	26	55	4	19	2
Quarter							
1990:1	100	17	5	78			
1990:2	100	19	6	75			
1990:3	100	13	8	79			
1990:4	100	13	10	77			
1991:1	100	19	12	70			
1991:2	100	18	16	66			
1991:3	100	15	22	63			
1991:4	100	12	17	71			
1992:1	100	17	20	63			
1992:2	100	20	31	49			

* First six months.
Source: Central Bank of Argentina.

Statistical Annex Table 2.12a. Argentina: Nonfinancial Public Sector Accounts
(Percentages of GDP at current prices)

Item	1977	1978	1979	1980	1981	1982	1983	1984	1985	1986	1987	1988
I. Current Resources	32.75	36.51	33.62	36.12	35.54	32.59	34.36	33.23	41.28	39.15	36.92	36.96
II a. Current exp. net of int.	22.58	27.78	26.74	30.96	31.98	29.25	34.10	32.60	35.02	32.75	32.57	34.79
II b. Net Capital exps.	12.87	12.19	10.25	9.20	9.40	8.07	9.45	7.58	6.82	7.28	7.95	7.91
III. Primary suplus (I-II)	-2.70	-3.46	-3.37	-4.04	-5.84	-4.73	-9.19	-6.95	-0.56	-0.88	-3.60	-5.74
IV. Interest	2.02	3.05	3.12	3.43	7.40	10.38	5.96	4.96	5.45	3.86	3.62	2.82
Domestic debt	1.39	2.47	2.61	2.64	5.17	5.72	0.94	0.80	0.78	0.37	0.58	0.45
Foreign debt	0.63	0.58	0.51	0.79	2.23	4.66	5.02	4.16	4.67	3.49	3.04	2.37
V. Financing needs (III-IV)	4.72	6.51	6.49	7.47	13.24	15.11	15.15	11.91	6.01	4.74	7.21	8.56

Source: Author's calculations based on data from the Secretariat of Finance.

Statistical Annex Table 2.12b. Argentina: Nonfinancial Public Sector Accounts. International Methodology, Excluding Provinces. Cash Basis.
(Percentages of GDP of the general budget for 1992)

Item	1989	1990	1991	1992
I. Current Resources	18.76	19.93	22.51	25.11
II a. Current exp. net of int.	17.08	15.97	20.06	21.98
II b. Net Capital exps.	2.99	2.10	1.49	1.53
III. Primary suplus (I-II)	1.39	0.49	1.49	1.25
IV. Interest	0.08	2.35	2.44	2.84
Domestic debt	12.76	6.89	6.06	5.69
Foreign debt	4.28	1.01	2.85	1.71
V. Financing needs (III-IV)	8.48	5.88	3.21	3.98
VI. Financing needs (IV-V)	12.68	4.53	3.61	2.87

Source: Carta Económica.

CHAPTER THREE

CHILE: THE ORIGINS
AND CONSEQUENCES OF
EXTERNAL CAPITAL

Manuel R. Agosin, J. Rodrigo Fuentes, and Leonardo Letelier[1]

The objective of this study is to analyze the determinants, the macroeconomic management, and the effects of external capital flows on the Chilean economy. This analysis is especially timely. In the 1982-87 period, the main obstacle to economic progress in Chile was the foreign exchange shortage caused by the debt crisis. Since then the country has had to deal with the opposite problem resulting from abundant external capital and its effects on the exchange rate and domestic investment. Perhaps the most significant result of the inflow of external capital has been its tendency to cause exchange rate appreciation. To counteract this, authorities implemented a series of measures that created a barrier between national and international short-term financial markets, thus discouraging international interest rate speculation. The objective has been to prevent a recurrence of the exchange rate appreciation experienced in the previous episode of capital inflows (1978-81), which adversely affected the steady expansion and diversification of exports, the cornerstone of Chile's economic growth in recent decades.

So far, the measures adopted have slowed the inevitable exchange rate appreciation caused by this new influx of external capital. In any event, the real exchange rate has fallen somewhat since early 1991.[2] It is impossible to deter-

[1] The authors are grateful for the invaluable comments of Professor Jorge Marshall and the project's two outside consultants, Robert Devlin and Ricardo Ffrench-Davis of ECLAC. Thanks also to Alejandro Fernández and Francisco Prieto; to Mauricio Cárdenas, Mario Damill, José Maria Fanelli, José Antonio Ocampo, and Willy Van Ryckeghem for their comments; and to Andrea Alvarado, Luis Figueroa, Carlos Oguín, and Eric Parrado for their help with the research.
[2] The real exchange rate is defined as the nominal price of the dollar, multiplied by the quotient of the applicable external inflation and the consumer price index (CPI). External inflation is calculated on the basis of the wholesale price indices (WPI), expressed in dollars, of Chile's main trading partners, weighted by their relative volume of trade with Chile, excluding petroleum and copper (see Feliú, 1992).

mine with any degree of accuracy what the impact of exchange rate appreciation has been on noncopper exports or on investments in exportable goods. What is certain, however, is that the output of new export products—as well as investments in such products—has a very strong inertial component. The fact that a sizable percentage of the external capital consists of direct foreign investment (DFI), much of which has gone to the export sector, may also explain why the flow of external capital and exchange rate appreciation have not slowed the growth of nontraditional exports. At any rate, it is vitally important that policies aimed at curbing exchange rate appreciation be pursued and, if necessary, reinforced with additional measures.

Although the focus of our analysis will be the 1987-92 period, constant reference will be made to the years 1978-81, when many of the regulations governing external financing were relaxed. Both periods were characterized by heavy capital inflows, but they were managed very differently by the economic authorities (see the third section of this study). Between these two periods, the Chilean economy was faced with a relative shortage of external resources. Most of the international loans obtained at this time were for the public sector and consisted of loans from international financial organizations and involuntary loans from private banks (debt restructuring and fresh loans or "new money").

This study is organized as follows. In the second section the capital flows are defined and their determinants analyzed. Special emphasis is given to three different types of flows: DFI, speculative capital, and new types of portfolio investment (mutual investment funds on the stock exchange and the flotation of Chilean securities on the New York Stock Exchange).

In the third section the management of capital flows is analyzed from the perspective of the fiscal, monetary, and exchange rate policies. With regard to monetary policy, the measures adopted in the second period of capital inflows (1987-92) are studied by comparing them with the approach taken in the 1978-81 period. A discussion of the steps taken with respect to the exchange rate follows and an econometric model is developed for the real exchange rate, as determined by the capital flows and other variables.

The effects of the capital flows on domestic investment are analyzed in the fourth section. One of the most significant findings of the study is that most of the capital flows have taken the form of DFI, representing as much as 40 percent of gross investment. Although not all of the DFI is new investment (in many cases it consists only of the purchase of existing assets), we will try to evaluate the real contribution of DFI to gross investment.

Some comments will also be made concerning the impact of the capital flows on investment via their effect on the exchange rate and the availability of credit in the private sector. There also is an assessment of the positive effect that the capital inflows may have had on domestic investment by driving up share prices and, consequently, lowering the cost of capital for Chilean corporations.

The final section of the study contains the conclusions, from which certain policy lessons are drawn for dealing with unexpected capital flows and real exchange rate appreciation.

Definition and Determinants of the Capital Flows

Over the course of the last two decades the orientation of the Chilean economy has shifted dramatically, with the result that the market is now recognized as the most efficient agent for resource allocation. This change is reflected in all spheres of economic policy. In the field of trade policy, between 1974 and 1979 all nontariff measures were eliminated and the tariff was reduced to a low, uniform rate (11 percent at present). Apart from certain refunds of customs duties paid on inputs, there are almost no export incentives. As far as the capital account of the balance of payments is concerned, most of the deregulation of capital inflows occurred in the 1978-81 period (although some controls were reinstated in 1991 to handle the enormous volume of foreign exchange). Capital outflows are still subject to certain controls, which were partially relaxed in 1991.

The driving force of the country's erratic economic growth has been exports, the share of which in the gross domestic product (GDP) has increased substantially (from less than 15 percent in 1974 to more than a third at present, at 1977 prices). New export products—including fruits and vegetables, forestry products, seafood (fish meal in particular), and an expanding range of manufactured products, including paper and cellulose—have experienced the fastest growth. Investment in fixed assets, however, was weak throughout the period, never exceeding 20 percent of GDP.[3] In addition, the manufacturing sector's share of total output shrank by nearly 5 percentage points. Many manufacturing companies that might have remained profitable, even with much lower tariffs than the ones in force before the reform, could not survive the shocks of sweeping trade reform, increasing overvaluation of the exchange rate, and the high interest rates associated with deregulation of the domestic financial market (see Ffrench-Davis, Leiva, and Madrid, 1991; and Mizala, 1992).

After the depression of 1982-83, during which GDP fell 15 percent, the Chilean economy grew steadily, with a slight interruption in 1990 as a result of policies to lower inflation caused by the sharp rise in spending in the final year of the military regime. This growth coincided with a boom in nontraditional exports, recovery of investment, and a heavy inflow of private external capital.

---

[3] A recent revision of the national accounts for the period since 1985 revealed a significant increase in the estimate of the rate of gross fixed capital formation in GDP (at 1986 prices) for the entire period, which, according to the new estimates, rose from 18 percent in 1985 to 25 percent in 1992 (see Banco Central de Chile, 1993).

Table 3.1. Capital Revenue in Chile, 1980-92
(Millions of dollars)

	1980	1981	1982	1983	1984	1985	1986	1987	1988	1989	1990	1991	1992[a]
Gross inflow	4,603	6,517	2,474	1,407	2,444	2,057	1,974	2,081	2,628	3,651	4,463	1,820	4,012
Debt amortization[b]	-1,438	-1,819	-1,259	-899	-504	-673	-1,233	-1,136	-1,619	-2,373	-1,171	-1006	-1,115
Net inflow	3,165	4,698	1,215	508	1,940	1,384	741	945	1,009	1,278	3,292	814	2,897
Direct investment from abroad	375	554	663	261	138	187	440	1,184	1,592	2,175	1,943	1,194	1,139
Direct investment abroad	-44	-21	-17	-3	-11	-2	-3	-7	-16	-10	-8	-98	-426
Portfolio investments	—	—	—	—	—	—	—	—	—	87	362	26	323
Public credits[c]	45	326	-458	-118	760	758	661	773	981	735	583	-124	754
Private credits	4,226	5,658	2,286	1,267	1,558	1,115	876	131	71	665	1,582	823	2,222
Long-term[d]	(3,379)	(4,919)	(2,347)	(1,809)	(1,110)	(882)	(618)	(266)	(191)	(219)	(301)	(433)	(616)
Short-term[e]	(847)	(739)	(-61)	(542)	(448)	(233)	(258)	(-135)	(-120)	(446)	(11,281)	(390)	(1,606)
												(300)[f]	(981)[f]

[a] Preliminary.
[b] Refers only to medium—and long-term debt.
[c] Loans from official bilateral and multilateral sources; includes short-term credits.
[d] Credits from international banks and suppliers. In the 1978-82 period, most of those benefited were in the national banking sector. In 1983, private bank flows went primarily to the Central Bank in the context of the periodic renegotiation of the debt.
[e] Commercial lines of credit and other flows to banks and the nonbanking private sector.
[f] Net of borrowing to constitute the reserve requirement on foreign credit.
Source: Central Bank of Chile.

The effects of the resumption of private voluntary capital flows began to be felt in 1987, when DFI increased substantially in response to the incentives created by the debt for equity program (see Table 3.1). From 1987 to 1990, capital inflows grew steadily. After a slump in 1991, they began another steep upward climb in 1992. The most important component was DFI, which represented between 28 percent (1992) and 60 percent (1988-89) of the gross inflows of capital (before deducting debt amortizations). Another significant component between 1988 and 1992 was private short-term loans, which represented between 21 and 40 percent of the gross inflows of capital. Medium- and short-term voluntary private loans (primarily from international banks and suppliers) became available again in 1991. In 1992, these loans constituted 15 percent of the gross inflows of external capital.

Portfolio investments, which appeared in 1989, are a new and interesting phenomenon. Although still representing only a relatively modest percentage of total capital inflows, they have grown considerably in the last two years. Most of these investments are channeled through a few U.S. and British mutual funds, created specifically for the purpose of investing in Chilean corporations. In addition, for the first time, shares of a growing number of Chilean companies have been floated on the New York Stock Exchange through ADRs.

Another recent development was the initiation in 1991 of a substantial flow of capital exports by Chilean companies, in the form of direct investments abroad, particularly in Argentina. In 1992, the flow of such investments totaled US$426 million.

Placing the capital flows of the 1987-92 period within the context of the trend of such flows since 1978 is an interesting exercise.[4] As indicated in Table 3.2, net capital inflows in the 1978-81 period (the previous episode of heavy private inflows) represented between 11 and 14 percent of GDP. If this same percentage is measured in 1977 prices and dollars (the year in which the dollar was at what might be considered a long-term "normal" or equilibrium level), it was between 11 and 18 percent.

Although the accumulation of international reserves was substantial, between 50 and 100 percent of the inflows financed large current account deficits (caused by increasing real appreciation of the peso). In the current period, the capital inflows have been far more modest, both in nominal terms and as percentages of GDP. The only year in which the inflows were similar to those experienced between 1978 and 1981 was 1990, when they represented nearly 12 percent of

---

[4] For an analysis of the management and impact of the capital flows in 1978-82, see Ffrench-Davis and Arellano (1981), Hachette and Cabrera (1989), Mizala (1985), Marshall (1990), Morandé (1988), Morandé (1991), and Ramos (1988).

Table 3.2. Chile: Summary of Balance of Payments, 1978-92
(Millions of dollars)

	Trade balance	Current account	Net capital revenue	Errors and omissions	Accrued reserves	Net capital flow to GDP	
						In nominal dollars	In 1997[a] dollars
1978	-426	-1,088	1,946	-146	712	12.6	11.9
1979	-355	-1,189	2,247	-11	1,047	10.8	11.2
1980	-764	-1,971	3,165	50	1,244	11.5	13.0
1981	-2,677	-4,733	4,698	102	67	14.2	17.9
1982	62	-2,304	1,215	-76	-1,165	4.8	5.5
1983	986	-1,117	508	68	-541	2.6	2.3
1984	363	-2,111	1,940	188	17	10.1	8.5
1985	884	-1,413	1,384	-70	-99	8.6	5.9
1986	1,092	-1,191	741	223	-228	4.4	2.8
1987	1,229	-808	945	-91	45	4.9	3.0
1988	2,219	-167	1,009	-110	732	4.6	2.8
1989	1,578	-767	1,278	-74	437	5.0	3.2
1990	1,273	-597	3,291	-326	2,368	11.9	7.6
1991	1,575	143	814	282	1,238	3.0	1.7
1992	749	-583	2,896	185	2,498	7.6	5.4

[a] GDP (in 1977 pesos) was converted to dollars at the average exchange rate for 1977. Capital revenue was deflated by the external price index for Chile.
Source: Central Bank of Chile.

GDP. Measured in 1977 prices and dollars, the inflows were even smaller, representing between 2 and 8 percent of GDP, figures which are not much larger than those recorded during the external credit squeeze caused by the drying up of private external capital. Unlike what happened in 1978-81, in the current period the trade balance still shows a surplus (although with a substantial decrease in 1992), the current account deficit has shrunk instead of increasing (also with the exception of 1992), and more than 70 percent of the net capital inflows have been added to the international reserves.

The composition of the capital inflows varied more noticeably than their total volume (see Table 3.1). In 1978-81, most of the capital inflows were in the form of medium- and long-term loans from international banks to Chilean banks. This was so partly because of the increasing relaxation of the limits placed on external borrowing by banks for the purpose of making loans in pesos and the guarantees that banks could grant on the foreign currency indebtedness of non-banking institutions;[5] it was also partly a response to the wide availability of

---

[5] These limits were completely eliminated in June 1979.

medium-term Eurocredits (at six-month adjustable rates) brought about by the recycling of the surpluses of oil-exporting countries.

Of particular importance during the adjustment to the disappearance of voluntary credits (1983-86) were credits from multilateral financial organizations and fresh, medium-term credits ("new money") from international banks to the Central Bank and the Treasury in the context of the periodic rescheduling of the debt.[6] It is interesting that Chile, unlike other Latin American debtor countries, had substantial flows of multilateral resources (as well as involuntary credits from international private banks), which facilitated the economy's far-reaching structural adjustment (Damill, Fanelli, and Frenkel, 1992). Both components gradually decreased and became insignificant in 1987, when the new period of voluntary private capital inflows began.

In short, since 1987, Chile has experienced a substantial inflow of international private capital. As Table 3.3 shows, although the capital account showed an improvement over the adjustment period (1983-86), the two periods are distinguished more than anything else by the shift in the composition of the capital flows toward private capital (primarily DFI and short-term flows), which more than compensated for the contraction of public flows, involuntary loans from international banks to the Chilean public sector in the context of debt rescheduling, and the increase in medium- and long-term debt amortization. Thus, with respect to the capital flows, the most important difference between the adjustment period and the new external capital boom is that in the former, much of the capital was used to amortize or refinance external debt, while in the latter direct investment and interest rate speculation have predominated.

Comparing the 1987-92 period with the years 1983-86 reveals a change in the sign of international reserves accumulation. This change can be attributed primarily to the current account and secondarily to the increase in capital inflows.

Following is an analysis of the most important components of the capital flows: DFI, speculative flows, and portfolio investments.

Direct Foreign Investment

It has already been mentioned that DFI has played a vital role in the current episode of capital inflows. Since 1974, DFI has been governed by Decree Law (DL) 600, which has been amended only slightly in the meantime. The basic principles of this decree are equal treatment for foreign investors, free access to domestic markets, and the near total elimination of state controls on the activities of foreign corporations or the sectoral allocation of their resources. It is now

---

[6] It should be remembered that the Central Bank assumed the external debt of private entities, exchanging it for debt in pesos.

Table 3.3. Chile: Balance of Payments, Annual Averages, 1983-86 and 1987-92
(Millions of dollars)

	1983-86	1987-92	Variation	% of total
Current account	-1,458	-463	995	69.4
Capital account	1,143	1,706	563	39.3
Net direct investment	195	1,444	1,249	87.1
Portfolio investment	–	133	133	9.3
Debt amortization	-770	-1,403	-633	-44.1
Public capital	515	617	102	10.3
Private capital				
Medium- and long-term	1,104	338	-766	-53.4
Short-term	109	578	478	48.0
Errors and omissions	102	-22	-124	-8.6
Accrued reserves	-213	1,220	1,433	100.0

Source: Central Bank of Chile.

possible to repatriate capital one year after an investment is made; before the amendments to DL 600 in March 1993 the waiting period was three years. Foreign investors are guaranteed the right to remit profits and may choose either the tax system applicable to Chilean companies or a fixed-rate tax on profits, guaranteed not to increase for 10 years.[7] A fixed-rate option also exists for customs duties on inputs and capital goods and for the tax on services. When the investments are for export projects larger than US$50 million, companies can hold bank accounts outside Chile for the purpose of paying interest, dividends, royalties, and for purchases of raw materials and capital assets. Since these benefits are not available to Chilean investors, it might be said that current legislation and regulations give foreign investors preferential treatment.

Another way of making direct investments in Chile is through the debt-for-equity program—Chapter XIX of the Compendium of International Exchange Regulations of the Central Bank—which has been in effect since the latter half of 1985. This program works as follows: an investor buys an instrument of Chilean external debt in the international markets (which, until 1990, could be obtained at substantial discounts) and exchanges it at face value (minus a discount negotiated with the debtor, generally the Central Bank) and at the official exchange rate for a note from the Central Bank (or other debtor) in national currency, which can be sold in the

---

[7] Since 1985, a 20-year fixed tax rate can be chosen for investments larger than US$50 million.

domestic financial market in order to make an investment authorized by the Central Bank (or converted into share capital of the private debtor). There are, however, some restrictions. In the case of large investment projects in the mining sector, only 10 percent of the investment can be made through debt-for-equity swaps. Between 1987 and 1990, the use of Chapter XIX was authorized for portfolio investments by mutual funds of Chilean shares (known as Chile Funds) traded on international stock exchanges (Desormeaux, 1989). When this program was first introduced, profits could not be remitted for four years and capital could be repatriated only after 10 years. As explained below, these restrictions were relaxed in order to alleviate the downward pressure on the exchange rate.

It should be noted that investments made under Chapter XIX are considerably more regulated than those covered by DL 600. The former are subject to approval on a case-by-case basis, while approval of the latter by the Foreign Investment Committee is merely a formality for registration and monitoring purposes.

The volume of DFI has been substantial since 1987. In nominal terms, DFI tripled in 1987, increased again by 80 percent between 1987 and 1989, and then fell to nearly half in 1991 (see Table 3.4). The importance of these figures for the Chilean economy can be appreciated when compared with the figures for GDP and gross capital formation, for example. Direct foreign investment represented 8.5 percent of GDP in 1989 and accounted for more than 40 percent of gross investment in 1988-89. Even after falling to more "normal" levels in 1991-92, it is still equivalent to 3 percent of GDP and 14 percent of gross investment.[8]

Apart from the long-term stability of the rules of play governing foreign investments and the proven stability of and excellent outlook for the Chilean economy in general, it is clear that the debt-for-equity program was a decisive factor in the rise of DFI. During the time it was in effect (1985-91), this program accounted for more than 44 percent of total DFI in Chile. There is a difficult problem to be solved with respect to the degree of "additionality" that these resources represent.[9] Certainly, companies that invested money in Chile under this program benefited from a substantial subsidy that was not available to those who used DL 600. Ffrench-Davis (1990) estimates that between 1985 and 1989, the implicit subsidy in the program was 46 percent of the value of the investments (obtained by dividing the value of the discounted notes used in the country by their purchase value in the international markets); in nominal terms, the subsidy totaled nearly US$900 million. Although it is impossible to determine with any

---

[8] Strictly speaking, gross investment and DFI cannot be compared since the former refers to an item in the national accounts and, therefore, reflects real investment processes, while the latter is a financial and balance of payments variable.

[9] Desormeaux (1989) offers a positive view of the program, while Ffrench-Davis (1990) is somewhat more critical.

Table 3.4. Foreign Direct Investment in Chile, 1978-92
(Millions of dollars)

	Decree Law 600	Nationali- zations	Chapter XIX (%)	Total	FDI/GDP (%)	FDI/Gross investment (%)
1978	235	(67)	—	168	1.1	6.1
1979	305	(57)	—	248	1.2	6.7
1980	305	(54)	—	251	0.9	4.3
1981	419	(44)	—	375	1.1	5.0
1982	384	(41)	—	343	1.4	12.0
1983	182	(40)	—	142	0.7	7.3
1984	160	(23)	—	137	0.6	0.4
1985	137	(9)	32	161	1.0	7.3
1986	184	(8)	213	390	2.3	15.8
1987	497	—	707	1,204	6.4	37.6
1988	787	—	856	1,643	7.4	43.8
1989	898	—	1,261	2,159	8.5	41.9
1990	1,531	—	412	1,943	7.0	34.6
1991	1,104	—	-37	1,067	3.8	20.2
1992	1,171	—	-32	1,139	3.0	14.1

Note: The figures in this table are not identical to those included in the balance of payments since the data published by the Central Bank are not exactly the same as those supplied by the Foreign Investments Committee.
Source: Central Bank of Chile and Foreign Investments Committee.

degree of certainty whether the Chapter XIX investments would have been made regardless, in which case the arrangement would only have represented an exchange "gift" for foreign investors, it is true that DL 600 investments did not decrease while Chapter XIX was in effect. On the other hand, it can be argued that DFI was abnormally low in 1985 and would have increased anyway, given the improvement in Chile's external position in 1987-89, chiefly as a result of the recovery of copper prices.

In any case, it is likely that the international publicity surrounding the launching of the program drew the attention of new investors to Chile. It also helped significantly to alleviate the external debt problem at a very opportune time. Partly because of the reduction of the debt balance (and partly because of the sharp increase in the volume of exports), the debt-export ratio fell from more than 5 in 1984 to less than 2 in 1990. The success of the program was evidenced by the rise in the price of Chilean debt instruments on the international markets, which meant that debt-for-equity swaps were no longer a good deal. In fact, since the second quarter of 1991, no new investments have been made using this option.

A sizable percentage of the DFI has gone to export sectors. Between 1985 and 1991, mining projects accounted for more than half of the flows covered by

Table 3.5. Chile: Direct Foreign Investment by Sector, 1985-91
(Percentage)

	Decree Law 600	Chapter XIX
Agriculture	1.1	10.9
Forestry	0.6	14.8
Fishing	0.3	4.4
Mining	50.9	11.9
Manufacturing	17.2	29.8
Foods	—	(5.9)
Paper and cellulose	—	(17.4)
Chemical products	—	(2.6)
Services	29.8 [a]	28.2
Communications	—	(5.3)
Banking, finance, and insurance	—	(12.5)
Generation of electricity	—	(2.3)
Hotels	—	(2.9)
Total	100.0	100.0
Total (millions of US$)	4,740.0	3,631.0

[a] Including construction.
Source: Central Bank of Chile and Foreign Investments Committee.

DL 600 (see Table 3.5). Only two large copper projects (La Escondida and La Disputada de Las Condes) represented a significant percentage of foreign investments in the 1987-90 period. The only other sectors of any importance are manufacturing and services. Although there are no disaggregated figures for the former, judging by the data available for investments larger than US$100 million, in the manufacturing sector most of the investments went to the forestry and paper and cellulose industries, both of which are oriented primarily toward the external markets. It may be, then, that nearly two-thirds of the DFI made through DL 600 was in export sectors. The evidence regarding DFI in services indicates that it was concentrated in the financial sector. In some cases where the percentage of the total is difficult to assess, these investments do not represent the creation of new assets but rather purchases of existing assets, which means that not all of the DFI contributed to increasing the level of gross investment. For example, the heavy foreign investments in La Disputada de Las Condes included the purchase and expansion of the mine and the construction of refineries.

There was greater sectoral selectivity in the investment policy under Chapter XIX, which produced a greater sectoral distribution of resources of this type. The strict limits on mining investments explain the small share of mining in these investments. In contrast, certain export manufacturing sectors (processed foods and paper and cellulose) and the forestry, fishing and agricultural sector (probably export) stand out. Investments in services were concentrated in telecommunications (recently privatized), pension fund administrators (AFPs), banks, health insurance companies (ISAPRE), power companies (also recently privatized), and hotels. In short, it may be that for investments covered by Chapter XIX as well, from one-half to two-thirds went to export sectors. These investments, unlike the DL 600 investments, were concentrated in the sectors responsible for the extraction or processing of nonmining raw materials. Manufactures not involving raw materials in which Chile has natural comparative advantages do not figure prominently either in the flows through DL 600 or in those through Chapter XIX.

It is impossible to determine accurately what percentage of the investments made through the two mechanisms was used to purchase existing firms and what percentage financed new investments. The purchase of existing assets was undoubtedly more significant in the case of Chapter XIX investments than among DL 600 investments. A sizable percentage of the Chapter XIX investments in the services sector were purchases of existing firms. Even in certain export sectors, some joint ventures with Chilean business groups included purchases of blocks of shares of Chilean companies. Ffrench-Davis (1990) estimates that in the 1985-89 period, purchases of existing firms represented between 25 and 56 percent of all debt conversions. This high percentage prompted the Central Bank in 1990 to give preference to new investments in tradable goods over the purchase of existing assets.

Speculative Flows

Until 1975, regulations governing the domestic financial market and the control of capital flows from abroad discouraged speculative flows into the country. Only in 1978, with the relaxing of the restrictions on the external indebtedness of banks, did speculative flows become a possibility. Later, and gradually during 1982, the country risk concept and the growing expectation of a devaluation of the peso (which occurred in June of that year) led to a significant reduction in the flows of private capital, which from then until 1986 were involuntary and generally went to the public sector. It was not until 1987 that significant volumes of private capital began to flow again, which included a considerable speculative component. Short-term private capital did not start increasing significantly until 1988. It can be concluded, therefore, that from 1978 to 1982 and from 1988 to the present, there were speculative flows into Chile.

Measuring speculative capital poses considerable statistical problems because such capital is usually hidden in both the current and the capital accounts. Except for credits to finance foreign trade, short-term capital (less than a year) is generally considered speculative. However, the fact is that flows under a year may not be speculative, while those over a year may well be. In any case, the short-term private flows represent an initial estimate of the amount of speculative capital.

When there are capital controls or measures discouraging short-term flows (as in Chile since mid-1991), the main routes for the entry of speculative capital are the underinvoicing of exports, the overinvoicing of imports, and the "leads and lags" in concluding foreign trade transactions (Reisen, 1992). Although the flows generated in this way can be quite large, especially in an economy such as Chile's where foreign trade represents a high percentage of total GDP, they are virtually impossible to measure.

Another channel through which speculative capital can enter the country is the informal exchange market. These flows are no doubt influenced both by the interest rate differential between Chile and the international financial markets (in particular, the rates on the dollar) and by expectations of appreciation or devaluation of the peso. The Central Bank prepares an estimate of these flows, which is included in an item of the capital accounts called "other assets."

The speculative flows are part of the short-term flows generated by the private and banking sectors and in direct commercial credit transactions. The latter, although not speculative themselves, obviously react to interest rate differentials. One way of estimating the speculative flows, then, is to add the short-term private flows included in the balance of payments to the "other assets" item. For the period between the fourth quarter of 1991 and the end of 1992 the balance of payments figures were decreased by the nominal values of the quarterly increase in the total cash reserves affecting these credits since the banks had to borrow abroad in order to form the required reserves. This borrowing did not, however, result in a net increase in the external capital available in the economy.

As Table 3.1 and Figure 3.1 show, the short-term private flows behave as expected and are extremely positive in 1980-81 and in 1989-92. The latter period was characterized by a widening gap between domestic and international interest rates (see the third section of this study), the perception among economic agents that the Chilean peso would appreciate in real terms (due to the abundance of external capital and the terms of trade improvement), and a significant reduction in the perceived country risk.

Portfolio Investments

It is interesting to analyze the determinants of the newest flows, portfolio investments, which enter the economy via the so-called Chile Funds and through the sale of shares on international stock exchanges in the form of ADRs. The latter are an alternative to the direct offering of shares by Chilean companies in the United States. The holder or owner of an ADR can sell it in the U.S. market or can exchange it for the securities it represents through a flowback operation. To make this latter option viable, the Chilean authorities have agreed to grant the holders of ADRs free access to the exchange markets. As Table 3.6 illustrates,

Figure 3.1. Chile: Short-term Capital Inflows
(Quarterly data in millions of U.S. dollars)

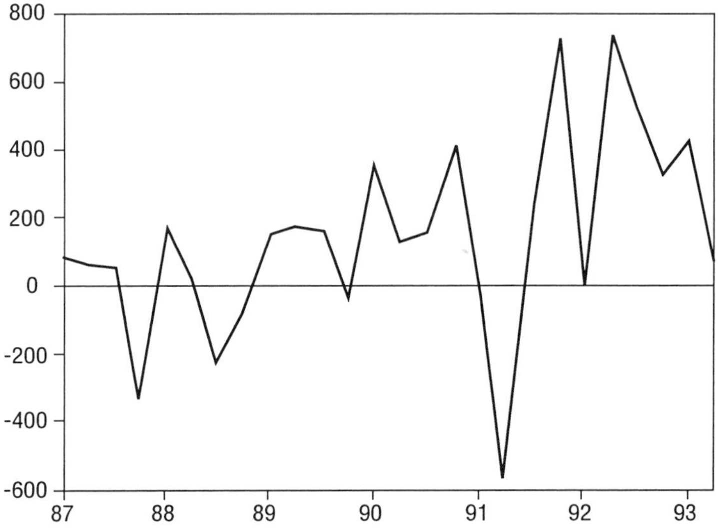

Source: Central Bank of Chile.

from 1989 to mid-1993, US$463 million entered the economy through invest-
ment funds and US$665 million through ADRs.

A monthly series of the Chile Funds is published by the Central Bank. The
inflows of this kind of capital have closely followed changes in the corresponding
legislation and, therefore, have been erratic. In September 1987 authorization was
granted for the creation of these investment funds and for the entry of capital through
the debt conversion program (Chapter XIX). In mid-1989 changes were made in
Chapter XIX which provided larger tax exemptions and shortened the waiting periods for the remittance of profits, making this method of investment more profitable. As mentioned above, in early 1990 the Central Bank announced more stringent rules for the application of Chapter XIX and excluded investment funds.

Macroeconomic Management of Capital Flows

Generally speaking, macroeconomic policy was fairly successful in cushioning
the impact of capital flows on the growth of aggregate demand and inflation. The
main instrument used to produce these effects was a monetary policy of sterilizing the increase in money supply caused by the exchange operations of the Central Bank. To accomplish this, the Central Bank sold its notes in the financial

Table 3.6. Foreign Portfolio Investment in Chile, 1989-92
(Millions of U.S. dollars)

	Investment funds	ADRs	Total
1989			
III	6	—	6
IV	81	—	81
1990			
I	194	—	194
II	24	—	24
III	34	99	133
IV	15	6	21
1991			
I	24	-1	23
II	7	-9	-2
III	5	-18	-13
IV	21	-3	18
1992			
I	11	83	94
II	9	38	47
III	16	108	124
IV	5	53	58
1993			
I	5	59	64
II	5	250	255
Total	462	665	1,127

Source: Central Bank of Chile.

market and varied the interest rate so that the market would absorb all of the securities it wished to sell.

One effect of this policy, together with the economic "boom" experienced since 1991, was that interest rates remained relatively high and tended to increase. On the other hand, the rise in interest rates made management of exchange rate policy difficult. To avoid a significant drop in the real exchange rate, the Central Bank was forced to initiate a series of exchange measures aimed at increasing the cost and risk of international interest rate speculation. This effort has been successful to date, since the measures adopted halted the appreciation of the peso that occurred between early 1991 and late 1992.

Monetary and Fiscal Policy

In the macroeconomic management of capital inflows, the preference has been to utilize monetary and exchange policies. The main objectives of fiscal policy were

Table 3.7. Chile: Source of Changes in the Base Money Supply
(Averages in billions of pesos)

Year	Changes in the supply [1]	Exchange transactions Foreign currency purchases	Others[2]	Domestic credit[3]
1977	14.3	7.5	—	6.9
1978	16.6	16.7	—	-0.2
1979	20.7	28.0	—	-7.3
1980	25.5	30.3	-6.0	0.7
1981	-6.4	-47.5	-0.8	41.8
1982	-23.5	-157.6	-29.3	163.3
1983	83.3	-174.8	0.1	183.0
1984	121.6	-201.9	6.4	207.8
1985	280.8	-476.1	20.5	483.7
1986	412.8	69.3	23.8	-51.9
1987	360.5	325.7	12.8	-302.5
1988	60.1	643.6	75.2	-658.7
1989	56.0	1,332.5	76.4	-1,352.9
1990	77.0	869.3	28.1	-820.3
1991	193.0	690.4	77.7	-575.1
1992	70.0	559.3	63.5	-550.8

[1] The base money supply includes coins and checks in circulation which were issued by the Central Bank, as well as the financial system's deposits in the Central Bank.
[2] Transactions in national currency valued in foreign currency.
[3] Includes financial and other sectors.
Note: The issue through exchange transactions does not exactly match the changes in the international reserves. The major sources of difference are: (1) the change in the reserves caused by changes in the autonomous foreign debt of the Central Bank, which has no monetary effects; (2) the changes in the composition of resident assets between national and foreign currency, which do not affect the international reserves but which do affect the exchange transactions of the monetary authority; (3) lags between movements of foreign currency and national currency in forward operations and futures contracts; (4) exchange rate variations in each period; and (5) differences between the interest received and the interest paid abroad by the Central Bank, which affect the reserves but have no monetary impact.
Source: Central Bank of Chile, *Síntesis Monetaria y Financiera del Banco Central e Informe Económico y Financiero* (various issues).

to maintain domestic stability and, at the same time, to increase social spending (especially on health and education). Consequently, fiscal policy responded only indirectly to the capital inflow, insofar as it was used to slow the growth of demand, caused in part by the increase in capital inflows. Since the onset of these inflows, the government has maintained a significant rate of savings and a sizable surplus. It was aided in this process by the high economic growth rate and the high copper prices between 1987 and 1992. The fiscal surplus (excluding the quasi-fiscal deficit of the Central Bank) ranged from 0.8 percent of GDP in 1989 to 2.5 percent in 1992. Of course, the economic "boom" in Chile was a key factor in the rise of tax revenues. The surge in aggregate demand also prompted a cautious approach to fiscal spending. In recent years, instead of increasing expenditures along with the growth in public revenues, the government has used part of its surplus to prepay its enormous debt to the Central Bank (largely generated in the recovery of the banking sector and its debtors after the crisis of 1982).

Monetary policy has been managed very differently in the current period of capital inflows than it was in the 1978-81 period. From 1977 to 1981, when the monetary approach to the balance of payments gained prominence in Chile, monetary policy was passive with regard to the accumulation of reserves, which was highly monetized. In 1981 a new policy was introduced, aimed at offsetting the monetary effects of changes in reserves with more or less equivalent expansions or contractions of domestic credit. In the current episode of external capital inflows, an aggressive and apparently successful sterilization policy has been followed.

This effect can be seen in Table 3.7—which shows the components of the variation in the currency issue—by comparing the Central Bank's exchange operations with the change in domestic credit. Note that in 1981, the changes in domestic credit were strictly (and negatively) related ($R^2 = 0.99$) to the exchange operations. This would seem to indicate that domestic credit was used to counteract the effects of foreign exchange purchases and sales in 1981. Table 3.7. also shows that sterilization was incomplete: in 1986, increases in the currency issue caused by exchange operations exceed the contractions of domestic credit.

Sterilization led to a steep rise in international reserves, which climbed from US$1.778 billion in late 1986 (or 57 percent of imports) to US$10.338 billion in September 1993 (approximately equivalent to Chile's annual imports, which are now much larger than in 1987). The basic problem posed by the monetary policy option of sterilizing the increases in liquidity caused by the accumulation of reserves was its adverse effect on domestic interest rates. As Figure 3.2 shows, in the second half of 1989 the domestic real interest rate was consistently higher than the LIBOR. The sharp increase in the rate differential in the first half of 1990 was the result of the implementation of restrictive monetary policies aimed at combating the inflationary surge of 1989-90. After a decline in domestic rates caused by the deliberate cooling of the economy, the rate differential increased again in early 1991, mostly because of the increase in domestic rates and the drop in dollar rates. The new surge in domestic rates was caused by the effort to curb inflation and the effect of sterilizing the accumulation of reserves.

We can conclude that the economic authorities, having abandoned the monetary approach to balance of payments in response to the crisis in the early 1980s, were relatively successful in their efforts to sterilize the flows of private capital. This led to increases in domestic interest rates, which put additional pressure on the exchange market by encouraging even larger capital inflows; exchange policy was used to deal with this problem.

Figure 3.2. National and International Interest Rates

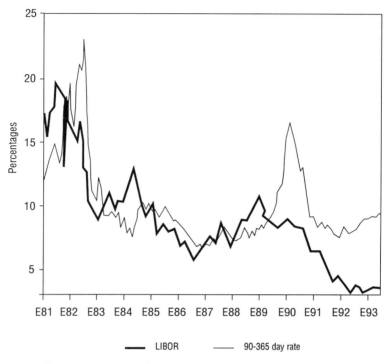

Source: Central Bank of Chile.

Exchange Policy

The exchange policy was amended extensively over time. At the start of the military regime, the objective was to offset the impact of trade reform with real devaluations of the peso. Starting in 1976, the nominal exchange rate was used to combat inflation. This policy culminated in 1979 when the dollar was fixed at $Ch39, and such parity was maintained until the 1982 crisis. Following a period of experimentation, a "crawling peg" exchange rate system was adopted, along with sharp real devaluations, a policy which remained in effect from 1983 to 1990. The Central Bank set a reference price for the dollar, with a flotation band of 2 percent on either side. The reference dollar was depreciated daily, based on the differential between the previous month's domestic inflation and estimated international inflation.

A series of measures was gradually introduced to handle the growing capital inflows—which, as early as 1988, began to eliminate the exchange shortage—and to prevent the new foreign exchange surplus from causing substantial real appreciation of the peso. In mid-1989 the dollar flotation band was expanded to

5 percent in both directions. In early 1991 the strict crawling peg exchange rate adopted by the monetary authorities was abandoned and in an effort to introduce "exchange noise," a modest appreciation was permitted, followed by a devaluation in subsequent months. In June 1991, together with a slight appreciation of the "reference dollar" (the reference exchange rate) and a tariff reduction to 11 percent, a cash reserve of 20 percent was established for short-term external credits. At the same time, the 1.2 percent tax on credits in domestic currency was extended to external credits. In January 1992 the price of the reference dollar was reduced 5 percent and the dollar flotation band in the formal exchange market was expanded to 10 percent in both directions. In May 1992 cash reserves for external credits were raised to 30 percent and in July of that year the dollar was replaced with a mix of currencies (consisting of the dollar, 50 percent; the German mark, 30 percent; and the Japanese yen, 20 percent) as the reference exchange rate.

The objective of these measures was to discourage speculation on the interest rate differential between the dollar and the peso and to create greater exchange rate uncertainty in the short term, while preserving a degree of certainty for investors in tradable goods, which the Central Bank will protect by supporting the long-term real exchange rate. Moreover, replacing the dollar with a mix of currencies for the reference exchange rate increased the stability of the value in pesos of exports, which are geographically well-dispersed, with the United States accounting for less than 20 percent of the total.

An effort was also made in 1992 to facilitate capital outflows as a means of alleviating downward pressure on the exchange rate. For example, the minimum waiting periods for repatriating capital or remitting profits on Chapter XIX investments were shortened, in some cases subject to the payment of a commission on the original investment. Moreover, AFPs were authorized to invest up to 3 percent of their funds abroad. Finally, Chilean banks were allowed to grant credit to support trade within Latin America to companies from other countries of the region and to purchase low-risk financial assets abroad. It is hardly likely that these measures will have a significant impact on the real exchange rate since the profitability of financial assets is sufficiently greater in Chile than abroad, which should also discourage substantial external investments by banks or AFPs. It is even likely that foreign investors will choose to reinvest their profits in Chile instead of repatriating their capital. Moreover, measures of this type, which facilitate the outflow of capital (or of profits, dividends, or interest) could have the opposite effect and encourage larger flows into the country (Williamson, 1992).

As Figure 3.3 indicates, the real exchange rate rose sharply from its low point in April 1982 until June 1988. After fluctuating randomly until February 1991, it took a downward turn that continued until December 1992. In its ascendant phase, between April 1982 and June 1988, the real exchange rate rose 133 percent. The decline in the period between February 1991 and December 1992 was 17 percent. It should also be noted that the real exchange rate toward the end

Figure 3.3. Chile: Real Exchange Rate Index
(1986=100)

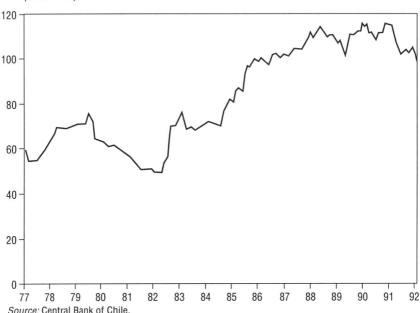

Source: Central Bank of Chile.

of 1992 remained well above the levels observed in the mid-1980s. In 1993, the downward pressures on the real exchange rate eased and there was a slight depreciation, due in part to the significant deterioration of the prices of Chile's major export products (copper, cellulose, fish meal, and some fruits and vegetables). Judging by the figures available to date (which cover only the first half of the year), capital is still flowing into Chile, although the short-term flows have dwindled significantly, possibly because the steps taken have had the desired effect.

One of the most important ways in which capital flows affect the economy is via their impact on the exchange rate, which is a factor in the allocation of investment resources between the tradable and nontradable sectors. To examine these effects, an econometric analysis was performed using the long-term equilibrium exchange rate, *TCR**, which is determined by the so-called "fundamentals" (Edwards, 1989). Thus, the variations in *TCR* are flows of the latter toward their equilibrium level, plus digressions from this level, which is a function of the macroeconomic disequilibria (*DESM*). Following is the equation for the variation observed in the real exchange rate:

$$\Delta TCR_t = \theta\,(TCR_t^* - TCR_{t-1}) + \lambda\,(DESM_t) + \gamma\,\Delta E_t \tag{1}$$

where ΔE represents the variation of the nominal exchange rate.

The equilibrium *TCR* is determined by the following equation:

$$TCR_t^* = \alpha_0 + \alpha_1 TI_t + \alpha_2 \tau_t + \alpha_3 \left(\frac{G}{Y}\right)_t + \alpha_4 FC_t + \alpha_5 Y \qquad (2)$$

where G is public spending, Y is domestic output, τ is the tariff level, TI is the terms of trade, and FC is a measure of the capital flows.
Replacing equation (2) in (1) and arranging terms gives equation (3):

$$TCR_t = \theta\alpha_0 + \theta\alpha_1 TI_t + \theta\alpha_2 \tau_t + \theta\alpha_3 \left(\frac{G}{Y}\right)_t + \theta\alpha_4 FC_t + \theta\alpha_5 Y_t$$
$$+ (1-\theta) TCR_{t-1} + u_t \qquad (3)$$

Because of the slight variance of tariffs in the period in question, a dummy variable *(DUM20UP)* was used, which has a value of 1 when the average quarterly tariff was 20 percent or more and 0 in the opposite case. Moreover, in implementing the model, the lag real exchange rate variable was replaced, a variable which is itself explained by lags of the independent variables, through a structure of lags of the latter. For this, the Almon polynomial lag technique was used (with second degree polynomials). This method was chosen because in estimating equation (3) in its original form, the one-period lagged real exchange rate is the only significant explicative variable and it tends to explain 95 percent of the total variation in the real exchange rate. Substituting backwards, we can replace the one-period lag real exchange rate with lags in the independent variables.

Therefore, the model we are looking for, in logarithms (L), is:

$$LTCR = \beta_0 + \beta_1 DUM20UP_t + \beta_2 D914 + \sum_{i=0}^{t} \alpha_{t-i} LTI_{t-i}$$

$$+ \sum_{i=0}^{k} \gamma_{t-i} LGFIS_{t-i} + \sum_{i=0}^{m} \theta_{t-i} FC_t + \sum_{i=0}^{p} \delta_{t-i} LPGB_{t-1} + u_t \qquad (3)$$

The results are shown in Table 3.8. The *D914* variable is a "dummy" with a value of 1 for the fourth quarter of 1991. One interesting result is the effect of the tariff variable. A rise in the uniform tariff beyond the 20 percent level lowers the real effective exchange rate by 7 percent. The *LTI* variable (log of the terms of trade) has a negative effect on the real exchange rate, which is statistically significant only with two or more lag periods. The long-term elasticity of the real exchange rate with regard to the terms of trade appears to be statistically significant at -0.27. The constant rise in the real exchange rate in the 1982-88 period was due in part to the increasing terms of trade deterioration.

Table 3.8. Chile: Estimate of the Real Exchange Rate Equation

	C	DUM20UP	D914	LTIL	GFIS	FC	LPGB
t	-1.10	-0.07	-0.30	0.01	0.14	3.0E-05	0.44
	(-0.40)	(-1.60)	(-5.18)	(0.17)	(2.47)	(1.29)	(1.91)
t-1				-0.04	0.08	-2.5E-05	0.12
				(-1.87)	(2.38)	(-1.30)	(2.99)
t-2				-0.07	0.02	-7.9E-05	0.07
				(-0.53)	(0.64)	(-4.08)	(2.55)
t-3				-0.83	-0.04	-1.3E-04	
				(-3.91)	(-2.14)	(-5.40)	
t-4				-0.08	-0.11		
				(-1.88)	(-2.97)		
Total				-0.27	0.09	-2.0E-04	0.63
				(-6.16)	(0.80)	(-3.77)	(2.64)

Adjusted R^2= 0.96; Durbin-Watson = 1.97; N = 36; *t*-statistic in parentheses.
Source: Author's estimates.

The lack of access to the financial market also contributed to the rise of the real exchange rate in this period. Despite official multilateral loans and involuntary loans from private banks, there was an obvious decline in the amount of capital entering the country in the 1983-87 period. This effect is demonstrated by the *FC* variable (capital flows, measured in current dollars and deflated by the External Price Index), the semi-elasticity of which appears in the above table. These flows have an impact with certain lags on the real exchange rate, and a long-term elasticity equal to -0.076,[10] which is fairly low.

The *LGFIS* variable (log of fiscal spending) is positive in the contemporaneous variable and in the first lag period, and negative in the third and fourth lag. Its long-term elasticity is low and statistically insignificant. There were considerable differences of opinion in Chile about the necessity of cutting government spending to reverse the decline of the real exchange rate. Presumably, the effect of public spending on the real exchange rate is negative because it has a nontradable component greater than private spending. Moreover, it has been argued that fiscal *savings* must be increased (by cutting spending) in order to lower interest rates and thus discourage capital inflows. Our findings are consistent with recent analyses indicating that the impact of public saving on the exchange rate is not particularly significant in quantitative terms.[11]

---

[10] This elasticity was calculated using the mean of the *FC* variable, which is 382.03.

The log *PGB* variable was included as a proxy of the demand for imported goods, which has a direct impact on the real exchange rate. This variable also yields fairly solid results. The estimated long-term elasticity of the exchange rate with regard to business activity is 0.62. This is very important for an economy such as Chile's which is experiencing steady growth and at the same time hopes to maintain a high real exchange rate. *Ceteris paribus*, this economy, which is growing at a rate of 8 percent per annum, should have an increase of approximately 5 percent per annum in the real exchange rate.

In conclusion, we can state that the model developed explains about 94 percent of the total variation in the exchange rate and that the trade policy variables (represented by the tariffs) and the international variables (represented by the terms of trade and the capital flows) significantly affect the trend of the real exchange rate. Improved access to financial markets has kept Chile's exchange rate lower than it would have been if the conditions of 1983 persisted. This is clearly visible in Figure 3.4, which presents a simulation of the real exchange rate, based on the assumption that the capital flows remain constant at the 1983 level. The profound effect of the capital flows on the economy is particularly interesting, given the differences between the log of the simulated exchange rate and the actual rate in certain periods. This is especially true of the period between the second quarter of 1990 and the fourth quarter of 1991, when the simulated exchange rate was from 6 to 24 percent higher than the actual rate.

Exchange management in the most recent period of heavy capital inflows has differed substantially from the approach taken in the 1978-82 period. Between July 1979 and April 1982 the real value of the dollar fell 35 percent, or twice the amount of exchange appreciation in the most recent period. If we compare the policies on external capital and the control of its effects on the economy in the current period with those adopted in similar circumstances in 1978-82, we are led to the conclusion that the macroeconomic policies followed since 1991 have been far more pragmatic and have yielded positive results.

First, the monetary authority succeeded in sterilizing the monetary effects of the heavy capital inflows and the attendant accumulation of international reserves. The cost of this policy has been high: the interest rates that the Central Bank has to pay on its bonds are much higher than the returns on its investments in foreign currency. It is estimated that the Central Bank's losses in this regard were approximately 0.5 percent of GDP in 1992.[12] Moreover, net sales of securities have kept interest rates higher than they would have been had such sales not occurred.

---

[11] See Arrau, Quiroz, and Chumacero (1992) for a discussion and empirical analysis of the effects of public saving on the exchange rate.

Figure 3.4. Chile: Actual and Predicted Real Exchange Rate
(Pesos per dollar)

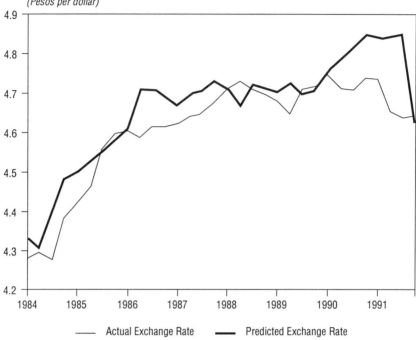

It should be noted that investment is still low—especially when compared to the rate in more rapidly developing countries—and that in order for it to rise significantly, real interest rates must fall.

As far as the impact of capital flows on the exchange rate is concerned, it can be concluded that the policies followed since the onset of the current foreign exchange boom have achieved their objective of preventing significant real appreciation of the peso. It is perhaps for this reason, as well as the predominance of DFI in the capital flows, that the probable effects of the capital flows on investment have been more positive than negative.

---

[12] The Central Bank estimates that losses in 1992 due to interest rate differentials on its assets and liabilities totaled $Ch130 billion (Banco Central de Chile, 1992, p. 51). At the average exchange rate for 1992 ($Ch362 per US$), this figure equals US$359 million, or approximately 1 percent of GDP. Roughly half of these losses were due to yield differentials between the reserves in foreign currency and the bonds that the Bank had to issue to sterilize the monetary effects of the accumulation of such reserves.

Table 3.9. Chile: Gross Formation of Fixed Capital, Domestic Savings, and Contributions from Foreign Savings, 1978-92
(Percentage of GDP at 1977 prices)

Year	GDP growth rate	Gross fixed capital formation		Domestic savings	Foreign savings[2]	Nonfinancial current account[3]
		Previous national accounts	Revised national accounts[1]			
1978	8.2	14.5	—	14.0	5.9	3.2
1979	8.2	15.6	—	14.4	8.5	5.2
1980	7.8	17.6	—	17.7	10.3	6.6
1981	5.6	19.5	—	14.7	17.9	12.9
1982	-14.1	15.0	—	11.4	8.1	0.1
1983	-0.7	12.9	—	13.4	3.5	-4.4
1984	6.3	13.2	—	17.5	6.3	-2.1
1985	2.4	14.8	17.7	20.3	1.2	-7.1
1986	5.7	15.0	17.1	21.7	0.5	-7.4
1987	5.7	16.4	19.6	23.1	0.3	-6.0
1988	7.4	17.0	20.8	21.9	1.7	-4.7
1989	10.0	18.6	23.9	23.7	2.7	-2.9
1990	2.1	19.5	24.6	24.7	-0.2	-4.9
1991	6.0	18.2	22.3	25.3	-1.6	-6.3
1992	10.4	19.8	25.1	25.9	0.4	-4.0

[1] At 1986 prices.
[2] Corresponds to the current account deficit.
[3] Net transfers for financing an import surplus of nonfinancial goods and services.
Source: Central Bank of Chile.

Effects on Investment

Investment Trends in the Last Decade

To fully understand the role of capital flows in the macroeconomics of Chile, these flows must be placed within the context of the savings-investment process. As indicated in Table 3.9, after the 1982-83 depression, when it fell to less than 13 percent of GDP, fixed gross investment recovered gradually and rose to nearly 20 percent of GDP (25 percent according to the recent revision of the national accounts). Domestic savings increased even more dramatically, but external savings (measured by the current account deficit of the balance of payments) contributed almost nothing to the financing of investment. In net terms, the capital inflow financed the debt service and the accumulation of reserves.

Regardless of the measure used, investment was extremely depressed throughout the first half of the 1980s and only began to recover in the middle of the

Table 3.10. Chile: Investment Indicators, 1981-92

	Construction starts (1981=100)	Real fixed gross investment[a] (1981=100)	Capital goods imports (Millions of 1981 US$)
1981	100.0	100.0	1249.7
1982	40.7	66.5	599.3
1983	47.1	56.2	366.3
1984	51.5	61.3	617.7
1985	63.7	70.3	664.4
1986	63.4	75.3	693.0
1987	94.2	87.5	942.0
1988	108.4	100.9	1097.9
1989	127.7	117.1	1581.1
1990	122.0	125.2	1686.3
1991	149.3	123.9	1475.8
1992[b]	192.7	149.0	1969.6

[a] Data in 1977 pesos.
[b] Preliminary.
Source: Author's calculations based on data from the Central Bank of Chile.

decade. As indicated in Table 3.10, which shows the trend of investment and its major components, investment remained below the 1981 level until 1989. The only exception was construction starts, which reached the 1981 level in 1988.

The investment recovery that began in the mid-1980s and is still in progress has affected every component of investment. Taking 1981 as a base, fixed gross investment in 1992 rose 56 percent, construction starts rose more than 90 percent, and capital goods imports rose just under 60 percent. Nevertheless, despite the growth of investment since 1988 and its acceleration in 1992, the Chilean economy is still generating surprisingly low aggregate investment ratios, given the high economic growth rates achieved in recent years and the substantial inflows of private external capital, much of which, as mentioned above, has taken the form of DFI. Given the sharp rise in investment in export sectors, especially those connected with foreign investments, the relatively slight gain in aggregate investment would seem to indicate that, except for exports involving raw materials, investment in other tradable sectors (especially the manufacturing sector) has fallen far behind.

Impact of Capital Flows

It is difficult to determine how much capital flows contributed to the growth of investment. Four major effects can be distinguished: (1) the direct, positive effect of DFI; (2) the possible impact of the easing of balance of payments constraints, which may have increased the country's ability to import capital goods; (3) if investment is limited due to lack of access to credit (in other words, if the interest rate alone does not balance the credit market), the increased liquidity brought about by the capital flows and the resultant accumulation of reserves could have favorably affected investment; and (4) the exchange appreciation caused by the capital inflows may have stimulated investment by lowering the cost of capital goods, most of which are imported.

Moreover, the effects of the capital flows on the allocation of investment between tradable and nontradable goods may have been considerable. Appreciation of the peso may have adversely affected investment in tradable goods (especially export goods, which have been the main impetus of economic growth in Chile since the mid-1980s). Exchange appreciation may also have had an expansive effect on short-term business activity (because it increases real income) and a negative effect in the longer term (by negatively affecting the profitability of the tradable sectors of the economy). Consequently, the accelerator effect should increase investment in the short term (and decrease it in the long term); the net effect is unclear.

Finally, capital flows may have positively affected investment in another, nontraditional way. The rise of share prices on the stock exchange may have had something to do with the heavy flows of capital into the country in recent years, and high share prices may have encouraged Chilean companies to issue new shares in order to finance investments.

A study of the determinants of investment conducted by Solimano (1990) sheds light on some of these effects. Solimano defines a model consisting of three, simultaneous equations for investment, the Tobin Q (approximated by the real share price index), and real income. The results of defining this model indicate that investment is affected by the level of credit in the private sector, but that the effect is not very important in quantitative terms. On the other hand, the impact of the exchange rate on investment is complex. In the short term, exchange overvaluation can increase the profitability of investment by lowering the price of replacement capital, giving rise to an explosion in investment that is not sustainable and that is concentrated in the "wrong" (nontradable) sectors. In the longer term, the impact of real depreciation can become more positive because it increases the value of capital in the tradable sector and this effect becomes greater than the impact of the increased replacement cost as the relative importance of the tradable sector of the economy grows and the dependence of investment on imported capital goods decreases.

It is unlikely that the impact of the recent capital flows on investment has been felt through the easing of the availability of foreign exchange or private sector credit. As explained above, the abundance of foreign exchange in the Chilean economy was due to a variety of factors, the most important of which was the improvement in the current account (see Table 3.3). As far as the avail-ability of credit in the private sector is concerned, there can be no doubt that external conditions have become much more favorable in recent years, seeing that Chilean debtors—banks and some large companies in particular—have gained access to international credit markets. If there was a credit squeeze that acted through some route other than the interest rate, the resumption of volun-tary loans to Chilean banks and companies might have helped alleviate it. How-ever, in reality, it is unlikely that such a route would have been of any great importance. On the one hand, external borrowing by companies and banks was discouraged by the imposition of progressively higher reserve requirements on external credits. On the other hand, the aim of monetary policy was to sterilize a large percentage of the increase in money supply caused by larger capital flows. This means that companies with no access to the international financial market did not enjoy more favorable credit conditions as a result of the in-creases in capital flows.

Apparently, the immediate impact of the flows via DFI was the most signifi-cant. As mentioned above, these investments substantially increased the capacity to produce exportable goods. It is also possible that the exchange rate apprecia-tion that occurred in early 1991 significantly affected investment in exportable goods, although this is nothing more than a conjecture at present. As we have seen, without the inflow of capital in the 1988-91 period, Chile might have had a considerably lower exchange rate than it did, and this could be affecting the rate of investment in the tradable goods sectors, especially in marginal projects in-volving the export of manufactures, the most dynamic of Chile's export sectors and one that relies heavily on the maintenance of a favorable exchange rate.

Finally, the sharp increase in share prices coincided with the inflow of external capital, although the timing of the two phenomena differed. The value of both speculative capital and investment funds peaked in 1990, whereas the largest increase in share prices occurred in 1991. Nor does it appear that there is any explicit relationship between share prices and new share offerings by Chilean corporations. The largest share offerings were in 1987 and 1988 within the context of the privatization program. Since then, new share offerings have decreased appreciably, despite the boom in share prices in the 1987-91 period as a whole and in 1991 in particular, when the price index of shares traded on the stock exchange rose more than 90 percent in real terms.

Impact of DFI on Gross Investment

This section contains an analysis of the role of DFI on gross investment (GI) in Chile. The period in question is 1983 to 1991. Quarterly data are used.

Two avenues can be identified to explain the relationship between DFI and GI. First, there is a direct effect related to the real investment component of DFI.

Table 3.11. Chile: Estimates from the Investment Equation

	LIED	LQ	LPIB
t	0.035		
	(2.85)		
t-1	0.034	0.0003	0.62
	(2.59)	(10.48)	(9.21)
t-2		0.00018	0.41
		(16.76)	(14.43)
t-3		0.00011	0.25
		(9.63)	(12.12)
t-4		5.4×10^{-5}	0.14
		(4.66)	(5.73)
t-5		1.8×10^{-5}	0.071
		(3.13)	(3.76)
Total of coefficients	0.069	0.00065	1.49
	(5.34)	(17.36)	(16.65)

Adjusted R^2 = 0.98; Durbin-Watson = 0.47; N = 32; t-statistic in parentheses.
Source: Author's estimates.

Second, because a sizable percentage of the capital account consists of DFI, and to the extent that some of it passes through the exchange market and increases the supply of foreign currency, it helps alleviate the foreign exchange and credit squeeze that could be limiting domestic investment. The following single-equation model was defined to cover both elements:

$$LIT = \alpha + \sum \beta_i \cdot LIED_{1-i} + \sum \gamma_i \cdot LQ_{1-i} + \sum \delta_i \cdot LPGB_{1-i} + \mu_i \qquad (5)$$

All of the variables are expressed in logarithmic terms (L). The variable Q is Tobin's Q (approximated here by the general price index of shares traded on the stock exchange, deflated by the CPI) and GDP is the quarterly gross domestic product. The model was defined using Almon polynomials. The results are shown in Table 3.11.

The best fit was obtained using a second degree polynomial for all variables. Two lags were set for DFI and five for Tobin's Q and GDP. In the latter two cases, the contemporaneous value was excluded. The long-term effect of the variables used is given by the sum of the individual coefficients for each lag. In our case, said elasticity is extremely low for the Q variable, a little less than 0.1 for DFI and close to 1.5 for GDP. The low value of GI elasticity as compared to DFI is a

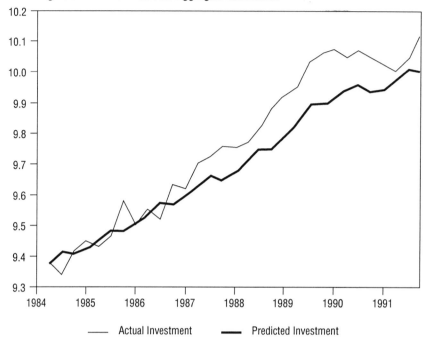

Figure 3.5. Chile: Predicted Aggregate Investment

consequence of the faster growth of the latter. As mentioned above, it is likely that a considerable percentage of DFI financed purchases of existing assets. Moreover, investments by Chilean companies in tradable sectors not exporting raw materials or their byproducts have fallen behind.

Finally, for the purpose of examining the role of DFI in the period in question, Figure 3.5 compares the effective growth of gross investment (LTI in logarithms), with a simulation of the same variable ($SLIT$), estimated on the basis of the results of the previous regression and assuming that DFI remains constant at the level of the fourth quarter of 1985 in all remaining cases. As the figure illustrates, gross investment would have been considerably smaller if DFI had remained at the 1985 levels. This simple model shows that gross investment would have been about 10 percent smaller in the 1987-91 period. In other words, the increase in DFI contributed more than 40 percent of the rise in gross investment between 1981 and 1991.

Impact on Investment in Exportable Goods

It is especially interesting to study the indirect effect of the flow of external capital on investment in exportable goods—manufactures in particular—via its impact on the exchange rate. Unfortunately, there are no data disaggregated by busi-

Table 3.12. Chile: Annual Growth Rates of GDP and Real Exports, 1973-92
(Percentages)

	GDP	Total exports	Intermed. goods exports[a]	Manufactures[b]	Exports/ GDP[c] (%)	Noncopper/ exports[c] (%)
1973-79	2.7	9.7	57.9	31.4	14.3	17.9
1979-83	-0.8	5.3	6.2	-3.6	22.3	49.6
1983-92	6.5	6.5	10.2[d]	14.4	25.2	53.2
1988	7.4	6.8	17.0	20.2	27.9	53.5
1989	10.0	6.4	14.9	24.6	29.4	52.1
1990	2.1	11.0	8.6	11.9	31.0	56.2
1991	6.0	5.5	8.0	17.9	33.0	61.9
1992[e]	10.4	12.3	—	19.8	33.5	61.1

[a] Nonmining products and nonmanufactures. Includes fish meal, wood, and wood products.
[b] Does not include fishmeal, wood, or wood products.
[c] The figures refer to the first year of each period.
[d] 1983-91.
[e] Preliminary.
Source: Central Bank of Chile.

ness sector for investment, much less for export sector investment. Economic development in Chile in the last two decades was closely linked to the expansion and diversification of exports. The most dynamic exports were noncopper raw materials and related semimanufactures. Exports of manufactures also soared, but from very low initial levels. The exchange rate was one of the basic variables explaining the trend of the exportable goods supply.[13] As can be seen in Table 3.12, which presents real export and real GDP growth rates, the only subperiod in which exports of manufactured goods contracted in real terms (and the growth of intermediate goods slowed dramatically) was from 1979 to 1983. Interestingly, it was in 1979-82 that substantial appreciation of the exchange rate occurred as a result of the inflow of private capital.

It can also be seen that in the current period of declining real exchange rates, no significant slowdown has yet been observed in the growth of these exports. It may be that the effects of exchange rate fluctuations are delayed, especially if it is believed that investment is the principal conduit for the impact of the exchange rate on these exports. This is why the authorities have assigned such a high priority to controlling exchange rate appreciation.

---

[13] Using quarterly data and a partial adjustment model, two supply functions of exportable goods were determined econometrically, one for raw materials other than copper (including wood products and fish meal) and the other for manufactures. The results reveal long-term export elasticities with regard to the exchange rate of approximately one and lags of about one year. Our findings coincide *a grosso modo* with those of Moguillansky and Tittelman (1993).

In a small, open economy such as Chile, appreciation affects not only the allocation of resources between the tradable and nontradable sectors, but also the long-term growth rate.[14] The growth of the nontradable sector (like that of the import substitution sectors) is strictly limited by the size of the domestic market. The growth of exports is generally not subject to such limitations, especially when accompanied by the diversification of both products and markets. Moreover, it is probably true that economies of scale and apprenticeship can be better exploited by exporting than by producing for the domestic market.

The Exchange Rate and Capital Goods Imports

The exchange rate can also affect investment via its impact on the cost of capital goods, most of which are imported in a small economy such as that of Chile. This effect can be the opposite of the one associated with investments in exportable goods: the higher the real exchange rate, the higher the replacement cost of capital goods, which could discourage investment. It is interesting to see how significant this effect can be. Even when exchange rate depreciation negatively affects investment (price effect of capital goods), if it leads to a higher growth rate, gross investment could increase (income effect of depreciation), even if the capital goods are lacking.

To analyze this question, quarterly figures were obtained for real capital goods imports in the 1981-91 period. The following formula was used for the demand for imported capital goods:

$$LM_t = \alpha_0 + \alpha_1 \cdot Le_{t-1} + \alpha_2 \cdot LY_t + \alpha_3 \cdot L\tau_t + u_t \qquad (6)$$

where M represents real capital goods imports; e, the real exchange rate (adjusted by the external price index); Y, the gross domestic product; and τ, the average tariff.

The results of the least squares regression were the following:

$$LM_t = 1.78 - 044 \cdot Le_{t-1} + 0.99 \cdot LY_t + 0.27\tau_t \qquad (7)$$
$$\quad\;\; (3.05)\;(-1.93) \qquad (9.98) \qquad (1.75)$$

where the t-statistic is in parentheses; the adjusted R^2 is 0.830; D.W. = 1.57; and N = 43.

---

[14] Obviously, we refer to appreciation not due to factors that affect the long-term equilibrium of the exchange rate. Usually, as the economy grows, the exchange rate appreciates because of a permanent improvement in the productivity of the factors.

The elasticities revealed by the model are all significant at the standard levels of significance. The income elasticity of capital goods imports is one and their elasticity with respect to the exchange rate is fairly low (0.44), which means that the principal effect is associated with the growth of GDP and not the cost of capital goods. Using the estimated coefficients of equation (7) and those obtained in the exchange rate equation (Table 3.8), it is seen that a GDP growth rate of 8 percent would produce a direct 8 percent increase and an indirect 2 percent decrease in capital goods imports (the latter owing to the exchange depreciation caused by the rise in GDP). On the other hand, it is very likely that real depreciation of the exchange rate, by impacting positively on exports and on goods substituting for imports, has a positive effect on investment via its effects on aggregate demand, despite the attendant rise in the cost of capital goods.

It should also be noted that higher tariffs are related to an increase in capital goods imports, despite the fact that the latter also drive up the costs of capital goods. As with adjustments in the exchange rate, the income effect (positive force) of a rise in average tariffs is apparently stronger than the price effect (negative force).

Conclusions

This study analyzed the flow of private external capital into the Chilean economy since 1987 and its effects on development. Emphasis was given to the changes that the inflow of external capital caused in the management of economic policy, monetary and exchange rate policies in particular.

The main component of the inflow of external capital in recent years has been DFI. This is apparently due to the continuing favorable conditions for foreign investment in Chile, especially in exportable goods in which it has natural comparative advantages. Another important factor has been the replenishment of DFI stocks, which were at unusually low levels in the mid-1980s. The debt capitalization program (Chapter XIX of the Compendium of International Exchange Regulations of the Central Bank) also had a positive effect on the level of DFI. A significant exchange subsidy was an indirect outcome of this program. There is continuing controversy in the literature about the actual effect of the promulgation of Chapter XIX. On the one hand, it is believed that DFI might have increased even without the debt conversion program and exchange rate subsidy. However, several arguments in this study support the theory that Chapter XIX helped increase the flows of foreign investment, alleviate the debt problem, and channel external investment resources to nonmining export sectors.

Another important component of the capital flows in recent years was speculative capital. It is difficult to define this concept and in this study several definitions are discussed, emphasizing their advantages and disadvantages. The definition we have chosen is closely linked to the flows of short-term private capital, both in the balance of payments and through the informal market. In "normal" conditions, these flows are heavily influenced by the difference between the domestic and international interest rates, corrected by devaluation expectations and the perception of country risk.

Two structural changes were fundamental in the flows of short-term capital since the early 1980s. The first is the debt problem, which was at its worst from 1982 to 1987, the year in which copper prices rose sharply and Chile successfully renegotiated its external debt. Between 1983 and mid-1987, the short-term external flows dwindled to almost nothing.

The second structural change is associated with the exchange measures adopted to discourage international interest rate speculation, in particular through the establishment of reserve requirements for short-term external credits. Such speculation was further discouraged by greater uncertainty about the price of the dollar, caused by the widening of its flotation band and the designation of a mix of currencies for determining its center point. These policies, adopted in June 1991, led to a significant decrease in short-term capital flows attracted by domestic interest rates far above the international rates.

Regarding monetary management of the capital flows, the differences between the former period of heavy capital inflows (1978-81) and the 1987-92 period were studied. The main difference between the two is that in the former, monetary policy was essentially passive and permitted monetization of the flows, while in the latter the monetary authority effectively sterilized much of the capital inflow. This led to interest rates substantially higher than what would have prevailed without sterilization and necessitated the use of the above-mentioned exchange measures to prevent an even larger flow of speculative capital.

Our analysis of the impact of exchange rate policy is based in part on the definition of an econometric model for the equilibrium real exchange rate. According to this model, the major variables affecting the real exchange rate are aggregate demand, the terms of trade, and capital flows. The necessity of increasing government savings in order to maintain the exchange rate has been much discussed in Chile. Our findings, however, corroborate studies showing that government savings have little effect on the real exchange rate. Even if an increase in government savings were to have some positive effect on the exchange rate via a possible reduction in interest rates, there are no good reasons for subordinating fiscal policy to exchange rate objectives, especially when there are other effective ways of managing the exchange rate.

No statistically meaningful relationship could be established between external capital flows and gross investment in the Chilean economy. The only variable significantly related to gross investment is DFI, although the elasticity of gross investment with respect to DFI is rather low. In other words, DFI has grown out of all proportion to the size of the Chilean economy, while gross investment has increased only modestly. This could be an indication of two complementary phenomena: (1) despite the increase in the rate of investment in the economy as a whole, investment continued to be weak in tradable sectors not associated with natural resources in which Chile has comparative advantages and which have not received DFI; and (2) a certain percentage of DFI—substantial, but difficult to determine quantitatively—financed the purchase of existing assets. In any case, a simulation using the equation for gross investment as a function of DFI (and other variables) indicates that gross investment in the Chilean economy would have been 10 percent less in the 1987-91 period had DFI remained at its 1983 levels. Between 1981 and 1991, the increase in DFI explains 40 percent of the rise in domestic investment.

Another interesting exercise analyzed the distribution of investment between tradable and nontradable goods. Although there are no figures for the sectoral allocation of investment, available analyses of the export/exchange rate relationship indicate that the exchange rate is a crucial variable in the maintenance of export growth, particularly with respect to the introduction of new products in the international markets. Consequently, investment in exportable goods other than copper seems to be determined largely by the exchange rate.

Our analysis also revealed that the principal determinant of capital goods imports is the rate of economic growth. A surge in growth should produce a directly proportionate increase in capital goods imports (income elasticity of demand near one). At the same time, the exchange rate depreciation caused by faster growth—because it drives up the replacement cost of capital goods in pesos— depresses capital goods imports somewhat, but the impact via this price effect is relatively small and far less significant than the effect of the rise in income.

These results suggest the following hypothesis. Economic growth in Chile has become increasingly dependent on the steady growth of exportable goods, which has clearly supplemented the latter's share of GDP. Because of this structural change, exchange depreciation has had an increasingly positive effect on investment. This is so partly because the capital stock in exportable goods has been expanding and, therefore, exchange rate depreciation is raising the value of capital in the economy (an effect discussed by Solimano, 1990). Moreover, the larger the export sector the greater the positive effect of real depreciation on investment. As the export sector grows, the increments of investment in it— prompted by the effect of depreciation on the relative prices of tradable goods— become larger than the decreases in investment in the nontradable sectors. In turn, the multiplier effect of the growth of exports on the economy as a whole could be exercising a positive income effect, even on the nontradable and import substitution sectors. It must also be kept in mind that investment in the export sector is not subject to the limitations imposed by a narrow domestic market (which is certainly the case with investment in nontradable goods), particularly if the growth of exports leads to the increasing diversification of products and markets. Therefore, the reallocation of resources to the export sectors would lead to higher rates of growth—and of gross investment—in the long term.

Moreover, although exchange rate depreciation has a negative price effect on imports of capital goods, it may be smaller than the positive income effect on such imports and on investment in general as a result of the stimulus to business activity provided by such depreciation.

These considerations justify the efforts of the authorities to contain the real appreciation of the peso caused by the inflow of private external capital in recent years. It is especially important for the Chilean development model that real exchange appreciation in excess of what has already occurred since 1991 be avoided. If the wide gap between domestic and international interest rates sparks new increases in speculative flows, despite the steps taken to date, it will be important to back them up with new measures. For example, consideration could be given to the temporary imposition of caps on the short-term external borrowing of banks for the purpose of making loans in national currency, and on such borrowing by nonbanking institutions with access to international financial markets. These policies are being pursued in many other countries and were the norm in Chile up to 1979.

One of the reasons that so much emphasis has been placed on the exchange rate is that the authorities have not had many other tools to work with. The radical trade liberalization undertaken by Chile nearly 20 years ago and the belief in neutral incentive policies make it difficult to formulate fiscal or financial measures to support the process of diversifying and expanding Chilean exports. The seesawing of the exchange rate, despite the efforts of the monetary authorities, suggests that more pragmatic policies could make a significant contribution to economic growth in Chile.

APPENDIX

NOTES ON THE VARIABLES USED

Real exchange rate: Series published by Banco Central de Chile, *Boletín Mensual*.

Nominal exchange rate: Banco Central de Chile, *Boletín Mensual*.

Gross domestic product: Banco Central de Chile, *Boletín Mensual*; Indice Mensual de Actividad Económica (IMACEC): Banco Central de Chile, *Informe Económico y Financiero*.

Interest rate: Annualized interest rate charged in 90- to 365-day indexed operations, published in Banco Central de Chile, *Boletín Mensual*; the quarterly value is the average of the monthly rates.

Tobin's Q: Calculated by dividing the monthly series of the General Share Price Index in nominal values, published by the Santiago Stock Exchange, by the wholesale price index (WPI), published by the Central Bank in its *Boletín Mensual*. The quarterly figures are the average of the index in the respective months.

Government spending: Figures published in the *Informe Financiero del Tesoro Público*; the deflator used is the CPI.

Average tariff: Ffrench-Davis, Leiva, and Madrid (1991), p. 34.

Capital goods imports: quarterly data in current dollars and deflators provided by the Central Bank.

Quarterly gross investment: Determined on the basis of annual figures published by the Central Bank, using the Chow-Lhin quarterization method, presented in the journal *Estudios de Economía* of the University of Chile, June 1987. The related series needed to use this methodology are the value added of construction, capital goods imports, and the seasonally adjusted gross domestic product (the source of all these series is the Central Bank).

Capital flow: Defined as the capital account less reserves; the deflator used was the External Price Index (excluding Latin America). The annual and quarterly balance of payments data were provided by the Central Bank. The External Price Index was taken from Feliú (1992).

Reserves variation: Banco Central de Chile, *Informe Anual de Balanza de Pagos*. Government savings: Determined using the income and expenditure figures published in the *Informe Financiero del Tesoro Público*; the deflator used was the CPI.

Direct foreign investment: Obtained using quarterly balance of payments data provided by the Central Bank, based on certain specific items: foreign investment under DL 600 and Chapter XIV, capitalization of external credits, investment with external debt instruments, and credits obtained under DL 600 and Article 15. The deflator used was an external price index published by the same institution.

Terms of trade: The export price index was constructed by weighting the top three export products in the period (copper, cellulose, and fish meal) according to their relative share of the total in 1985-87. The average prices for each product were obtained from the Banco Central de Chile, *Boletín Mensual*. The index for imports was provided by the International Monetary Fund, *International Financial Statistics*.

Bibliography

Arrau, P., P. Quiroz, and R. Chumacero. 1992. *Ahorro fiscal y tipo de cambio real.* Programa Post-Grado de Economía ILADES-Georgetown University, Serie de Investigación I-44. Santiago.

Banco Central de Chile. 1992. *Evolución de la economía en 1992 y perspectivas para 1993.* Santiago.

Banco Central de Chile. 1993. *Cuentas Nacionales de Chile 1985-1992.*

Damill, M., J.M. Fanelli, and R. Frenkel. 1992. *Shock externo y desequilibrio fiscal. La macroeconomía de América Latina en los ochenta. Chile.* Santiago: ECLAC.

Desormeaux, J. 1989. *La inversión extranjera y su rol en el desarrollo de Chile.* Working Document No. 119. Instituto de Economía, Pontificia Universidad Católica de Chile. Santiago.

Edwards, S. 1989. *Real exchange rates, devaluation, and adjustment.* Cambridge, Mass.: The MIT Press.

Feliú, C. 1992. *Inflación externa y tipo de cambio real: nota metodológica.* Serie de Estudios Económicos Nro. 37. Santiago: Banco Central de Chile.

Ffrench-Davis, R. 1990. Debt-Equity Swaps in Chile. *Cambridge Journal of Economics.* Vol. 14.

———, and J.P. Arellano. 1981. *Apertura financiera externa: la experienca chilena en 1973-80.* Colección Estudios CIEPLAN. 5.

———, P. Leiva, and R. Madrid. 1991. *La apertura comercial en Chile: experiencias y perspectivas.* Estudios de Política Comercial Nro. 1. Geneva: UNCTAD.

Hachette, D., and A. Cabrera. 1989. *The Capital Account Liberalization in Chile, 1974-82.* Working Document No. 120, Instituto de Economía, Pontificia Universidad Católica de Chile. Santiago.

Marshall, E. 1990. *La apertura financiera en Chile y el comportamiento de los bancos transnacionales.* ECLAC Studies and Report No. 78. Santiago.

Mizala, A. 1985. *Segmentación del mercado de capitales y liberalización financiera.* Notas Técnicas Nro. 69. Santiago: CIEPLAN.

————. 1992. Las reformas económicas de los años setenta y la industria manufacturera chilena. Colección Estudios CIEPLAN. 35. Special Issue.

Moguillansky, G., and D. Tittelman. 1993. *Estimación econométrica de funciones de exportación en Chile.* Estudios de Economía. 20 (1). Santiago: Department of Economics, University of Chile.

Morandé, F. 1988. Apreciación del peso y entrada de capitales externos. ¿Cuál viene antes? Chile, 1977-82. In *Del auge a la crisis de 1982,* eds. F. Morandé and K. Schmidt-Hebbel. Santiago: ILADES.

————. 1991. Flujos de capitales hacia Chile, 1977-1982 : una nueva mirada a la evidencia. In *Movimientos de capitales y crisis económica: los casos de Chile y Venezuela,* ed. F. Morandé. Santiago: ILADES.

Ramos, J. 1988. Auge y caída de los mercados de capitales en Chile. In *Del auge a la crisis de 1982,* eds. F. Morandé and K. Schmidt-Hebbel. Santiago: ILADES.

Reisen, H. 1992. Financial Opening and Capital Flows. Paris: OECD Development Centre. Unpublished document.

Solimano, A. 1990. *Inversión privada y ajuste macroeconómico. La experiencia chilena en la década de los 80.* Colección Estudios CIEPLAN.

Williamson, J. 1992. *Acerca de la liberalización de la cuenta de capitales.* Estudios de Economía. 19 (2). Santiago: Department of Economics, University of Chile.

CHAPTER FOUR

THE MACROECONOMIC
EFFECTS OF EXTERNAL CAPITAL:
COLOMBIA

By Mauricio Cárdenas S. and Felipe Barrera O.

Colombia, like other Latin American countries, has lately experienced an inflow of private capital that is without precedent in its recent economic history.[1] In fact, the accumulation of international reserves (net) was $634 million in 1990 and $1.875 billion in 1991. In 1992 the increase in reserves was $1.347 billion, bringing the overall balance to $7.92 billion, or approximately 1.5 times the annual volume of imported goods (i.e., 18 months of imports). For 1992, new reserves approaching $800 million are projected.

The source of this capital is uncertain and has sparked an interesting debate (Garay and Cárdenas, 1993). An unarguably dominant factor is the repatriation of Colombian capital, prompted by high yields, both real and financial.[2] The structural reform process—including, in particular, deregulation of the capital account and tax amnesties—has also played an important role.

The importance of exogenous factors such as the steep (but probably temporary) decline in the profitability of various investments in the United States (short-term interest rates, real estate, corporate profits, etc.) cannot be overlooked, however. Another notable factor in this regard is the greater access of Latin American agents to international stock markets and to the portfolios of institutional investment funds.

Given the significance of external factors, which could be reversed in the medium term, the Colombian authorities have intervened in the exchange market

---

[1] For an analysis of the Latin American experience, see Calvo, Leiderman, and Reinhart (1993) and Cárdenas (1992).

[2] Nevertheless, part of the capital "boom" is undoubtedly due to the presence of new foreign investors, who have changed their perception of the level of risk and profitability in Colombia.

to prevent appreciation of the currency.[3] Nevertheless, a comparison of the real exchange rate index (multilateral) in the final quarter of 1990 with its current level reveals an appreciation of nearly 14 percent.

As in other Latin American countries, the monetary effects of the intervention have been sterilized, which has led to increases in interest rates (especially in 1991) and in the liabilities of the monetary authority. The quasi-fiscal deficit, therefore, has grown by amounts ranging from 0.7 percent to 1.7 percent of GDP.

The purpose of this paper is to analyze the major causes and consequences of the recent flow of capital into Colombia. More specifically, the objectives are: (i) to identify the source, size, composition, and determinants of those flows; (ii) to evaluate their macroeconomic impact and to analyze the effectiveness of monetary, fiscal, and exchange policy in stabilizing the additional inflows of foreign exchange; and (iii) to estimate the medium- and long-term effects of the capital flows, especially those received in the form of productive investment.

The case study for Colombia contains several interesting details. First, the capital flows are distorted by the influx of foreign exchange from drug trafficking, the dynamics of which can transcend simple economic rationality. Second, unlike recent experiences in Argentina, Mexico, and Venezuela, among others, in Colombia there is no correlation between the capital flows and the privatization process (which has been modest by Latin American standards). Finally, and closely linked to the above, the inflow of capital has not eased the public sector budget constraint; quite the opposite, the stabilization policy has necessitated a substantial fiscal adjustment.

This study is divided into six parts. Following this introduction, the second section describes, in very general terms, certain aspects of the process of structural reform in progress in the Colombian economy in the last three years. Special emphasis is given to the major features of the trade, exchange, and financial reforms, which have a direct impact on the capital flows. The focus of the third section is the quantification of this capital, which requires a special methodology because of the unique characteristics of Colombia's external accounts. This section also presents the results of various econometric exercises seeking to identify the determinants of the capital flows.

The fourth section concentrates on policies aimed at the macroeconomic stabilization of the capital flows. It presents a discussion of the need to stabilize the inflows of foreign exchange and analyzes the effectiveness of both the

---

[3] From a conceptual viewpoint, the government's ability to intervene successfully in the exchange market is limited, especially if the capital inflow continues. In fact, in economies characterized by freely mobile capital (especially in the developed countries), the policy of "leaning into the wind" has not been very effective. See, in particular, Domínguez and Frankel (1988); Obstfeld (1982b and 1988); Rogoff (1984); and Weber (1986).

"microeconomic" policies (e.g., withholdings, reserve requirements, tax surcharges, etc.) and those of a macroeconomic nature such as monetary, exchange, and fiscal management.

The fifth section contains a discussion of the impact of the flows on capital formation in the Colombian economy. In this regard, several indicators of investment performance are analyzed, such as capital goods imports and the qualitative responses to major opinion polls. Also studied are the connection between the capital flows and the stock market, as well as the relationship between investment and capital flows. The sixth and final section summarizes the major findings and policy recommendations of this study.

Structural Reforms in the Colombian Economy, 1990-92

In the past three years the Colombian economy has been subjected to a series of far-reaching structural reforms that have involved profound changes in the development model and, consequently, in the functioning of the labor, financial, and exchange markets, as well as in the production of internationally tradable goods and services. In short, the aim of the structural reform process has been to increase the openness of the economy, promote competition and economic efficiency, and encourage the development of private initiative. Unquestionably, these changes have created a far more hospitable environment for the repatriation of capital.

The trade reform eliminated the quantitative restrictions applicable to 99 percent of the tariff items and reduced the level of nominal protection (tariff and surcharge), which, on average, fell from 43.7 percent in December 1989 to 11.7 percent in March 1992. In addition, the tax incentives for exports were lowered, procedures were simplified, and the advance deposit for imports was abolished. The reform was gradual at first but then gathered momentum in 1991 due to the sizable accumulation of reserves (see Lora, 1990; and Ocampo, 1992).

The financial reform (Law 45 of 1990) made it easier for new economic agents (both domestic and foreign) to gain access to the system. To introduce greater competition in the system, the law also promoted the shift from specialized to full-service banking through the creation of trusts, leasing companies, pension administration funds, etc. In addition, the level of forced investment and bank reserve requirements was reduced in order to lower the brokerage margin, and the process of reprivatizing nationalized banks was set in motion (see Lora, 1991; Arboleda, 1991; and Villegas, 1991).

The exchange system, in existence since 1967 and characterized by a series of daily minidevaluations and tight control of foreign exchange transactions, was substantially modified in 1990. As part of the strategy to internationalize the economy, decentralization of the exchange market was considered essential. To achieve this, the legal prohibition against holding assets denominated in foreign currency was partially lifted (amnesty was granted and foreign bank accounts of up to $20,000 were permitted) and financial and stock brokers were authorized to buy and sell foreign exchange. Even so, the Bank of the Republic still intervenes heavily in the system by purchasing foreign exchange with Exchange Certificates (bonds denominated in dollars), which have a term of one year and a redemption price determined daily in dollars. The secondary price of the certificates at the time of issue determines the price of the dollar on the free market. Through this mechanism (in force since June 1991), the Bank of the Republic maintains tight control over the price of the currency.

The objectives of the foreign investment regulations were to provide greater incentives for (and increased access to) technology transfers, to promote competition in certain domestic industries of a monopolistic nature, and to facilitate the process of integration with other economies and markets. To this end, complete investment freedom was guaranteed, except in the case of investments in public services (for which prior approval from the National Planning Department [DNP] is required) and in the mining sector (which is regulated by the Ministry of Mines), and a series of minor limitations of an informational nature in the financial sector. Similarly, the barriers and restrictions against the remittance of profits were removed, with remittances now being subject only to taxation, and the tax rate was lowered from 44 percent to 38.4 percent.

Lastly, advances in the privatization process were marginal, in part because of political opposition. Among the few examples worth noting are the sale of various financial institutions nationalized in the 1980s and the stock market offering (through the Industrial Development Institute) of the government's holdings in several joint ventures.

Capital Flow Measurements and Determinants

As mentioned in the introduction, the quantification of external capital flows in Colombia is difficult because of the illegality of certain foreign currency transactions. This, however, is the result of two clearly discernible forces. First, strict exchange controls in Colombia between 1967 and 1991 forced transactors to seek ways and means of concealing capital flows (e.g. over- and under-invoicing goods and services) prohibited by legislation. Second, as is well known, some of the proceeds from drug trafficking enter the economy through the official market under some heading that is not the real reason for such transactions.[4]

---

[4] There is a tendency to view the estimated inflow of drug money as a capital flow, whereas in the strictest sense, it is a mixture of current transactions and capital inflows generated by the divestiture of external assets acquired with drug money.

These two factors explain the existence of a black—or parallel—market, which is the conduit for some illegal transactions. Measuring the capital flows that enter (or leave) the economy through the black market is virtually impossible. Consequently, the quantities indicated in this paper are limited solely to the figures reported in the official market.

It is possible, however, that the official figures are a good approximation since the two markets are not entirely segmented. In fact, as will be seen below, there is constant switching, so that when the exchange premium (the percentage difference in favor of the official rate) increases, the incentives for conducting illegal transactions in the official market also increase. By legalizing many foreign exchange transactions, the exchange reform of 1990 reduced but did not eliminate the black market.

Moreover, despite liberalization of the exchange system, there is still an incentive to conceal the capital flows among the current transactions in the official accounting. The tax provisions (which apply to the capital flows) increase the attractiveness of other items (such as tourism) that are tax-exempt or which might more easily escape detection in subsequent tax audits.

The Official Figures

According to the balance of payments (Table 4.1), the recent accumulation of international reserves is due essentially to the performance of the current account. In fact, the capital account showed a deficit in 1990 and 1991. In 1992 the balance was positive as a result of greater direct foreign investment in the petroleum sector. Of particular note in the current account are the recent jump in unilateral transfers and the trade surplus, especially in 1991.

Nevertheless, the annual balance of payment figures do not permit analyzing the short-term trends in external transactions. The information needed for this is found in the foreign exchange balance, which is a daily record of foreign currency transactions carried out by the Bank of the Republic.[5] Table 4.2 shows the quarterly trend of the foreign exchange balance in the 1987-92 period.

The data show that the steady accumulation of reserves began in the first quarter of 1990, apparently as a result of the change in the services and transfers account from persistent deficits to considerable surpluses. The trade balance also improved in 1990, as did the private capital account, which has had sizable positive balances since early 1991. As a whole, and viewed in terms of the foreign exchange balance, the accumulation of reserves seems more than anything to be determined by the performance of the current account.

---

[5] There are substantial differences between this accounting item and the balance of payments, but the overall balance is the same. For an analysis of these differences, see Cárdenas (1989).

Table 4.1. Colombia: Balance of Payments
(Millions of dollars)

	Trade balance	Services balance	Net transfers	Current acct.	Foreign investment	Public capital	Private capital	Capital acct.	Reserve variation
1978	667	-410	73	330	66	99	-23	140	660
1979	537	-127	102	512	103	567	348	983	1611
1980	13	-74	165	104	51	651	270	945	1235
1981	-1333	-631	242	-1722	228	1074	640	1916	242
1982	-2076	-978	169	-2885	337	997	637	1964	-701
1983	-1317	-1673	164	-2826	514	853	-197	1138	-1723
1984	-404	-1983	299	-2088	561	1019	-633	944	-1261
1985	109	-2156	461	-1586	1016	1394	-189	2220	284
1986	1922	-2244	785	463	562	822	-336	1079	1464
1987	1461	-2482	1001	-21	287	-221	-123	-9	-22
1988	827	-2006	964	-215	186	615	164	938	360
1989	1474	-2570	898	-198	547	579	-641	485	162
1990	1957	-2452	1027	532	471	-217	-267	-174	626
1991	2972	-2327	1693	2453	419	-219	-986	-788	1919
1992*	1454	-2100	1636	990	722	n.a.	n.a.	536	1347

*Preliminary
n.a. Not available
Source: Balance of Payments, DANE, FEDESARROLLO calculations.

Measuring the Capital Flows

Clearly, one of the components of current transactions is a capital flow. It is essential, then, that a method of measuring capital inflows be developed. The traditional approach, based on the balance of the private capital account, is simply unrealistic. This problem is a matter of daily concern to economic analysts in Colombia. The point of departure is identifying those items of the current account that might contain capital flows. This is the case with the services and transfers account, and even with certain items of the commercial account such as exports of goods produced by the private sector. It is well known that over-invoicing textile exports to the Caribbean is a surreptitious method of repatriating capital.

Probably the most exact measurement of the capital flows in these items is that of Steiner, *et al.* (1992), who employ a Beveridge-Nelson type methodology to distinguish the permanent and temporary components of the corresponding time series. The assumption is that the temporary component of the series is a good proxy for the capital flows.[6]

---

[6] Other studies make no such distinction, however, and assume that for certain items of the current account, the aggregate value and the implicit speculative component behave identically.

Table 4.2. Colombia: Foreign Exchange Balance
(Millions of dollars)

	Trade balance	Services balance & transfers	Current account	Private capital	Public capital	Capital account	Reserve variation
1987:1	23.4	-88.1	43.8	-34.2	-260.8	-265.0	-221.2
1987:2	182.6	-121.8	164.5	10.0	-120.0	-107.2	57.3
1987:3	26.6	-58.8	104.3	16.4	-172.1	-157.4	-53.1
1987:4	223.6	-9.8	364.2	-29.3	-166.2	-176.2	188.0
1988:1	-3.9	-207.2	-85.4	9.7	-125.5	-139.4	-224.8
1988:2	77.9	-196.7	10.4	22.8	753.3	739.3	749.7
1988:3	71.7	-100.1	126.5	5.2	-361.9	-430.8	-304.3
1988:4	170.3	11.2	337.0	-26.6	-94.5	-189.4	147.6
1989:1	-68.5	-139.1	-81.3	-158.6	-281.2	-300.2	-381.5
1989:2	146.5	-16.2	270.3	-69.7	-294.6	-349.9	-79.6
1989:3	159.9	-99.5	189.1	-48.2	-190.7	-291.8	-102.7
1989:4	143.7	-88.1	206.3	32.8	488.3	506.9	713.2
1990:1	53.1	-182.7	9.9	-36.0	120.3	-53.5	-43.6
1990:2	361.1	-172.9	348.4	-33.7	-250.3	-370.8	-22.4
1990:3	215.8	-48.8	344.1	6.0	57.8	50.0	394.1
1990:4	245.0	-4.6	385.7	31.1	-326.1	-133.7	252.0
1991:1	64.7	213.2	411.7	-61.4	-219.4	-420.4	-8.7
1991:2	363.6	198.1	64.4	108.2	-282.8	-149.5	614.9
1991:3	601.7	227.9	74.2	90.2	-254.9	-184.9	789.3
1991:4	27.9	3.3	154.9	21.9	213.0	431.5	586.4
1992:1	29.6	418.0	565.3	201.8	-146.9	-116.9	448.4
1992:2	2.5	388.3	486.5	222.3	-160.5	13.8	500.3
1992:3	-389.2	223.2	-43.8	148.5	100.0	97.2	53.4
1992:4	-415.7	58.2	-228.8	182.7	-322.7	504.7	75.9
1993:1	-501.5	119.1	-215.1	84.6	-300.3	220.0	176.4
1993:2	-600.7	304.1	-6.8	181.2	-199.2	376.4	433.7

Source: Foreign Exchange Balance, Bank of the Republic.

The method of disaggregating time series has certain drawbacks. Actually, there is no good argument to prove that the temporary component of such a series constitutes a capital flow: temporary fluctuations in the price or quantity of a good or service produced for export cannot be considered a capital flow. Moreover, the longer temporary shocks continue, the more permanent any change in the series—such as a speculative flow—tends to become (which is contradictory).

Of course, the choice of methodology is crucial in measuring the flows. The method used in this paper identifies the flows filtered through the current account by means of a different procedure. First, the flows of commercial indebtedness are calculated by comparing the trade balance of both the foreign exchange

Figure 4.1. Colombia: Capital Flows Weighted by Balance of Trade
(Millions of dollars)

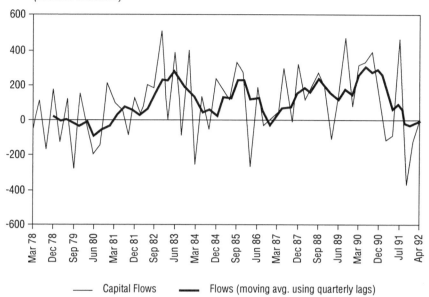

———— Capital Flows   ▬▬▬ Flows (moving avg. using quarterly lags)

balance and the balance of payments. Second, the capital flows implicit in the services and transfers account of the foreign exchange balance are distinguished. Finally, the private sector capital flows obtained directly from the capital account of the foreign exchange balance are examined.

Flows of Commercial Indebtedness

The foreign exchange balance records foreign currency transactions in the Bank of the Republic, while the balance of payments includes all transactions between residents and nonresidents (whether foreign currency is involved or not). Commercial operations financed abroad are not included in the foreign exchange balance.

The difference between the trade balance of the foreign exchange balance and that of the balance of payments (excluding oil transactions) was used to measure the flows of commercial credit[7]. The resultant series (Figure 4.1) reveals a very erratic and somewhat "counterintuitive" behavior since capital inflows are observed in the 1980-82, 1983-85, and 1986-90 periods.

---

[7] When the trade balance of the balance of payments is -$500 and the foreign exchange balance is in equilibrium, the existence of commercial credits totaling $500 can be inferred.

Capital Flows in the Balance of Services

This section presents the results of a methodology aimed at identifying the speculative component implicit in the service transactions and transfers of the foreign exchange balance. The exercise is based on quarterly data for the 1978-92 period, grouped under five major headings: (i) tourist income; (ii) other income (the sum of labor income, transfers and the "others" item); (iii) private interest expenditures; (iv) travel expenditures; and (v) other expenditures (the sum of students, freight, profits, dividends, and other expenditures).

For each of these groups of transactions the "fundamental" determinants are identified and the corresponding regressions are estimated. Any part not explained by the models is considered a capital flow. In other words, it is assumed that any change in the series not covered by the regressions constitutes a capital flow.

In an exercise on the determinants of the services account, Correa (1984) includes as explanatory variables the level of external activity (for income) and the level of domestic activity (expenditures), in addition to the real exchange rate, the interest differential, the exchange premium, and a measurement of the quantitative restrictions. It is obvious that some of these variables, while they successfully explain the behavior of the corresponding series, do so because they include the speculative component (i.e., the capital flow implicit in the series). Therefore, in our disaggregation exercise, neither the yield spread nor the exchange premium nor the real exchange rate is considered a "fundamental" variable. Other variables are included, however, that may help to explain the nonspeculative component of the series.

The real exchange rate is excluded because, as Steiner *et al.* (1992) point out, devaluation expectations (an essential component in calculating the yield spread) are closely related to the level of the real exchange rate. When the currency is overvalued (in relation to the level of equilibrium), the public expects a devaluation. By analogy, a revaluation is expected when the currency is undervalued.

The nominal series were deflated using the CPI of the developed countries since, in most cases, the variables used were also defined in real terms (except in the interest expenditures equation). The resultant series of flows was multiplied by the price index to express it in nominal terms. All of the regressions are estimated in logarithms.

Tourist Income

There was a sharp decline in tourist income in 1982 following the maxidevaluation in Venezuela. There was a significant recovery in 1990, however, with a record high in the second quarter of 1991 (Figure 4.2). The total number of tourists entering the country (data from the Corporación Nacional de Turismo) was selected as a basic determinant of tourist income, on the assumption that real per capita spending remains unchanged over time. Of course, the larger the number of tourists entering the country, the higher the level of tourist income. The results of the regression were the following:

$$IT = -16.72 \quad + \quad 1.33 \, TE \tag{1}$$
$$(-3.95)^{***} \quad (3.82)^{***}$$

with an R^2 of 0.20 (*** 99 percent significant). The residuals indicate two definite periods of capital flows, 1978:01-1981:04 and 1990:04-1992:02, as expected.

Other Income

The other income account—which includes labor income, transfers and the "others" item—remains somewhat stable until 1985, followed by an upward trend within a period of relative instability. The basic determinant used for this income was the volume index of the imports of developed countries, a proxy for the level of business activity in the rest of the world. Of course, as the income of the rest of the world rises, labor income and transfers also increase. The corresponding regression provided the following results:

$$OI = \quad -3.00 \quad + \quad 0.93 \, Yex \tag{2}$$
$$(-6.50)^{***} \quad (8.34)^{***}$$

The R^2 of the regression was 0.55.

The estimated values (Figure 4.3) suggest the presence of capital outflows in the 1989:01 and 1990:03 periods. Capital inflows are also observed between 1990:04 and 1992:02.

Private Interest Expenditures

The payment of interest on private external debt is another channel through which capital flows occur. To identify this component, a regression was estimated utilizing the external interest rate (LIBOR) and the balance of private external debt as explanatory variables. Since there are no figures for the quarterly balance of private external debt, the total of this debt at the end of 1977 was added to the (private) capital account of the foreign exchange balance for each quarter. The estimate provided the following results:

$$EINT = -4.57 \quad + \quad 0.51REX \quad + \quad 1.03DP \tag{3}$$
$$(-4.85)^{***} \quad (5.04)^{***} \quad \quad (8.36)^{***}$$

Figure 4.2. Colombia: Tourism Inflows, Balance of International Payments
(Millions of dollars)

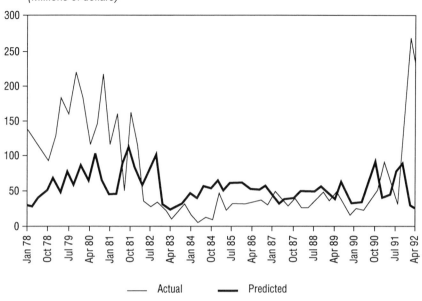

Figure 4.3. Colombia: Other Inflows, Balance of International Payments
(Millions of dollars)

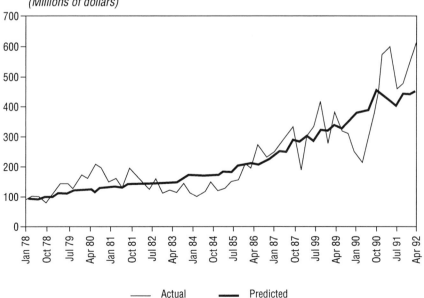

with an R² of 0.63. As expected, Figure 4.4 shows that in the 1980-84 period, sizable outflows of capital occurred. However, outflows are also observed in the 1990-94 period, which is a "counterintuitive" result.

Tourist Expenditures

As Figure 4.5 shows, tourist expenditures were highly stable throughout the period in question, except in the 1982-84 subperiod. As expected, the basic determinant of these expenditures is the number of tourists leaving the country, again on the assumption that real per capita spending (in dollars) remains constant. The regression provided the following results:

$$ETUR = -7.63 \quad + \quad 0.51 \; PS \tag{4}$$
$$(-2.83)^{***} \; (2.31)^{***}$$

with an R² of 0.09. The exercise suggests the presence of heavy capital outflows between 1982:01 and 1984:03.

Other Expenditures

Finally, the "other expenditures" item (which includes the total of students, freight, profits, dividends, and other expenditures) is considered a function of the volume of imports. In this case, the results were the following:

$$OE = \quad -1.15 \quad + \quad 0.64 \; IMP \tag{5}$$
$$(-1.67)^* \qquad (2.29)^{**}$$

with an R² of 0.09.

Despite the considerable instability of this item, the corresponding estimate (Figure 4.6) indicates the presence of substantial capital inflows since late 1991.

Capital Flows in the Services Account: Synthesis

The total residuals of the above regressions (with a negative sign in the case of expenditures) represent the flow of capital through the services account. Despite the fact that in two instances the regressions evince downward adjustments (perhaps because other significant determinants such as the exchange rate were excluded), the series provides highly plausible results. In fact, as Figure 4.7 shows, the series indicates the presence of capital inflows in the 1978:01-1981:01 period. Then, from 1981:03 to 1986:02, in the midst of the exchange crisis, a con-

Figure 4.4. Colombia: Private Interest Payments, Balance of International Payments
(Millions of dollars)

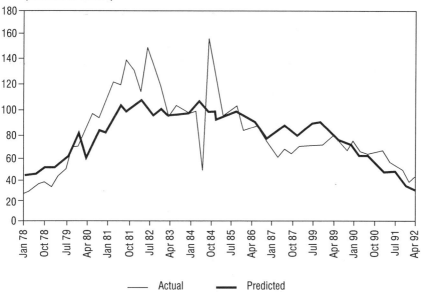

Actual   Predicted

Figure 4.5. Colombia: Tourism Payments, Balance of International Payments
(Millions of dollars)

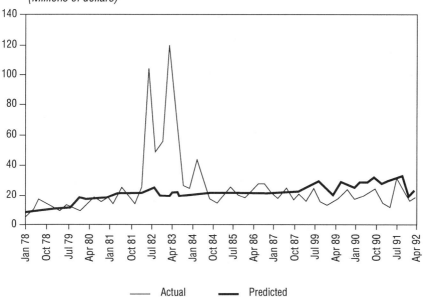

Actual   Predicted

siderable outflow of capital occurred. The series also reveals a period of heavy inflows in the second quarter of 1990. When the private capital balance of the foreign exchange balance is added to the above series (Figure 4.8), a global estimate of the capital flows is obtained.

Determinants of Capital Flows: Yield Spread and the Exchange Premium

When bonds denominated in foreign currency and bonds in domestic currency are perfect substitutes, so that the only difference between them is the unit of denomination, interest parity is achieved. In other words,

$$r_t = r_t^* + \hat{S}_t^e \tag{6}$$

where $\hat{S}^e$ is the projected rate of devaluation of the local currency, r is the domestic interest rate and r^* is the interest rate on bonds denominated in foreign currency (dollars). Conversely, when assets are not perfect substitutes, or when there is some level of imperfection that limits the degree of capital mobility, or when errors are made in measuring devaluation expectations, the aforementioned equivalence may not always occur. In these conditions, a yield spread or exchange premium (relative) on the local currency will result (d_t), so that the above equation becomes:

$$r_t = r_t^* + \hat{S}_t^e + d_t. \tag{7}$$

Figure 4.9 shows the trend of the financial yield spread in Colombia in the 1978-92 period. Given the existence of a spread statistically different from zero, it can be inferred that domestic financial assets and external financial assets are not perfect substitutes. In calculating the spread, it was assumed, based on the theory of rational expectations, that the projected rate of devaluation is the same as the actual rate of devaluation. The exchange rate used was the one in effect in the official market, i.e., the official exchange rate up to mid-1991 and the so-called "representative" rate from that point on.

When an agent decides to execute a speculative transaction (presumably because of the trend of the differential), he may opt to buy (or sell) foreign exchange in either the official or the black market. The higher the premium in the official market the greater the incentive to filter the transaction through some item in the official accounts. But the existence of a positive premium does not guarantee that the transaction will be carried out in the official market. There may be accounting and legal implications in the latter that simply do not exist in the black market.

Figure 4.10 describes the trend of the exchange premium during the period in question. For a very long time (from September 1982 to December 1990), the price in the official market was lower than the black market price.

Figure 4.6. Colombia: Other Payments, Balance of International Payments
(Millions of dollars)

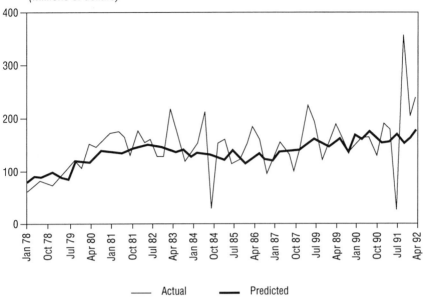

——— Actual   ■■■ Predicted

Figure 4.7. Colombia: Capital Flows, Weighted by Balance of Services
(Millions of dollars)

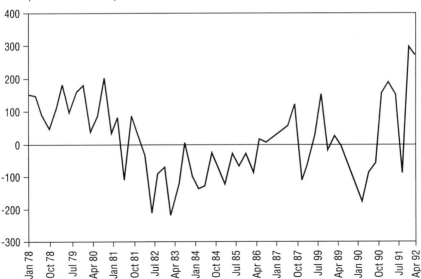

Figure 4.8. Colombia: Capital Flows, Weighted by Balance of Services and Private Capital
(Millions of dollars)

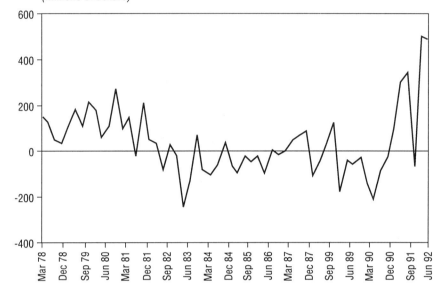

Figure 4.9. Colombia: Rate of Return Differential, Predicted Exchange Rate (Rational Expectations)
(Percentages)

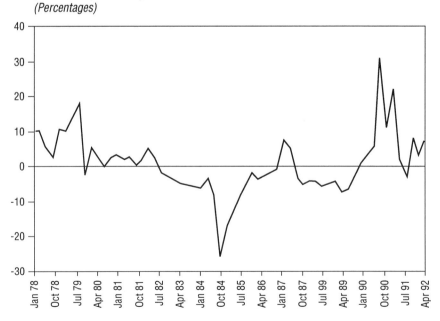

Figure 4.10. Colombia: Exchange Rate Surcharge, Predicted Exchange Rate/ Secondary Market Exchange Rate
(Percentages)

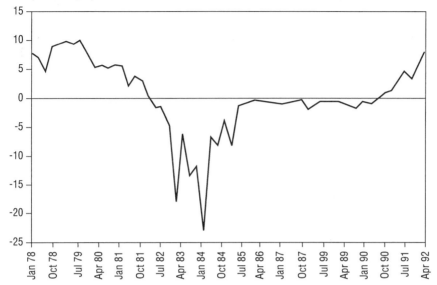

Determinants of Capital Flows: Summary of the Literature

Most of the econometric studies conducted in Colombia concur that the interest differential, corrected for devaluation expectations, is the principal determinant of capital flows.[8] For example, Steiner *et al.* (1992) find that the flows are closely related to the capital gains potential generated by disequilibria in the real exchange rate and the interest differential. Herrera (1991) obtains similar results. Urrutia and Pontón (1993) also note a significant correlation between the flow of capital, a measurement of interest differential, and the exchange premium. These authors also consider other flow determinants such as the amnesty for the repatriation of flight capital in 1990 and the liberalization of the exchange system.

---

[8] It should be noted that there are significant differences in nearly all of the studies, in terms not only of their flow measurements (as discussed in the previous section) but also in their definition of devaluation expectations, a variable that cannot be directly observed. For example, Steiner, *et al.* (1992) use the official devaluation observed and, as an alternative measurement, the deviation of the real exchange rate from its point of equilibrium. Cárdenas (1993), on the other hand, uses the devaluation observed in the representative market and past devaluation in both the official and representative markets.

Table 4.3. Colombia: Determinants of Capital Flows, 1978:1-1992:4

Dep. Var.	Comm. Indebt. Flow			Flow through Services Account			Private capital account			FK2	
C	-350.00 (-2.63)**	-296.00 (-0.79)		8.23 (0.69)	7.84 (0.68)	25.70 (3.12)*	25.10 (3.04)*	27.60 (3.29)*	34.06 (2.32)**	34.04 (2.17)**	35.45 (2.34)**
DIF	-1.49 (-0.44)	-0.48 (-0.12)	3.40 (2.20)**	1.95 (1.27)		3.37 (3.05)*	2.54 (2.31)**		6.78 (3.38)*		
DIF(-1)										4.50 (2.20)**	
DIF(-2)					3.63 (2.40)**			3.04 (2.77)*			6.67 (3.37)*
PC	-4.99 (-1.08)	-6.05 (-1.08)	9.65 (4.6)*	10.73 (5.08)*	9.88 (4.99)*	-1.33 (-0.9)	-0.44 (-0.29)	-0.22 (-0.15)	8.32 (3.06)*	10.29 (3.66)*	9.66 (3.72)*
IMP	0.46 (3.39)*										
BK/IMP		1,138.00 (1.05)									
R² Adj.	0.19	0.02	0.47	0.43	0.46	0.12	0.07	0.11	0.44	0.37	0.43
D.W.	2.40	2.23	1.62	1.75	1.62	0.86	1.14	0.94	1.5	1.78	1.51
Q (21)	0	0.16	0.76	0.85	0.98	0	0	0	0.36	0.72	0.7
N	58	50	58	57	56	58	57	56	58	57	56

FK2 = Flow through Services Account + Private Capital Account.
DIF = Profitability Differential; PC = Exchange Premium.
IMP = Imports excluding oil; BK/IMP = Capital goods imports/Total imports.
Q = Level of Q statistic significance.
* Significant.
** Highly significant.
Source: Author's calculations.

Moreover, Cárdenas (1993), in an analysis of weekly data, finds that although the correlation between interest differential and flows is positive, its predictive value is negligible since the regressions yield low R^2s, suggesting that there are other flow determinants.

In another connection, much of the discussion about flows in Colombia has centered on the direction of causality between capital flows and interest differential. Most of the studies assume (implicitly) that yield spreads generate capital flows. Another interpretation raises the possibility of a reverse direction of causality: a higher level of (exogenous) flows kindles revaluation expectations and, therefore, results in a positive differential. Carrasquilla (1993) finds evidence supporting flow-to-differential causality in the 1985-92 period. Cárdenas (1992), however, finds no causality in either direction.[9]

A final group of studies analyzes the source of said capital for the specific purpose of gauging the importance of drug trafficking. In particular, Urrutia and Pontón (1993) question the theory that a sizable percentage of the capital inflows can be attributed to this activity. Their argument is that drug profits have declined in recent years. This suggests that the inflows of foreign exchange are associated in large measure with overseas sales of Colombian and foreign assets (prompted by the interest differential), which in the past may have been acquired with illegal funds. O'byrne and Reina (1993), however, believe just the opposite. Based on data collected from various sources, the authors suggest that drug trafficking is more profitable than ever, mostly because of the appearance of new crops such as *amapola* (poppy) and the penetration of new markets, including Europe.

Determinants of Capital Flows: Results

This section presents some of the econometric results obtained using the definitions of capital flows, yield spread, and exchange premium given in the preceding sections. The models prove the hypothesis that an increase in the spread in favor of financial investments attracts external capital. Similarly, a higher exchange premium causes a swing toward the official market.

The principal results are presented in Table 4.3. First, the flows of commercial indebtedness seem to depend neither on the yield spread nor on the exchange premium. The only significant variable in this case is the value of imports, the coefficient of which indicates that every dollar of imports generates 46 cents of financing. It does not appear to be true that the weight of capital goods imports increases the volume of commercial financing.

---

[9] All three tests are based on the Granger method. It should be noted that the econometric test conducted by Carrasquilla reveals no level of acceptable significance and that in the work of O'byrne and Reina (1993), it is found that causality exists, going from differential to flow for the 1980-84 period.

Table 4.4. Colombia: Determinants of Capital Flows, 1978:1-1992:4

Dep.Var.	Flow through services account			Private capital account			FK2		
C	4.49 (0.39)	6.41 (0.53)	4.63 (0.42)	20.63 (2.66)*	22.96 (2.73)*	25.00 (3.19)*	25.13 (1.81)***	29.38 (1.87)***	29.60 (2.20)**
DIF	1.06 (0.53)			0.84 (0.62)			1.90 (0.78)		
DIF(-1)	0.91 (0.47)				0.91 (0.67)			1.83 (0.72)	
DIF(-2)			1.10 (0.64)			0.98 (0.80)			2.08 (0.99)
PC	10.74 (5.02)*	11.05 (5.14)*	10.37 (5.51)*	-0.15 (-0.10)	0.06 (0.04)	0.17 (0.12)	10.59 (4.03)*	11.12 (3.97)*	10.54 (4.58)*
D	5.08 (1.85)***	2.44 (0.86)	7.60 (2.70)*	5.49 (2.92)*	3.84 (1.94)**	6.17 (3.07)*	10.58 (3.14)*	6.28 (1.70)***	13.78 (4.00)*
R² Adj.	0.49	0.43	0.52	0.23	0.12	0.23	0.52	0.39	0.55
D.W.	1.67	1.88	1.70	0.91	1.43	1.10	1.63	2.13	1.80
Q (21)	0.55	0.83	0.70	0.00	0.00	0.00	0.26	0.78	0.40
N	58.00	57.00	56.00	58.00	57.00	56.00	58.00	57.00	56.00

FK2 = Flow through Services Account + Private Capital Account.
D = Dummy Interaction 1990:03-1992:04 with corresponding DIF.
DIF = Profitability Differential; PC = Exchange Premium.
IMP = Imports excluding oil; BK/IMP = Capital goods imports/Total imports.
Q (n.s.) = Level of Q statistic significance.
*Significant.
** Very Significant.
*** Extremely Significant.
Source: Author's calculations.

Regarding the capital flows hidden in the services account, the results indicate that both the differential (contemporaneous and delayed) and the premium are significant and have the expected sign. These two variables alone explain nearly 45 percent of the change in the dependent variable. In the case of the actual flows of private capital from the foreign exchange balance, the differential has the expected effect. Of particular note is the fact that the exchange premium seems to have no effect on this item of the foreign exchange balance. Consequently, the explanatory power of the regression is less than in the preceding case.

A global estimate of the capital flows is obtained by adding the capital flows "hidden" in the services account to the flows of private capital. The econometric exercise for this balance indicates that a 10 percent increase in the differential is associated, on average, with a capital inflow (private) of $67.8 million per quarter.

This figure is consistent with other studies. For example, Steiner, et al. (1993) suggest a range of $39.5 million to $72.7 million for this same increase and period. Herrera (1991) obtains a larger estimate, $418 million annually, while Urrutia and Pontón (1993) mention $6.7 million per month.

The exchange premium also seems to have a positive and significant effect on the inflow of capital. In fact, as our results show, a 10 percent rise in the official rate over the parallel rate, *ceteris paribus,* leads to an increase of $8.3 million in the capital inflows recorded in the official accounts.

To what extent the capital flows respond to the differential may be skewed, however, by what occurred in the third quarter of 1990 at the start of the process of structural reform in the Colombian economy. In fact, it is quite possible that the increase in capital mobility dates from that period. To prove this hypothesis, a variable was added to the regressions to distinguish the effect of the differential in the 1990:03-1992:02 period.[10]

The results, shown in Table 4.4, clearly demonstrate that the impact of the differential on the capital flows was negligible in the 1978:01-1990:02 period. Following this latter quarter, however, the effect is positive and significant (so that the results presented in the table, in which the sample is not subdivided, are determined by the recent structural changes). According to the new measurements, a 10 percent increase in the differential is associated with a capital inflow of $105.8 million per quarter since 1990:03 (the figure is identical for an equivalent rise in the exchange premium). For the preceding period (1978:01-1990:02), the effect is insignificant.

A simulation exercise based on the econometric results shows that the change in the average differential alone, from a negative 4 percent in 1990 to a positive 12 percent in 1991, explains the $693 million capital inflow in 1991. In 1992, the

---

[10] More specifically, the variable is defined as the differential (with the corresponding lag) multiplied by a dummy for the final subperiod.

Table 4.5. Colombia: Granger Causality Test

A. Differential causes capital flow

	CS	CP	FK2	
			(a)	(b)
F statistic	1.74	2.30	2.35	1.59
P.C.	83%	92%	92%	81%
Q( )	92%	93%	80%	91%

B. Capital flow causes differential

	CS	CP	FK2
F statistic	2.13	0.56	1.03
P.C.	90%	36%	62%
Q( )	91%	99%	99%

CS = Flow through Services Account.
CP = Private Capital Account.
FK2 = CS+CP.
P.C. = Probability of casuality .
Q = Level of Q statistic significance.
(a),(b) = 3 and 4 lags, respectively.
Source: Authors' calculations.

differential fell to 7 percent, signifying a drop of approximately $200 million in the capital inflow as compared to 1991.

Of course, the above analysis rests on the assumption that the differential *causes* the capital inflow (when, in theory, the opposite may be true), which seems to be confirmed by the Granger-type causality tests. In fact, as Table 4.5 shows, the hypothesis that the differential does not cause the flow of private capital can be rejected with 92 percent certainty. When the latter flow is added to the flow filtered through the services account, the same thing happens (although for this latter item the hypothesis cannot be rejected). Causality in the opposite direction (from flows to differential) can be ruled out entirely, except in the case of flows through the services account.[11]

---

[11] The criterion for selecting the order of lags (3) was the "whiting out" of errors, which is verified through the Q-statistic.

Economic Policy and External Capital

Stabilization of the economy in the wake of capital inflows has been the chief objective of recent economic policy in Colombia. In particular, the authorities have tried to avoid revaluation of the currency and the acceleration of inflation by controlling the growth of credit supply. Similarly, a number of mechanisms have been developed to discourage the repatriation of capital. An integral part of this strategy has been the lowering of interest rates.

Given the recent opening of the economy, the authorities have tried to avoid revaluation of the currency in order to protect the competitiveness of national industry. From a theoretical viewpoint, the argument is based on the existence of economies of scale in production and marketing, so that productivity increases as more experience is gained in the production of a certain good (i.e., if the technology includes a "learning by doing" component).[12]

One possibility is intervention in the exchange market by the central bank.[13] In this case, the monetary authority maintains the desired exchange rate by purchasing international reserves with high-powered money. In doing so, it sacrifices monetary policy by losing all control over the monetary base. The risk in this instance, of course, is that the prices of goods not tradable internationally will react to changes in the money supply, unleashing an inflationary process.[14] To avoid the inflationary effects, the authorities can opt for a sterilized intervention, in which the purchase of foreign exchange is combined with open market transactions offsetting the monetary effect of the accumulation of reserves.[15] This type of operation actually constitutes a forward sale of domestic currency by the central bank. The cost of this policy is the quasi-fiscal deficit it generates.

Exchange Intervention in Colombia: Exchange Certificates

In Colombia there is a long tradition of exchange intervention. The type of intervention, however, has changed with the passage of time. During the period of strict exchange controls (1967-90), the Bank of the Republic held a monopoly on the purchase and sale of foreign exchange. The monetary authority set the exchange rate on a daily basis, in accordance with a program of minidevaluations aimed at

---

[12] Krugman (1987) maintains that a company's productive history is essential to understanding its competitiveness.

[13] For an excellent summary of the methods of intervention in the G-7 countries, see Obstfeld (1988).

[14] In free trade conditions, arbitrage pressures guarantee observance of the law of one price for tradable goods, so that changes in the prices of these goods depend on exchange rate fluctuations and not on changes in the money supply.

[15] The Colombian model is ingenious since the central bank combines the two operations (intervention and sterilization) by purchasing foreign exchange with exchange certificates.

controlling the real exchange rate, which itself is (to a certain extent) considered a tool, rather than a result, of economic policy. Moreover, some analysts have pointed out that, on occasion, the cost of keeping the real exchange rate at a certain level was loss of control over inflation. This interpretation assumes, of course, that the pace of devaluation is an important determinant of inflation (see Carrasquilla, 1992).

As mentioned above, the method of exchange intervention in Colombia is ingenious because it combines intervention and sterilization in a single operation. This may be why the system seems complex and why it is often misunderstood. The Bank of the Republic purchases foreign exchange with exchange certificates, which are bonds denominated in dollars with a term of one year. They have often been used in periods when foreign exchange was plentiful.[16] The redemption price in pesos of these instruments is set each day by the Bank of the Republic at the official exchange rate. This price is not, however, a true exchange rate since it is merely the redemption price in pesos of a security denominated in dollars at maturity.

Upon issue, exchange certificates are sold in the secondary market at a discount varying from 5.5 to 12.5 percent. As Cárdenas (1993) shows, the discount is equivalent to the difference between the interest rate (deposit) and the projected devaluation. The price of this security in the secondary market is the same as the price of the dollar, which has been called the *representative rate*. As Figure 4.11 illustrates, this rate varies within the bands comprising the limits set by the monetary authority for variation of the discount rate. If the latter exceeds 12.5 percent, the agents sell the exchange certificates to the Bank of the Republic, so that the discount is reduced.

The representative rate varies within the band, however, causing uncertainty among the agents who execute foreign currency transactions. For example, if the rate moves from its lower limit to the upper limit (i.e., the peso is devalued 7 percent) within a period of two months, this represents an annual devaluation of 50 percent (or a revaluation of 50 percent if the flow is in the opposite direction). This volatility is harmful for two major reasons. First, it increases the level of risk in export activities, without there being any hedging mechanisms available in the market. Second, and contrary to the general perception, the volatility of the representative exchange rate can attract speculative capital. Any investor knows that if the rate is near the lower limit of the band, the probability of accelerated devaluation is high. In this sense, the greater "noise" in the representative rate does not act as a barrier to speculative capital. It is likely that just the opposite occurs.

---

[16] Exchange certificates redeemable at 80 days for exports of services were reintroduced in late 1990. In mid-1991 they became more generally available and the term was extended to 90 days. The term was expanded to 360 days in October of that year and a yield of 9.5 percent was imposed on certificates in circulation, which implied a nominal revaluation of 5 to 8 percent.

Figure 4.11. Colombia: Official and Market Exchange Rates
(Colombian pesos per dollar)

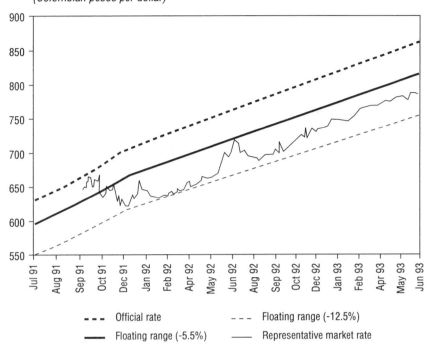

- - - Official rate   - - - Floating range (-12.5%)

——— Floating range (-5.5%)   ——— Representative market rate

In the long term, however, the pace of devaluation of the representative rate more closely mimics the official rate, which is subject to a highly regular series of minidevaluations. Consequently, agents who can afford to wait can avoid being harmed by the volatility of the representative rate. Finally, it would not be surprising if, in the near future, hedging mechanisms were to become available, which would make the system more efficient by generating profits for the buyers and sellers of this type of contract.[17]

Sterilized Intervention in Colombia: Other Instruments

Since late 1990, growth of the credit supply has been tightly controlled in Colombia by means of open market operations carried out by the Bank of the Re-

---

[17] There is also a parallel market for off-the-books transactions. The prices in this market maintain a certain correlation (which does not preclude the possibility of arbitrage profits) with prices in the legal (representative) exchange market, as well as with the tax rates imposed on transactions in the latter, prominent among which is a 10 percent withholding (3 percent up to July of this year).

public, the volume of which has at times exceeded the total money supply. In 1991, however, the placement of these securities caused a sharp hike in interest rates. In fact, the bank borrowing rate went from 29.2 percent in March 1991 to 38.5 percent in December of that year, while the lending rate was 47.9 percent in April 1991.

Monetary contraction has also been attempted by raising the bank reserve ratio (which, incidentally, limits the scope of the financial reform). At first, in 1990, the ordinary reserve ratio was raised; then, in January 1991, this policy was reinforced with the establishment of a marginal reserve ratio of 100 percent. However, in September of that year, this measure was abolished, but the ordinary reserve ratio was raised 5 points. Other monetary instruments have been used for the same purpose. For example, in the second quarter of 1991 it was established that the "own-account position" of financial institutions had to be at least 30 percent.[18] Later, in March 1992, this percentage was raised to 45 percent. Another measure commonly used in Colombia is modification of the time periods allotted for advanced import deposits. In the current business cycle, for example, those periods were shortened twice (in late 1990 and in June 1991).[19] In the latter instance, the period was three months.

The authorities can also try to solve the problem by reducing the relative yield of domestic financial investments.[20] The lowering of domestic interest rates, as well as microeconomic measures such as taxing speculative capital (which is difficult to identify), are ways of accomplishing this. The difficulty lies in the assumption that the direction of causality is from the yield spread to capital flows and not vice-versa. If the opposite were true, i.e., if the capital flows were attributable to exogenous factors, the yield spread would be an endogenous variable since the larger the inflow of foreign exchange, the greater the expectation that a revaluation will occur. Thus, the efforts of the monetary authorities to lower interest rates are canceled out in the market by endogenous changes in devaluation expectations.

In September 1991, when the new board of directors of the Bank of the Republic was installed, an important qualitative change occurred in the orientation of monetary and exchange policy. A decision was made to slow the accumulation of reserves by closing the yield spread. Thus, the aggressive control of monetary aggregates was replaced by control of the interest rate. In May 1992

---

[18] The "own-account" position is defined as the excess of assets over liabilities, in foreign currency, which financial intermediaries must maintain, expressed as a percentage of technical net worth.

[19] The two measures differ from one another with respect to the type of goods levied and in that the former imposes a maximum registration period and the other directly limits the time of the import.

[20] In August 1991, in order to remove the uncertainty surrounding imports, it was decided that the pace of trade liberalization should be substantially quickened. This step was taken to attack the problem of stabilization directly by slowing the accumulation of reserves.

Figure 4.12. Colombia: Exchange Certificates (OMAs) and Accumulated Reserves
(Billions of dollars)

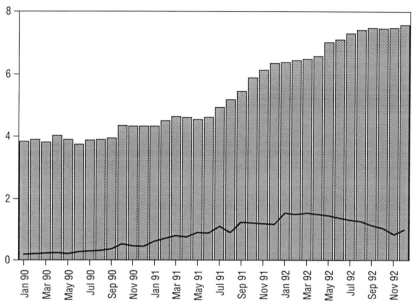

the authorities imposed a restriction on the lending rate of financial institutions, consisting of a ceiling of 35 percent on the average lending rates of banks and savings and loan associations (36.5 percent on finance companies and commercial financial corporations).

As Figure 4.12 shows, the open market operations (the so-called equity securities) and the exchange certificates had a decidedly contractive effect in 1990 and 1991. The balance of these securities rose from nearly $200 million in January 1990 to an average of $1.797 billion (28 percent of the reserves) in 1991. A high of $2.3 billion was reached in January 1992 and it was then that the effects of the change in monetary policy began to materialize. Taken as a whole, the balance of the nonmonetary liabilities of the economic authority decreased, indicating that these operations contributed to the growth of the monetary base.

Other microeconomic measures can help check the forces that encourage speculation. For example, in April 1991, a 5 percent charge was established for sales of foreign exchange to the Bank of the Republic. A three percent withholding at source was also imposed on external flows (other than legitimate exports) which, in July 1992, was raised to 10 percent. In that same month a cap of $25,000 was imposed on the amount of foreign currency that can be brought into the country by tourists, to stop the use of this channel for speculative purposes.

In summary, sterilized intervention coupled with a rise in interest rates was the strategy favored by the Colombian authorities until August 1991. Although the sterilization efforts have not been completely abandoned, closing the yield spread has been the strategy followed by the authorities since 1992.[21] The method of accomplishing this has consisted of controlling lending interest rates and curtailing the placement of equity securities and other open market operations of the Bank of the Republic (which undoubtedly dominate the market).

The Effectiveness of Sterilized Intervention in Colombia

When the authorities are successful in controlling the exchange rate, they may have a third instrument (in addition to the monetary and fiscal policies) with which to regulate the economy. Evidence from the rest of the world, however, is not very encouraging as far as influencing the exchange rate is concerned.[22]

One way of evaluating the effectiveness of the sterilization effort and the degree of monetary autonomy is to estimate the offset coefficient—the percentage of monetary contraction offset by the accumulation of reserves in a given period. For example, in the extreme case in which domestic and foreign securities are perfect substitutes (Mundell, 1968), the offsetting of the capital account by domestic credit measures is total and immediate.[23] In these circumstances, the monetary base is determined independently of the actions of the central bank, through the public's savings and investment decisions. For example, a domestic credit squeeze forces agents to repatriate capital in order to restore their monetary balances. In this extreme case, sterilization is ineffective in controlling the credit supply and only affects the composition of the monetary base.

For some authors (e.g., Herrera, 1991; and the references cited therein), the evidence suggests that the degree of integration of the Colombian economy with the rest of the world (even with exchange controls in place) precludes autonomous management of the monetary policy. In other words, the agents can, through the market, unravel any attempt by the authorities to regulate the money supply.

---

[21] In practice, the economic policy has been a combination *sui generis* (and very much in the Colombian style) of both approaches. From a theoretical viewpoint, it is highly questionable whether the authorities will manage to control both the credit supply and interest rates.

[22] For example, Frankel (1982a, 1982b) finds that German and U.S. bonds are perfect substitutes, based on monthly data from January 1974 to October 1978. Dooley and Isard (1983) obtain similar results with quarterly data. Rogoff (1984) finds a high degree of substitutability between bonds denominated in Canadian and in U.S. dollars, based on weekly data from March 1973 to December 1980. Evidence to the contrary has been presented by Danker, *et al.* (1985) and Loopesko (1983).

[23] However, the lack of substitutability is not itself a guarantee of monetary autonomy. For example, Obstfeld (1982a) shows that when the public correctly assimilates the public sector budget constraint (including the interest on nonmonetary liabilities), open market operations have no effect on interest rates or on the money supply.

Since this is an extreme situation and one that is highly relevant to the conduct of economic policy in Colombia, it is worth determining the offset coefficient using the reduced form developed by Koury and Porter (1974), based on the degree of equilibrium in the money and bond markets and the central bank balance sheet. The specific equation is:

$$\Delta R_t = \alpha_0 + \alpha_1 \Delta DC_t + \alpha_2 \Delta r_t + \alpha_3 \Delta Y_t + \alpha_4 D_t + u_t \tag{8}$$

where ΔR is the change in international reserves; ΔDC is the change in domestic credit; Δr^* is the change in the external interest rate; ΔY is the change in the level of nominal income; D is a "dummy" variable that assumes a unit value in the final quarter of each year; and u_t is a random error with a mean of zero. The offset coefficient is measured through $-\alpha_1$ (the offset is complete when $a_1 = -1$).

As Obstfeld (1982b) points out, the reduced-form method has a serious flaw in that the ΔDC variable is endogenous when sterilization policy is adopted (in which case domestic credit is determined by the external sector). Because of this, ΔDC is correlated with the errors and, as a result, the OLS estimators are inconsistent. Therefore, it is better to use instrumental variables and to formulate the above equation using a two-stage least squares (2SLS) procedure.

Moreover, given the special characteristics of the Colombian economy, the exercise utilizes three alternate definitions of the change in international reserves. The first consists of data from the balance sheet of the Bank of the Republic. The second is the change in reserves indicated by the foreign exchange balance (converted to pesos at the quarterly average exchange rate).[24] The third is a variant of the preceding definition, based on the sum of the current account and the private capital account. This latter definition is interesting since it excludes capital flows from the public sector, which are probably determined by factors other than the investment decisions of agents.

Table 4.6 summarizes the principal results of the estimates for the 1978:01 to 1992:3 period.[25] Despite the fact that in every case the offset coefficient $(-\alpha_1)$ is not 1, its value appears to be sensitive to the method of measuring the change in the reserves. In the upper panel, which uses the monetary figures, the largest ratio occurs but its confidence interval (± 2 standard deviations) does not reach

---

[24] These measurements of international reserves include a "valuation" effect due to devaluation of the nominal exchange rate, which should not be a factor in this exercise. However, separating the reserves from this effect is extremely difficult.

[25] Domestic credit is the difference between the monetary base and international reserves; the external interest rate is the 3-month LIBOR (Bank of the Republic figures); and real quarterly income is taken from Herrera (1991) and multiplied by the CPI (since there is no implicit quarterly deflator).

Table 4.6. Colombia: Offset Coefficient Estimate (Reduced Form)
(Period: 1978:1-1992:3)

A. Dependent variable: Absolute variation in net reserves

Procedure	Constant	DC1	REX1	Y1	D1	R² Adjust.	D.W.	RHO
OLS	-32730.47	-0.6	-1181.79	0.5543	76431.8	0.876	2.04	
	(-3.16)	(-13.74)	(-0.34)	(10.66)	(3.97)			
CORC	-33939.65	-0.6025	-1394.19	0.5567	77741.41	0.874	2	-0.03
	(-3.24)	(-13.34)	(-0.39)	(10.62)	(3.92)			(-0.22)
2SLS	-45034.43	-0.7105	6099.416	0.5711	97867.44	0.849	2.12	
	(-3.21)	(-5.01)	(0.51)	(4.54)	(2.68)			

B. Dependent variable: current account + capital account

Procedure	Constant	DC1	REX1	Y1	D1	R² Adjust.	D.W.	RHO
OLS	-48386.08	-0.156	737.74	0.62	47337.17	0.59	1.06	
	(-3.04)	(-2.32)	(0.14)	(7.76)	(1.59)			
CORC	-46905.52	-0.152	1840.354	0.619	42506.19	0.673	1.99	0.47
	(-2.06)	(-3.07)	(0.48)	(7.18)	(1.89)			(-3.7)
2SLS	-54352.75	-0.294	14167.41	0.554	81035.39	0.502	1.31	
	(-2.52)	(-1.35)	(0.78)	(2.87)	(1.45)			

C. Dependent variable: current account + private capital account

Procedure	Constant	DC1	REX1	Y1	D1	R² Adjust.	D.W.	RHO
OLS	-39043.57	-0.409	-692.0	8 0.493	27716.49	0.723	1.45	
	(-3.00)	(-7.44)	(-0.161)	(7.53)	(1.14)			
CORC	-39532.92	-0.404	-667.53	0.5018	23394.97	0.739	1.95	0.274
	(-2.46)	(-8.47)	(-0.177)	(7.047)	(1.07)			(1.93)
2SLS	-44916.03	-0.372	-1993.52	0.569	16899.7	0.715	1.46	
	(-2.77)	(-2.27)	(-0.146)	(3.91)	(0.401)			

Source: Author's estimates.

one. In the lower panels the ratio is considerably smaller (between 0.15 and 0.40), suggesting that in Colombia (temporary) stabilization policy is viable.[26]

Stabilization and Fiscal Policy

In Colombia, fiscal policy has traditionally been assigned an anticyclical role, given the fluctuations in the external sector. Thus, during external booms, monetary sterilization is the result of a fiscal surplus. The surplus is generated through the increase in current revenue, which, in the case of the coffee and oil booms, was automatically boosted. Of course, in these conditions the adjustment effort is not based on greater direct and indirect taxation, nor necessarily on a lower level of public spending. It should be noted that when large inflows of foreign exchange are attributable to flows of external capital (routed primarily to the public sector), as occurred in the 1979-82 period, there are no significant stabilization problems. In fact, as Cárdenas (1991) shows, external indebtedness in Colombia has been anticyclical, so that external borrowing partially offsets the negative external shocks that affect the current account of the balance of payments.

The present circumstances are entirely different since the capital inflow is a predominantly private phenomenon, without there being any increase in government revenue. Consequently, monetary sterilization through the government would inevitably require higher taxes or cuts in public spending. Moreover, since public investment is the most flexible component, it is likely that the responsibility for generating a fiscal surplus would fall disproportionately on this item.

Another important consideration is that monetary sterilization via open market operations is costly for the government. In Colombia, the yields paid on OMAs, together with the losses caused by the exchange differential, represented 0.78 percent of GDP in 1990, 1.51 percent in 1991 and 1.35 percent through October 1992. The monthly cost was approximately $60 million in mid-1990, with a downward trend in late 1992 (Figure 4.13).

Given inflexible fiscal goals, this cost will necessitate a fiscal adjustment, thereby generating certain equity problems that must be addressed. When the accumulation of reserves is the result of an export boom (coffee or oil), the greatest burden in terms of generating savings undoubtedly falls on the sector that is directly benefited (which is easily identifiable). Conversely, if there is a surplus in the private sector balance of payments, as in the present circumstances, it is much more difficult to distribute the savings effort equitably. It is not unlikely in such circumstances that the groups least benefited by the positive external shock will be forced to increase their savings through indirect taxation.

---

[26] These results are compatible with those of Fernández and Candelo (1983) and Rennhack and Mondino (1989).

Figure 4.13. Colombia: Fiscal Cost of Sterilization, Interest and Exchange Rate Losses
(Millions of dollars)

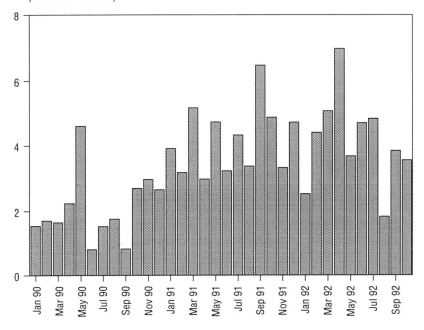

Table 4.7. Colombia: Consolidated Public Sector
(Percentage of GDP)

	1985	1986	1987	1988	1989	1990	1991	1992
Total income	0.22	0.21	0.24	0.23	0.24	0.26	0.26	0.32
Current payments	0.18	0.17	0.18	0.19	0.20	0.20	0.21	0.24
Investment payments	0.10	0.07	0.06	0.07	0.07	0.05	0.06	0.08
Total deficit	-5.43	-3.38	-1.19	-2.40	-2.10	-0.47	-0.46	0.03

Source: National Planning Department and FEDESARROLLO calculations.

When the effects of reducing the fiscal deficit (or generating a surplus) are highly regressive, it is essential that the advantages of such a policy be questioned. What are the real benefits of generating a fiscal surplus? It has been argued that the generation of public savings would have very beneficial effects. First, the monetary base is reduced, either through the decrease in international reserves (if the government uses the surpluses to pay external debt) or in net domestic credit (if the central government makes deposits in the Bank of the Republic). Second, the trend toward lower interest rates is reinforced, insofar as the demand for loanable funds contracts. Third, as a result of the foregoing, the pressures tending toward revaluation of the currency are alleviated. It is obvious, however, that if these variables are to be significantly affected, the change in public finances must be substantial and that, in fact, such change is being promoted by the subjection of fiscal policy to variations in the external interest rates applicable to Colombia.

Moreover, the arguments in favor of generating a fiscal surplus (although valid) are based on purely financial considerations and fail to take into account the effects of fiscal policy on business. In fact, in the Keynesian model for determining the exchange rate (Mundell-Flemming), increased public spending can create an external deficit (i.e., depreciation) if the mobility of capital is restricted.

From the onset of the massive inflow of capital the authorities have pushed for reduction of the fiscal deficit as a means of generating domestic savings consistent with the external surplus. To accomplish this, spending cuts have been unavoidable (thus slowing modernization of the economy). Even so, the fiscal adjustment has fallen short of expectations because the new constitution requires that the government make many new transfers to the various territorial entities.

According to Table 4.7, which shows the balance of the consolidated public sector, the deficit was reduced so substantially during the external boom of 1991-92 that fiscal balance was achieved in the latter year. The recovery was due for the most part to improvements in the collection of taxes made possible by the tax reform of June 1992, which increased the base and the rate of the value-added tax.

Productive Investment and Capital Flows

Figure 4.14 shows the trend of the investment/GDP ratio (total, public, and private) in the 1965-93 period. As can be seen, the ratio is low by international standards, as is the growth of real investment (3.9 percent per annum). Moreover, the cyclical component of investment, which is not small, maintains a close correlation with the external cycle (Cárdenas, 1991).

Upward trends in the external accounts are generally associated with unprecedented levels of investment. The most frequent interpretation of this result (in the tradition of the two-gap model) reveals the importance of the external constraint as a determinant of investment. When the constraint eases, it is possible to import the

Figure 4.14. Colombia: Investment-to-GDP Ratios
(Percentages)

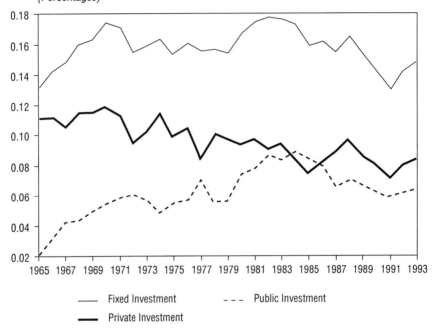

——— Fixed Investment   – – – Public Investment

——— Private Investment

capital goods needed to carry out investment plans. An additional factor is the increase in the relative price of nontradable goods when foreign exchange is plentiful. The profit margin in the construction sector increases, and the supply of such goods responds positively to the growth of demand (attributable to the income effect).[27]

There are, however, great differences between the performance of public investment and private investment.[28] Although the latter is procyclical (due to the aforementioned effect), the former is anticyclical because of the stabilizing role of public finances when fluctuations occur in the external sector.[29]

The recent capital inflows have had a positive effect on investment, especially in 1992. In any case, the steep decline in investment in 1991, despite the

---

[27] On average, during the 1970-90 period, the shares in aggregate investment of housing and of other construction were 15 percent and 32 percent, respectively. Machinery and equipment represented 34 percent, only 6 percent of which was of national origin.

[28] In the seventies, public investment accounted for 36 percent of the total. In the eighties, this figure increased by approximately 10 percentage points.

[29] Consequently, it is not surprising that in the exercises measuring the degree of complementarity between the two types of investment, negative ratios are often found in the short term and positive ratios in the long term. For more information on this subject see Sánchez and Lora (1992).

Figure 4.15. Colombia: Gross Formation of Fixed Capital
(Billions of 1975 Colombian pesos)

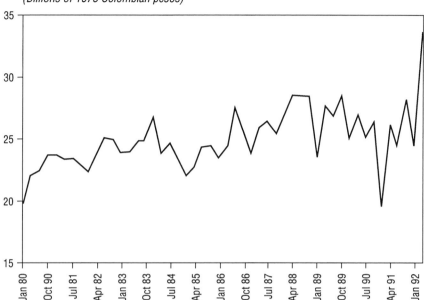

heavy inflows of capital, is paradoxical. In fact, both the data in Figure 4.14 and the quarterly series of the National Planning Department (Figure 4.15) show a sharp drop in the first quarter of 1991 followed by a recovery.

Recent Performance of Investment

There are theoretical arguments to suggest that the buoyancy of private invest-ment in the current circumstances of capital inflows is greater than that normally associated with an export boom. First, the inflow of capital not only eases the external constraint but also eliminates the credit squeeze (the effect of which on investment is fully documented). This latter effect is not necessarily present dur-ing coffee (or oil) booms, when, by definition, resources flow to the public sector and monetary sterilization negatively affects private sector financing.[30] Second, with the increase in the size of the stock market (especially in terms of new share issues and the creation of instruments such as mutual funds), it is possible that there was an improvement in the efficiency of the savings intermediation mechanisms.

---

[30] Traditionally, the stabilization of export booms has been partly based on raising reserve require-ments and imposing heavy restrictions on external indebtedness.

Figure 4.16. Colombia: Imports of Capital Goods
(Millions of dollars)

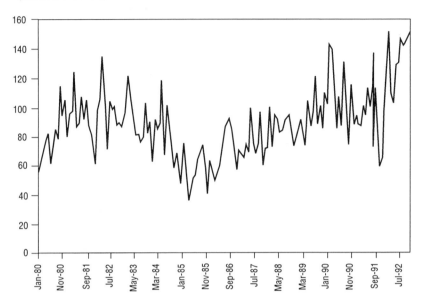

Figure 4.17. Colombia: Area Approved for Construction
(Millions of square meters)

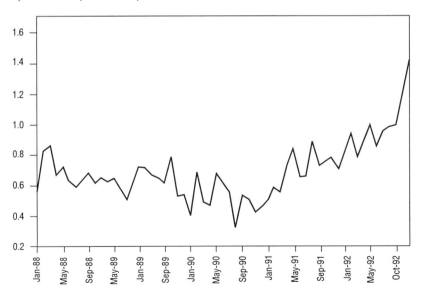

Figure 4.18. Colombia: Real Value of Share Transactions on the Country's Three Stock Exchanges

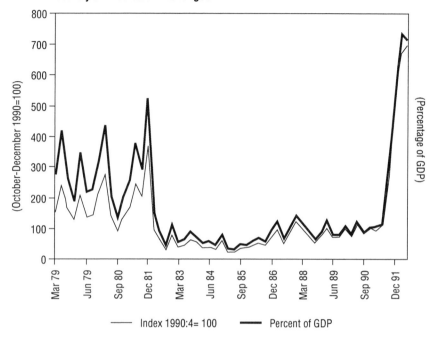

——— Index 1990:4= 100   ▬▬▬ Percent of GDP

The various indicators of capital formation seem to confirm the positive effect of the inflow of capital. In fact, imports of capital goods for industry (Figure 4.16) reveal a sustained recovery since late 1991, when the tariff reduction process culminated.

Regarding loans delivered and approved for construction, an upward trend is observed from 1988 to March 1991, when a significant upsurge occurred. On the other hand, the data on the area approved for construction show a decline between January 1988 and August 1990. Then a growth cycle begins, which is especially strong after October 1992 (Figure 4.17).

Recent data on direct foreign investment suggest another upturn, following a setback reminiscent of the end of the last decade.[31] The main impetus of this process, however, is the discovery of new oil deposits, since DFI in other sectors is moderate. Another source of information about the performance of investment

---

[31] DFI in petroleum represents approximately 75 percent of the total. DFI in other sectors (the most important of which is manufacturing) is fairly modest (the highest level of investment in the period under study is $182 million in 1990).

Figure 4.19. Colombia: Real Index of the Bogota Stock Exchange
(Deflator: CPI)

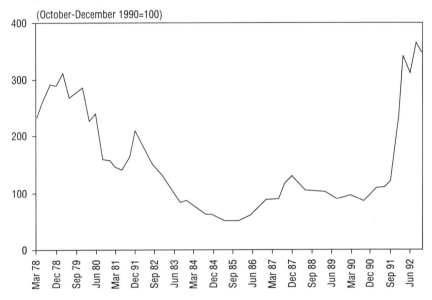

(October-December 1990=100)

Figure 4.20. Colombia: Nominal Index of the Bogota Stock Exchange: Top 20 Shares by Volume
(January 2,1991=100)

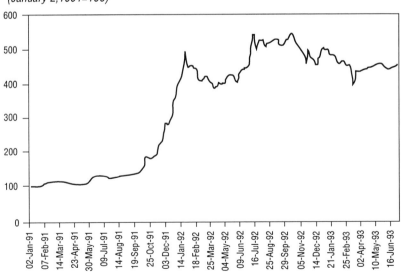

is the Business Opinion Survey conducted periodically by FEDESARROLLO among a group of 350-400 medium- and large-sized companies. One surprising finding is the excellent performance of investment plans reported by the companies throughout the 1990-92 period.

The Stock Market

Despite its recent growth, the Colombian stock market is extremely small by international standards. Figures 4.18 and 4.19 show, respectively, the trend of the real value of shares traded on the country's three stock exchanges and the index of average real prices on the Bogota Exchange. As the figures indicate, this market experienced a severe crisis in the last decade (the transactions represented a slight 0.2 percent of GDP), following a certain buoyancy in the late 1970s. The recent boom has meant a rise of six to seven times in the real value of transactions. Its share of GDP, therefore, is now about 1.8 percent, which is still very low for Latin America. Moreover, although the Index of the Bogota Exchange (IBB)[32] reached its highest point ever in real terms in 1992, it was not much higher than it was in 1978-79. Looking at the daily prices, the boom appears to be concentrated in the brief period between mid-October 1991 and February 1992 (Figure 4.20).[33]

The stock market is one of the conduits through which capital flows can affect investment. According to Tobin's "Q theory," in a world without taxes, firms invest until the last peso spent on the purchase of capital increases the firm's market value by more than a peso. Tobin assumes that, up to a certain point, the market value of an additional unit of capital equals the average market value of the existing capital. In other words, the average Q—the ratio of the market value of the capital stock to its replacement cost—is a good approximation of the marginal Q of an additional peso of investment. Therefore, it is natural to assume that investment is an increasing function of Q.[34] Moreover, when there

---

[32] The IBB is a (weighted) average of the share prices of the 20 companies with the largest traded volume. In January 1991 the method of compiling the index was changed. Between 1978 and 1990 the shares listed were the 20 most heavily traded in the immediately preceding two-year period (weighted according to their market share during that period). The new index, which is calculated daily, revises the listing of shares and weightings twice a month. To splice the two series, the growth of the new index is applied to the old.

[33] Concerning the sectoral composition of the shares traded, industry heads the list (approximately 60 percent for the 1978-92 period), followed by financial institutions (31.4 percent). However, in the last two years (1991-92), the latter have increased their share (40.2 percent) at industry's expense (54.5 percent).

[34] The Q theory is essentially a supply theory, according to which companies make production and investment decisions simultaneously (contrary to the premise of most investment theories in which output is predetermined).

are imperfections in the credit market, the company may be able to negotiate larger loans when its market value increases.

In short, the theory postulates that there is no reason to invest if an additional peso of investment does not increase the market value of the capital by more than a peso. Of course, given the natural delay between deciding on an investment program and implementing it, the response is probably not immediate. It is possible, using Tobin's formulation, to write an equation for investment:

$$I = (\frac{V}{K}) K \tag{9}$$

$$I(1) = 0 \quad I'>0.$$

where I represents gross investment and V/K is the Q ratio of market value to replacement cost. As in the case of other profitability indicators, the direct measurement of Q is a difficult task. An approximation, suggested by Solimano (1989), uses the share price index (IBB) as an indicator of the market value of capital goods and the producer price index (or any other aggregate that includes domestic and imported capital goods) as an indicator of their replacement cost.

Capital Flows and Investment: Econometric Results

The capital flows/investment ratio has been studied using very general indicators such as net international reserves (Chica, 1984) or total external credit (Ocampo, 1988). The Inter-American Development Bank (1989) disaggregates public sector credit, private sector credit, and direct foreign investment. Thus, there are no studies that use a finely-tuned measure of capital flows.

The model presented in this section, which is a variant of Solimano (1989), uses quarterly data to assess the importance of four possible determinants of investment. The first is investment yield, given by Tobin's Q. The second element is a capacity utilization variable, which is given by the deviation of output from its trend (i.e., the cyclical component of output). The third element is uncertainty and risk, which are measured using the variance of Tobin's Q and income.[35] The fourth element is a financing constraint, which is obtained by adding domestic credit to the capital flow. Real domestic credit (deflated by the CPI) was defined as the difference between international reserves and M2. The capital flow used was the sum of capital received through the services account and the private capital account, also deflated by the CPI.

---

[35] In this case, the random variance for two periods defined as $var(x,x_{-1})$ at each point in time.

Capital flows affect investment via two different routes. First, as mentioned in the preceding section, a correlation may exist between Tobin's Q and the inflow of capital. Second, one of the objectives of credit policy is to offset the monetary effects of the capital inflow. Consequently, the flow of external capital is used as an instrumental variable.[36] The variables are defined in real terms and are express in logarithms, so that the coefficients measure the corresponding elasticities, except in the case of total credit. The equation is as follows:

$$INV = f(Q_{t-1} , Y_t , \sigma_Q , \sigma_y , CT_t) \tag{10}$$
$$\quad\quad + \quad + \quad - \quad - \quad +$$

where the lag structure for Q was determined using the best adjustment.
The best estimate of the model was the following:

$$INV = 9.79 + 0.15{\bullet}Q_{t-1} + 0.75{\bullet}Y_t - 0.76{\bullet}\sigma_Q - 37.34{\bullet}\sigma_y + 0.28E\text{-}05{\bullet}CD_t \quad (11)$$
$$(159)^* \quad (4.27)^* \quad (2.45)^*\,(-1.16) \quad (-1.88)^{***}(5.88)^*$$

with an R^2 of 0.49, D.W.=2.02 and a Q-statistic significance level of 11 percent.
To establish the relationship between Tobin's Q and the capital flow, an equation was formulated to explain Q in terms of cyclical income (the higher the income the greater the projected yield), the interest rate (which adversely affects Q), and the flow measurement mentioned above. The result of the regression was the following:

$$Q_t = -0.42 + 3.39{\bullet}Y_{t-1} + 0.8E\text{-}4{\bullet}FK_t + 0.13{\bullet}R_t \tag{12}$$
$$(-0.23) \quad (2.30)^{**} \quad (4.55)^* \quad\quad (0.25)$$

$R^2 = 0.44$; D.W.= 0.78.

As seen, both the capital flow and the cyclical component of output are significant and have the correct sign, while the interest rate appears not to affect Q (various lags were used without success). The results of this equation justify the use of an instrumental variables technique due to the endogeneity between Q and investment, since the capital flows simultaneously affect both variables.

---

[36] A measurement of the flows—in millions of pesos and deflated by the CPI (at the official exchange rate)—was obtained by adding the inflow, estimated on the basis of the services account, to the private capital account.

A simultaneous estimation of the two equations (using a three-stage procedure), wherein capital flows, interest rate, cyclical income, and investment risk factors are considered, yields similar results:

$$INV = 9.76 + 0.18 \bullet Q_{t-1} + 0.76 \bullet Y_t - 1.04 \bullet \sigma_Q - 37.04 \bullet \sigma_y + 0.3E\text{-}05 \bullet CT_t \quad (13)$$
$$(125)^* \quad (3.19)^* \quad (2.65)^* \, (\text{-}1.52) \quad (\text{-}1.95)^{**} \, (5.01)^*$$

$R^2 = 0.47$; D.W.=2.03; Tobin's Q=8 percent.

According to the coefficients obtained, capacity utilization has a greater effect on investment than the yield variable. In fact, the elasticity of investment vis-à-vis Tobin's Q is 0.18, which means that an increase of 10 percent in this variable is associated, on average, with a gain of 1.8 percent in investment (quarterly), while the same increase in cyclical income sparks a rise of 7.6 percent in investment. The results are not clear with regard to the risk factors: the variance of Q is insignificant and the variance of Y is significant, but the effect is very slight. Finally, the results for the financing constraint factor are as expected: the impact on investment of an increase in domestic credit, whether as a result of internal financing or capital inflows, is positive and highly significant.

Conclusions

The Colombian economy has changed greatly in the last three years. In particular, since 1990 the current administration has promoted a series of structural reforms aimed at modernization of the production apparatus. The objectives have been to increase the openness of the economy, to limit intervention in certain markets, and to promote the development of private initiative.

These reforms have created a climate of optimism about the future of the economy. Partly as a result of extremely positive expectations concerning the economy's future performance, an across-the-board increase in the real profitability of investments has been observed in recent years. In fact, the rise in value of real estate and of the stock market, as well as the improvement in the financial balance sheets of the nation's largest companies, have been extraordinary.

These factors, together with the worldwide recession, low external interest rates and high financial yields in Colombia, attracted a massive inflow of capital. In fact, the (net) accumulation of reserves was $626 million, $1.919 billion, and $2.024 billion in 1990, 1991, and 1992, respectively. According to balance of payments statistics, the accumulation of reserves is due primarily to the performance of the current account. Thus, a great deal of the "capital" inflow resulted from goods and services transactions, owing to the illegality of certain transactions in foreign currency. The recording (and overinvoicing) of fictitious exports was widely used to repatriate capital obtained illegally abroad and to evade certain tax audits.

The study, utilizing a method of identifying the speculative component of services transactions, concludes that the total inflow of capital through this account was approximately $400 million in 1991. The data up to June 1992 suggest an amount close to $560 million. When the inflows "filtered" through the current account are added to the flows from the private sector capital account, aggregate balances of $649 million, $545 million, and $868 million are obtained for 1990, 1991, and 1992, respectively.

Not surprisingly, the accumulation of reserves caused serious macroeconomic stabilization problems, the most significant of which was real appreciation of the currency. To prevent a serious loss of competitiveness in the production of tradable goods, the monetary authorities intervened actively in the foreign exchange market. The methods of intervention, however, changed as time passed. Initially, until late 1991, the monetary effects of the intervention were fully sterilized via open market operations of a contractive nature. The scope of the sterilization effort generated high quasi-fiscal costs, which, in the presence of inflexible fiscal goals (as well as the anticyclical use of public finances), necessitated the adjustment of public spending and a rise in taxes. Moreover, the original policy led to an unnecessary hike in interest rates, further increasing the incentives to repatriate capital.

A basic change in the focus of the monetary policy occurred in 1992 with the reduction in the extent of sterilization. An effort was also made, as an explicit policy objective, to lower domestic interest rates and thus virtually to close the yield spread encouraging financial investments in the country. As a result of the new strategy, the credit supply expanded significantly, to levels consistent with the increased demand for money.

The effects of the intervention were successful as far as the exchange rate is concerned. In fact, the authorities managed to keep variations in the representative exchange rage within a range of 7.5 percentage points (although at first there were wide fluctuations within the band). Moreover, in recent months the representative rate has been extremely stable, with an annual rate of devaluation of about 15 percent.

Concerning the real exchange rate, the nominal rate of devaluation has brought about real appreciation over the 1990 level, but a certain stability when compared with the 1986 level, which has come to be viewed as the "equilibrium" level.

Finally, identifying the sectoral distribution of the resources obtained as a result of the external boom is extremely difficult. Nevertheless, this study presents some evidence that the capital inflow has had positive effects on investment. It is to be hoped, therefore, that although in the short term the capital inflow has not had significant revitalizing effects, in the long term its benefits will materialize in terms of growth of the Colombian economy.

Bibliography

Arboleda, S. 1991. La reforma financiera y de seguros. *Ejecutivos de Finanzas* 14.

Avella, M. 1982. Los acontecimientos recientes del sector financiero en perspectiva. *Coyuntura Económica*, October.

Bilsborrow, R. 1968. The Determinants of Fixed Investment by Manufacturing Corporations in Colombia. Doctoral thesis, University of Michigan.

Branson, William H., and Dale W. Henderson. 1985. The Specification and Influence of Asset Markets. In *Handbook of International Economics,* Vol. 2, eds. Ronald W. Jones and Peter B. Kenen. Amsterdam: North-Holland Publishing Company.

Calvo, G.A., L. Leiderman, and C. Reinhart. 1993. Capital Inflows and Real Exchange Rate Appreciation in Latin America: The Role of External Factors. IMF Staff Papers. Unpublished.

Cárdenas, Mauricio. 1989. El sector externo. In *Introducción a la Macroeconomía Colombiana,* eds. José A. Ocampo and E. Lora, Tercer Mundo-FEDESARROLLO.

————. 1991. Coffee Exports, Endogenous State Policies and the Business Cycle. Doctoral dissertation, University of California, Berkeley.

————. 1992. Flujos de capitales, tasa de cambio real y coyuntura macroeconómica en América Latina. *Coyuntura Económica.* September.

————. 1993. Flujos de capitales y mecanismos de estabilización macroeconómica en Colombia: 1991-1992. In *Op. cit.,* eds. Garay-Cárdenas.

Carrasquilla, A. 1992. Estabilización macroeconómica y tasas de interés en Colombia: ¿se agotó otro modelo? In *Apertura: Dos Años Después,* ed. Astrid Martínez, Asociación Bancaria y de Entidades Financieras de Colombia.

————. 1993. Acumulación de reservas y política macroeconómica: Colombia: 1990-1992. In *Op. cit.,* eds. Garay-Cárdenas.

Chica, R. 1983. El desarrollo industrial colombiano. *Desarrollo y Sociedad* (No. 12).

———. 1984. Un diagnóstico de la crisis de la acumulación de la industria colombiana. *Desarrollo y Sociedad* (No. 22).

Correa, P. 1984. Determinantes de la cuenta de servicios de la balanza cambiaria. *Ensayos sobre política económica* 6, December.

———. 1992. Paridad entre la tasa de interés real interna y externa: notas sobre el caso colombiano. *Coyuntura Económica,* April.

Cumby, Robert and M. Obstfeld. 1981. A Note on Exchange Rate Expectations and Nominal Interest Differentials: A Test of the Fischer Hypothesis. *Journal of Finance,* June.

Danker, Deborah J. *et al.* 1985. Small Empirical Model of Exchange Market Intervention: Applications to Germany, Japan, and Canada. *Staff Study* 135. The Board of Governors of Federal Reserve System.

Díaz-Alejandro, C.F. 1983. Stories of the 1930s for the 1980s. In *Financial Policies and the World Capital Market: The Problem of Latin American Countries,* eds. P. Aspe, R. Dornbusch, and M. Obstfeld. Chicago: University of Chicago Press-NBER.

———. 1984. *Latin American Debt: I Don't Think We Are In Kansas Anymore.* Brookings Papers on Economic Activity 2. Washington, D.C.: The Brookings Institution.

Departamento de Planeación Nacional. 1991a. *Programa Macroeconómico.* DNP-2507-UMACRO, January 21.

———. 1991b. *La revolución pacífica, Plan de desarrollo económico y social 1990-1994.*

Domínguez, K., and J. Frankel. 1990. Does Foreign Exchange Intervention Matter? Disentangling the Portfolio and Expectations Effects for the Mark. Mimeo.

Dooley, M.P., and P. Isard. 1980. Capital Controls, Political Risk and Deviations from Interest Rate Parity. Journal *of Political Economy* 88, April.

———. 1983. The Portfolio Balance Model of Exchange Rates and Some Structural Estimates of the Risk Premium. *IMF Staff Papers* 30, December.

————. 1982. A Portfolio-Balance, Rational Expectations Model of the Dollar-Mark Rate: May 1973-June 1977. *Journal of International Economics* 12, November.

Edwards, S. 1991. Flujos de capitales, tasas de interés y tipo de cambio en Colombia. December. Mimeo.

Fainboim, I. 1990. Inversión, tributación y costo de uso del capital en Colombia: 1950-1987. *Ensayos sobre Política Económica* (No. 18).

Fernández, J. and R. Candelo. 1983. Política monetaria y movilidad de capitales en Colombia. *Ensayos sobre Política Económica* (No. 3).

FEDESARROLLO. 1991. Reformas para la modernización de la economía colombiana. *Coyuntura Económica* (11,1).

Flavin, M. 1983. Excess Volatility in the Financial Markets: A Reassessment of the Empirical Evidence. *Journal of Political Economy,* December.

Frankel, J.A. 1982a. A Test of Perfect Substitutability in the Foreign Exchange Market. *Southern Economic Journal* 49, October.

————. 1982b. In Search of the Exchange Risk Premium: A Six Test Assuming Mean-Variance Optimization. *Journal of International Money and Finance* 1, December.

Garay, L.J. and M. Cárdenas, eds. 1993. *Macroeconomía de los Flujos de Capital en Colombia y América Latina.* FEDESARROLLO, Tercer Mundo y FESCOL.

Herrera, S. 1991. Movilidad de capitales y la economía colombiana. *Banca y Finanzas,* July-September.

————, and Juan M. Julio. 1992. La demanda de dinero en el corto y en el largo plazo en Colombia. Banco de la República. Mimeo.

Hodrick, R.J. 1987. The Empirical Evidence on the Efficiency of Forward and Futures Foreign Exchange Markets, *Fundamentals of Pure and Applied Economics* (No. 24).

Inter-American Development Bank. 1989. *Economic and Social Progress in Latin America.* Washington, D.C.: Inter-American Development Bank.

Kouri, Pentti, J.K. 1980. Monetary Policy, the Balance of Payments, and the Exchange Rate. In *The Functioning of Floating Rates: Theory, Evidence, and Policy Implications*, eds. D. Bigman and T. Taya, Cambridge.

————, and Michael G. Porter. 1974. International Capital Flows and Portfolio Equilibrium. *Journal of Political Economy*, May/June 82.

Krugman, P. 1987. The Narrow Moving Band, The Dutch Disease, and the Competitive Consequences of Mrs. Thatcher. Notes in the Presence of Dynamic Scale Economies. *Journal of Development Economics*, 27: 41-55.

Loopesko, B.E. 1983. Relationships Among Exchange Rates, Interventions, and Interest Rates: An Empirical Investigation. *Staff Study 133*. The Board of Governors of the Federal Reserve System.

Lora, E. 1990. Las encuestas arancelaria y la apertura económica. C*oyuntura Económica* (10,2).

————, ed. 1991. *Apertura y modernización: las reformas de los noventa*. Tercer Mundo-FEDESARROLLO.

————. 1992. El fortalecimiento del sector financiero en el proceso de ajuste: liberación y regulación en el caso colombiano. Research Centers Network Project.

Mankiw, N.G., D. Romer, and M.D. Shapiro. 1985. An Unbiased Reexamination of Stock Market Volatility. *Journal of Finance*, July.

Marsh, T., and R. Merton. 1984. Dividend Variability and Variance Bounds Tests for the Rationality of Stock Market Prices. *Sloan School Working Paper* (No. 1584-84), August.

Mundell, R. 1968. *International Economics*, New York.

Obstfeld, M. 1982a. The Capitalization of Income Streams and the Effects of Open-Market Policy under Fixed Exchange Rates, *Journal of Monetary Economics* 9, January.

————. 1982b. Can We Sterilize? Theory and Evidence. *American Economic Review*, May.

————. 1983. Exchange Rates, Inflation, and the Sterilization Problem: Germany, 1975-1981, *European Economic Review* 21, March-April.

————. 1988. The Effectiveness of Foreign-Exchange Intervention: Recent Experience, NBER Working Paper No. 2796.

O'byrne, A. Mauricio Reina. 1993. Flujos de capitales y diferencial de intereses en Colombia: ¿cual es la cuasalidad? In *Op. cit.*, eds. Garay-Cárdenas.

Ocampo, J.A. 1988. Una nota sobre la relación entre financiamiento externo, ahorro e inversión. *Ensayos sobre Política Económica* (No. 19), June.

————. 1989. El proceso de ahorro e inversión y sus determinantes en Colombia. In *Macroeconomía, Mercado de Capitales y Negocio Financiero*, ed. Carlos Caballero. Asociación Bancaria de Colombia.

————. 1992. La internacionalización de la economía colombiana, CLADEI-CIID, FEDESARROLLO. Mimeo.

Ocampo, J.A., J.L. Londoño, and L. Villar. 1985. Ahorro e inversión en Colombia, *Coyuntura Económica,* June.

Rennhack, R., and G. Mondino. 1989. Movilidad de capitales y política monetaria en Colombia. *Ensayos sobre Política Económica* (No. 15), June.

Rogoff, K. 1984. On the Effects of Sterilized Intervention: An Analysis of Weekly Data, *Journal of Monetary Economics* 14.

Sánchez, F., and E. Lora. 1992. Ahorro, inversión y perspectivas de crecimiento en Colombia. FEDESARROLLO.

Serven, L., and A. Solimano. 1992. *Private Investment and Macroeconomic Adjustment.* The World Bank Research Observer (7,1).

Solimano, A. 1989. *How Private Investment Reacts to Changing Macroeconomic Conditions.* Working Papers 212.

Steiner, R., R. Suescún, and F. Melo. 1992. Flujos de capital y expectativas de devaluación, *Coyuntura Económica,* June.

Shiller, R. J. 1984. *Stock Prices and Social Dynamics.* Brookings Papers on Economic Activity, 1984: 2. Washington, D.C.: The Brookings Institution.

Urrutia M., and A. Pontón. 1993. Entrada de capitales, diferenciales de interés y narcotráfico. In *Op. cit.*, eds. Garay-Cárdenas.

Villegas, L.B. 1991. Elementos económicos de la reforma financiera, *Ejecutivos de Finanzas* 14, April.

Weber, W. E. 1986. Do Sterilized Interventions Affect Exchange Rates? *The Federal Reserve Bank of Minneapolis Quarterly Review* 10, Summer.

Zuleta, L. A. 1991. Una reforma financiera para la década del noventa. In *Apertura y Modernización. Las Reformas de los Noventa*, ed. Lora. Tercer Mundo-FEDESARROLLO.

CHAPTER FIVE

FINANCIAL MARKETS
AND CAPITAL FLOWS
IN MEXICO

Jaime Ros[1]

One of the most remarkable phenomena that occurred at the start of the 1990s in Latin America was the resurgence of capital flows to the region. Mexico has occupied a prominent position in this process, having received nearly half of those flows.[2] As in other Latin American countries, this development has included new forms of access to international markets and the repatriation of significant amounts of capital.

Although the flows ended the previous decade's severe external credit squeeze and are, to some degree, a positive response on the part of foreign and domestic investors to the process of economic reform and structural adjustment initiated in Mexico in the mid-1980s, they have also been a source of concern, for three different reasons. First, to the extent that they cause appreciation of the real exchange rate and greater fluctuations thereof, their impact on exports and the import-substitution sectors is negative, thus creating new macroeconomic adjustment problems in the medium term. This subject is of particular importance in the current climate of trade liberalization.

If, in addition, the flows are concentrated in highly liquid financial assets, the process of real exchange rate appreciation must be dealt with in conditions of growing financial instability. Finally, they may be inadequately regulated and

[1] The author is indebted to Germán Echecopar for his assistance in preparing the data base and for his innumerable comments and suggestions concerning an earlier version of the text. Thanks are also due José Casar (ILET, Mexico City), Randolph Gibert (ECLAC, Mexico City) and José Alejo Hernández (Banco de México) for their help in developing the statistical base. The comments and concerns of José Casar forced the author to clarify the conclusions of this study.
[2] See Banco de México (1993), Calvo, *et al.* (1992), United Nations (1993), and World Bank (1993).

thus result in a poor allocation of resources (between consumption and investment, financial and physical assets, and among various economic sectors). This amounts to nothing less than the actual and potential contribution of the flows to the process of investment and growth, a subject of vital importance following a decade of sluggish economic growth.

The organization and objectives of this study are as follows. The first section documents the new institutional and external environment in which the recent episode of capital inflows unfolded. The next analyzes the nature and determinants of the flows; its objective is to assess the role of various factors in generating the flows as well as the extent to which macroeconomic policy can be used to respond to the changes that have occurred. The subsequent section examines the macroeconomic adjustment processes associated with the flows, both in the financial and the commodities markets, as well as in the savings and investment process. The final section summarizes the principal research findings and their economic policy implications.

Institutional Reforms and Capital Flows

The recent episode of massive capital inflows occurred in an economic and institutional environment quite different from the conditions prevailing throughout most of the previous decade. The last few years have witnessed the consolidation of the structural reform program launched by the Mexican government in the mid-1980s: the reform of foreign trade policies, the easing of restrictions on foreign investment, the privatization of public enterprises, and the deregulation of domestic business activity, including the financial sector.

Following the difficult macroeconomic adjustment necessitated by the debt crisis and the ensuing high inflation and economic stagnation, the macroeconomic climate took a turn for the better in 1988. The stabilization program adopted in late 1987—the Economic Solidarity Pact—quickly helped slow inflation and was a factor in 1992 when the rate of economic growth, although still quite modest, exceeded the rate of population growth for the fourth consecutive year.[3]

The processes of structural reform and macroeconomic stabilization were accompanied by other internal and external changes that facilitated the country's re-entry into the international financial markets: the opening of the stock market and the money market to foreign portfolio investment (in 1989 and 1991, respectively), the Brady plan for restructuring and alleviating the external debt burden in 1989 and, since the spring of 1990, the changes anticipated under the North American Free Trade Agreement (NAFTA).

---

[3] For an analysis of the processes of adjustment and reform in the 1980s, see Lustig (1992), OECD (1992), and Ros (1992), among others.

In this section we will examine this new environment. The emphasis will be on the measures and events that have had a direct impact on capital flows.

The Privatization Program

The privatization of state enterprises began shortly after the De la Madrid administration took office, although it was not until February 1985 that the government officially announced its intention of divesting itself of nonpriority and nonstrategic companies.[4] The program was accelerated in December 1987 in accordance with the Economic Solidarity Pact.[5] In 1989 the new administration continued the divestment process, while at the same time expanding the opportunities for private sector participation in the economy (in the banking system and in infrastructure projects such as the construction of toll highways, bridges, and hydroelectric dams).

The privatization process has consisted of two major stages. The first, from 1983 to mid-1990, was characterized by the sale, transfer, or liquidation of small and medium-size companies acquired or created by the state with little social or economic justification. Other than the fact that the actual number of state enterprises dropped from 1,155 to 310 between early 1983 and July 1990, their disappearance had little effect on the economic importance of the public sector and did not involve any major sums of external capital.[6]

The second stage, which had the greatest impact between late 1990 and mid-1992, included the sale of companies and banks with much larger assets than in the prior period. As Table 5.1 illustrates, revenue from the sale of assets totaled approximately $22 billion between 1989 and 1992. The privatization of TELMEX, acquired by a group of Mexican and foreign investors in 1990-91, and the sale of

---

[4] This program was part of a broader divestment policy that included both the sale and the merger or liquidation of state entities, the objectives of which were microeconomic efficiency and easing the state's financing constraints.

[5] The government announced that upon completion of the privatization program, the state would retain ownership and control in the following areas only: oil extraction, exploration, and refining and the basic petrochemical industry (PEMEX); electricity (Comisión Federal de Electricidad); railroads (Ferrocarriles Nacionales); food distribution (Conasupo); radioactive minerals and nuclear energy; satellite communications; and postal service. This meant, then, that the state would basically keep the "Big Four" public companies (PEMEX, CFE, Ferrocarriles Nacionales, and Conasupo) and would withdraw from the communications sector (TELMEX), aviation (Mexicana de Aviación and Aeroméxico), steel production, transportation equipment, chemicals and fertilizers, mining, sugar, and a host of other industrial and service activities.

[6] An overwhelming majority of the companies sold to private investors (93 percent) were acquired by Mexican investors. Concerning the fiscal impact of this initial stage of the privatization process, it has been estimated that government transfers were made to 22 companies in 1988, as compared to 49 in 1983. This contributed to the decrease in transfers—an important aspect of the fiscal adjustment in 1986—from 2.5 percent of GDP to 1.3 percent in the same period. For more information on this topic, see Gasca Zamora (1989) and USITC (1990).

Table 5.1. Mexico: Sources of Privatization Income
(Billions of dollars)

	1989	1990	1991	1992	1989-92	% of total 1989-92
Total[1]	0.78	3.13	10.78	6.82	21.51	100.00
Banks	0.00	0.00	7.44	4.93	12.37	57.50
TELMEX	0.00	2.10	2.75	1.40	6.25	29.10
Investors:						
Foreigners[2]	0.00	0.00	2.35	1.24	3.59	16.70
Nationals	0.00	2.10	0.40	0.16	2.66	12.40
Others	0.78	1.03	0.59	0.49	2.89	13.40

[1] Amounts are expressed in accruing terms and converted using the market exchange rate (quarterly average).
[2] Includes the options to buy exercised by Southwestern Bell International Holdings and France Cable et Radio, as well as the series "L" stocks which were acquired by foreign investor (May 1991 and May 1992).
Source: Author's own calculations based on SHCP (May 1993).

Table 5.2. Mexico: Uses of Privatization Income

	% of GNP		Billions of dollars			% of total
	1991	1992	1991	1992	1991-92	1991-92
Total [1]	3.3	3.3	9.42	10.74	20.16	100.0
Financial deficit [2]	1.4	0.1	4.02	0.28	4.30	21.3
Net reduction of debt	1.9	3.2	5.39	10.46	15.85	78.6
External	1.5	0.8	4.39	2.55	6.94	34.4
Banco de México	1.9	0.2	5.49	0.70	6.19	30.7
Private sector [3]	-1.6	2.2	-4.48	7.21	2.73	13.5
Residents [4]	1.8	1.5	5.03	4.94	9.97	49.5
Nonresidents [4]	-1.2	-2.7	-3.54	-8.77	-12.31	-61.1
Commercial banks	-2.1	3.4	-5.97	11.04	5.07	25.1

[1] Includes cash receipts (or amortization of Bank Privatization Bonds) and the reduction of internal or external public sector debt from reclassifying Teléfonos de México as a private enterprise. This number differs from that in Table 5.1, which expresses income in accruing terms.
[2] Accrued financial deficit. Includes accrued unpaid interest, which is only counted in the financial cash deficit upon liquidation.
[3] Financial and nonfinancial (including nonresidents).
[4] Nonfinancial. Calculated as the residual from the reduction of private sector debt.
Source: Author's own calculations based on Banco de México, *Informe Anual* (1991 and 1992, tables on the financing of the public sector deficit and on the balance of payments).

Table 5.3. Mexico: Privatization Income, Portfolio Investment, and Net Worth of the Private Sector

(Billions of dollars)

	1990:3-1991:2	1991:3-1992:2	1992:3-1993:1
Privatization income	5.9	13.6	1.0
Foreign investment in the stock market	4.0	6.5	2.7
Change in the position of private sector local assets:			
Government securities [1]	4.7	-12.8	-8.3
Net external assets [2]	-3.2	-8.4	-1.4
Errors and omissions in the balance of payments	-0.2	1.0	-2.4

[1] Holdings of governments securities by commercial banks and the private sector (excluding foreign portfolio investment in the money market, which corresponds to securities held by nonresidents).
[2] Assets in the capital account (excluding foreign debt guarantees) minus private sector debt (excluding that of enterprises with foreign participation) and commercial bank debt.
Source: Author's own calculations based on SHCP (1993), Banco de México, *Economic Indicators.*

commercial banks to local financial groups in 1991-92 represented the largest share of the revenue. TELMEX alone accounted for nearly 30 percent of the proceeds, while the sale of 18 banks contributed nearly 58 percent.[7] Most of these funds were added to the treasury in just two years, 1991 and 1992, during which time they represented between 82 and 94 percent of the total (depending on whether the figure is expressed in actual or accrued terms). In both years the revenue from privatization totaled an amount equivalent to 3.3 percent of GDP (see Table 5.2).

Both the sale of these assets and the method of privatization affected the nature and the size of the capital flows, as will be seen below. First, however, it must be remembered that this effect and the subsequent macroeconomic impact are not unrelated to the use the government made of the revenue from privatization. In addition to financing the deficit or acquiring other physical assets, the government can use these flows for three things: 1) reduction of its net external debt; 2) reduction of its debt with Banco de México; 3) reduction of its domestic, private

---

[7] Two of them (Banco Nacional de México and Banco de Comercio) accounted for half of this amount. Prominent among the rest of the companies sold (the "others" column in the table, accounting for 13.4 percent of the total revenue) were Mexicana de Aviación and Aeroméxico in mid-1989 and Compañía Minera de Cananea and Mexicana de Cobre, the two largest state copper companies.

sector debt. As Table 5.2 shows, nearly two-thirds of the total revenue from privatization received in 1991 and 1992 was used to retire external debt and domestic debt with Banco de México (roughly in equal parts). The remaining third (13.5 percent) was used to reduce domestic, private sector debt (including nonresidents) or to cover the public sector financial deficit. The latter represented 21.3 percent of the total, although it decreased as time passed (the financial deficit for 1992 as a whole was nearly zero).

Table 5.3 shows the changes in foreign portfolio investment in the stock market and in the position of private sector assets from mid-1990 on. The effect of the privatization process on foreign portfolio investment is apparent in the similar distribution of these two flows over time. The concentration of portfolio investment in the initial period (relative to the temporal distribution of the revenue from privatization) is probably explained by the large amounts of foreign capital involved in the privatization of TELMEX (which occurred, for the most part, in the initial period).

Regulation of Foreign Investment and Deregulation of Financial Markets

The law of 1973, which restricted investment in certain activities and established as a "general rule" a 49 percent cap on foreign investment, remains the basic legal reference for regulating foreign participation in the economy.[8] However, the De la Madrid administration in 1984 and the Salinas administration in 1989 eschewed a restrictive interpretation of the law. The new regulations established since then open up new areas of investment previously reserved for the state or for Mexican citizens (e.g., petrochemicals, financial services, and telecommunications), eliminate restrictions on majority shareholding by foreigners in numerous sectors, and simplify the administrative procedures for the approval of investment projects.[9]

---

[8] The "law to promote Mexican investment and regulate foreign investment," enacted in 1973, divides economic activities into four categories: a) those reserved for the state (such as petroleum, basic petrochemicals, electricity, and railroads); b) those reserved exclusively for Mexicans (in communications, transportation, forestry, radio, and television); c) those in which foreign investment is subject to specific limits (such as the ceiling on foreign ownership of 40 percent of the total capital in the secondary petrochemical and automobile parts industries, as well as any other activity subject to percentages indicated in specific laws); d) all other activities, in which foreign participation is limited to 49 percent. However, the National Commission for Foreign Investment (Comisión Nacional para la Inversión Extranjera, CNIE) was empowered to modify the 49 percent general rule applicable to all other activities and to authorize a higher percentage when such investment was considered beneficial for the economy. In practice, the law applied to new foreign investment projects since the CNIE allowed businesses wholly owned by foreigners to retain the capital structure they had prior to the passage of the law.

[9] In 1993, the Executive submitted to Congress a foreign investment bill incorporating recent changes in regulations and provisions of NAFTA concerning national treatment of external capital.

The greatest change so far was the decree of May 1989 ("Regulations of the law to promote Mexican investment and regulate foreign investment") which abolished all existing administrative provisions and resolutions and set forth an extremely liberal interpretation of the law of 1973.[10] With the implicit objective of raising direct foreign investment (DFI) as a percentage of total investment from the 1988 level of 10 percent to 20 percent, the new regulations provide for automatic approval of 100 percent foreign participation in investment projects of less than $100 million that satisfy a series of conditions, in addition to investments in nonclassified activities.[11] Among the latter are a number of industries in which certain administrative provisions had restricted majority shareholding by foreigners (such as glassmaking, cement, cellulose, iron, and steel) in other words, sectors formerly dominated by Mexican companies, both private and public.

Deregulation of the financial markets in 1988 was a pivotal factor in the growth of foreign portfolio investment.[12] The decree of May 1989 liberalized the neutral investment system (introduced in 1986) to promote the participation of foreign investors in the Mexican stock market by allowing companies listed on the exchange to issue "N," or "Neutral," series and to exchange "A" series for "N" series.[13] In addition, in late 1990 the restrictions on nonresident purchases of fixed-yield securities (essentially government securities) were abolished. The rapid growth in placements of ADRs on the New York Stock Exchange and of country funds on the U.S. stock markets was also fueled by changes in the regulations governing the U.S. financial markets (the "S Regulations" and the "144A" Rule),

---

[10] For more on this subject, see Lustig (1992) and USITC (1990).

[11] The conditions established by the decree, in addition to the requirement that the total assets not exceed $100 million, take into account the following criteria: the balance of payments (all of the funds must originate abroad and the expected flows of foreign exchange must remain constant during the first three years of operation of the project); regional development (the plants must be located outside the most heavily-populated urban areas: Mexico City, Guadalajara, and Monterrey); employment and human resources training (the investment must create permanent jobs and must establish training and personnel development programs); and the environment (appropriate technologies must be used). Nonclassified activities are those activities not mentioned in the decree and that fall outside the areas reserved by the law of 1973 for the state and for Mexican citizens or those that are subject to specific percentages of foreign participation. Such nonclassified activities number 547, or 73 percent of the 754 activities included in the Mexican Catalog of Economic and Productive Activities. Of the remaining 207 activities (which are classified and listed in the decree), the decree mentions 40 wherein 100 percent foreign participation is permitted subject to prior CNIE authorization.

[12] Other aspects of the financial deregulation such as the elimination of mandatory reserve requirements and interest rate caps are summarized in Table 5.4.

[13] See SECOFI (1993). The decree also introduced the temporary investment system, making it possible for foreign investment to participate indirectly, through temporary investment trusts, in activities that were formerly closed or subject to a predetermined limit. Another factor promoting expansion of the stock market in the recent period was the tax reform of 1987, which eliminated the bias against share capital investments.

which facilitated the access of Mexico and other developing countries to the international financial markets.[14]

The effects of these measures are illustrated in Figure 5.1, which shows the cumulative flow since late 1988 in various activities. Particularly noteworthy is the recent growth of portfolio investment in the stock market and the money market. The performance of these flows and of the external liabilities of the private sector will be examined in detail in the following sections. The figure also reveals the vitality of DFI, which is a result of the recovery observed in 1984 following the sharp contraction of 1982 and 1983. Whether this recovery represents a departure from the historic trend (and, if so, whether it can be attributed to the impact of the new regulations) will be discussed in a subsequent section.

Factors Specific to Mexico

Several of the changes in this period occurred not only in Mexico but in other Latin American countries as well. Some, however, particularly in the more recent past, are specific to Mexico. One of the most important is the agreement for restructuring and reducing the government's external debt burden, concluded in early July 1989 and signed with the creditor banks in February 1990.[15] Together with the retirement of external debt (shown in Figure 5.1)—financed with the revenue from privatization and the fiscal adjustment—and the recent decline in international interest rates, the debt restructuring agreement led to a substantial decrease in interest payments as a percentage of exports. This indicator, generally used to evaluate the country risk, recently fell below the levels reached in the mid-1970s. Figure 5.1 also shows the recent trend of an indicator of the country risk premium.

Another important aspect was the mid-1990 opening of NAFTA negotiations with the United States and Canada. The heads of state of the three countries signed the agreement in December 1992, and the negotiation of parallel agreements on labor and environmental standards ended in August 1993. Following approval by the legislative bodies of the three countries in 1993, the agreement will enter into force in January 1994. The prospect of greater economic integration in North America has often been cited as one of the elements contributing to the inflow of capital into Mexico.[16] At the same time, however, the ups and downs of the negotiating process have affected the stability of the flows. Although we

---

[14] On this latter subject, see El-Erian (1992) and Banco de México (1993).

[15] For an analysis of the agreement, see Lustig (1992).

[16] In particular, this is a result of the "padlock" effect on the economic reforms of the De la Madrid and Salinas administrations. For an analysis of this subject, see Lustig, Bosworth, and Lawrence (1992) and Hufbauer and Schott (1993).

Figure 5.1. Mexico: Capital Flows, 1989:1-1993:1
(Flows accumulated since year-end 1988, in billions of dollars)

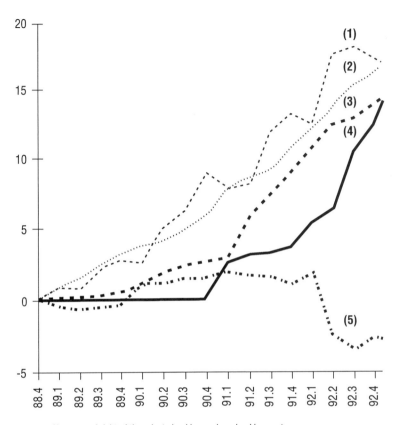

(1) Net external debt of the private banking and nonbanking sectors.

(2) Direct foreign investment.

(3) Portfolio investment in the stock market.

(4) Portfolio investment in the money market.

(5) Public external debt.

Source: Bank of Mexico, *Economic Indicators* (various issues).

will refer to this subject in other sections, it may be of interest to note here that the vitality of certain items in mid-1990 (and the slowdown in the second quarter of 1992) may be a reflection of this phenomenon (Figure 5.1).

Determinants of Capital Flows

The Capital Account: An Overview

The traditional presentation of the capital account in the balance of payments distinguishes financial transactions with the rest of the world by the type of financial assets involved (short- and long-term) and by the sector of the local economy (public or private) making them. The inclusion of foreign investment in the private sector account has always raised some doubt, however, since unlike the other items of the private capital account, neither DFI nor the indebtedness of foreign companies changes the net external asset position of the local private sector (although they do change the external asset position of the country).

Generally, but not always, local sector transactions with the rest of the world create foreign currency obligations. Thus, external indebtedness has always had a dual connotation: the liabilities are with nonresidents, and the debt is paid in foreign currency. With the opening of the stock market to nonresidents, there are now transactions that create national currency obligations as well: the purchase of government securities by nonresidents (called portfolio investment in the money market) and nonresident purchases of shares in Mexican companies (called portfolio investment in the stock market). These transactions do not change the external liabilities position (in foreign currency) of residents, although they do change the net liabilities position with the rest of the world.

The above discussion is intended merely to clarify the analytical framework used in the remainder of this study. For the purposes of this and the next section, an initial distinction is made between endogenous flows and those that can be considered exogenous in a short-term analysis. The latter include the traditional external borrowing of the public sector and DFI (together with the external borrowing of foreign companies). These foreign investment flows can be considered exogenous in the short-term insofar as they are correlative with long-term expectations and are less sensitive than other external capital flows to daily changes in the prices of financial assets. Distinguishable among the endogenous flows are those that change the external liabilities position of the public sector (portfolio investment in the money market) and those that change the net liabilities position of the private sector (net external liabilities as traditionally defined and portfolio investment in the stock market). These various flows are shown in Table 5.4, where we follow the convention of including DFI in the private sector account.

Table 5.4. Mexico: Capital Account in the Balance of Payments
(Billions of dollars)

	Annual averages		1989	1990	1991	1992
	1980-88	1989-92				
Public sector	4.866	2.817	0.79	-0.87	4.47	6.87
Nonfinancial (net) [1]	2.924	-2.59	-0.49	-5.50	-1.19	-3.17
Financial [2]	1.941	2.33	1.28	4.63	2.12	1.27
Domestic debt with nonresidents [3]	0	3.077	0	0	3.538	8.77
Private sector	0.088	12.54	2.39	9.03	19.67	19.08
Nonfinancial (net) [4]	-2.214	1.13	-1.57	-0.276	1.14	5.22
Financial [5]	0.81	2.82	0.98	4.25	5.25	0.80
Foreign investment	1.49	8.59	2.98	5.05	13.27	13.06
Stock market	0.00	3.40	0.49	2.00	6.33	4.78
Direct	1.71	3.98	3.18	2.63	4.76	5.37
Debt of foreign enterprises	-0.22	1.21	-0.69	0.43	2.18	2.91
Errors and omissions	-2.184	0.33	3.31	2.18	-2.21	-1.97
Capital account plus errors and omissions	2.769	15.684	6.48	10.35	21.93	23.98
Change in reserves	0.295	3.235	0.396	3.23	8.14	1.173
Current account deficit	2.474	12.449	6.085	7.11	13.79	22.809

[1] Net external debt, adjusted for external debt guarantees.
[2] Banco de Desarrollo and Banco de México.
[3] Foreign portfolio investment in the money market.
[4] Private debt minus the acquisition of assets abroad. Does not include the debt of enterprises with foreign participation.
[5] Debt of commercial banks.
Source: Author's own calculations based on SHCP (1993); Banco de México, *Economic Indicators.*

A Short-term Model of Asset Markets

In this section we present the results of developing an aggregate model of the asset markets, a model which has two basic characteristics. First, it is a portfolio adjustment model with imperfect capital mobility, both in the sense that domestic and external assets are imperfect substitutes in resident and nonresident portfolios and in the sense that the adjustment of the capital stocks to the desired levels is not instantaneous.[17] Second, it is a short-term model since, in addition to treating the external interest rate and the nominal exchange rate as exogenous variables, monetary factors have no contemporaneous impact on real variables or price levels. The asset markets attain equilibrium solely through changes in the domestic interest rate, changes in the quantity of money, and changes in the net external assets involved in the reorganization of the portfolios of private investors.[18]

The estimations refer to the reduced form of the equations for the domestic real interest rate (r) and the total external liabilities of the private sector (F), due to the endogenous determination of these variables. The first equation expresses the interest rate as a function of the rates of return of the alternative assets (the rate of inflation, π, and the external interest rate, i^*, adjusted for the expected devaluation, f); a proxy for the exogenous component of the risk premium (pr); the level of GDP (y); private wealth (R); the contemporaneous supply of bonds $(D_g\text{-}Bc$, where D_g is the total public sector domestic debt and Bc, the debt holdings of the central bank); and the delayed effects of the demand for bonds among residents and nonresidents $(Bp_{-1}$ and Bx_{-1}, respectively).[19]

$$r = r[(D_g - Bc),\ \pi,\ (i^* + f),\ pr,\ y,\ R,\ (Bp + Bx)_{-1}] \tag{1}$$

The effect of each of the exogenous variables on the interest rate depends on how conditions in the bond market change. Thus, an increase in the supply of bonds due to a decrease in the holding of central bank bonds has a positive effect on the interest rate. An increase in the external interest rate or in the risk premium raises the interest rate by causing capital outflows and reducing the demand for bonds. The interest rate is negatively affected by the rate of inflation and positively affected by the level of real income due to the substitution effect between money and bonds. An increase in wealth lowers the interest rate by increasing the demand for bonds. Finally, the capital stocks ratio of the preceding period includes the delayed (and negative) effects of a greater demand for bonds.

The second equation expresses the external liabilities of the private sector as a function of its financial wealth and the rates of return of the various assets. Since this is the reduced form of the equation, the domestic interest rate is expressed through its exogenous determinants. For example, an increase in the

---

[17] For a review of the bibliography on this subject, see Branson and Henderson (1984). A discussion of the subject as it concerns Mexico can be found in Cumby and Obstfeld (1983).

[18] For more information on this subject see Kouri and Porter (1974).

[19] A more complete explanation of the exogenous and endogenous components of the risk premium is presented in a later section.

supply of bonds or in the level of GDP, by raising the interest rate in the bond market, leads to an increase in the demand for external liabilities.[20]

$$e.F^*/p = F[\pi, i^*+f, pr, y, R, (e_{-1}.F_{-1}^*/p_{-1}), (D_g - Bc), (Bp + Bx)_{-1}] \qquad (2)$$

In this equation, F^*, e, and p are the end-of-period values of the dollar balance of net external liabilities (F^*), the nominal exchange rate (e, pesos per dollar), and the price index in Mexico (p). In addition to the usual variables, we include two dummy variables in order to include the effects that money market deregulation and privatization have on investment decisions involving a choice between domestic and external assets. The first (D_1) has a value of 0 until 1990:4 and a value of 1 following deregulation of the money market in 1991:1. The second (D_2) is 0 until 1989:1 and 1 in 1989:2, when the privatization of large enterprises was first undertaken.[21]

For the purpose of investigating the effects of these variables on foreign portfolio investment in the stock market, a second version of equation (2) was developed, which includes the cumulative flow of shareholder investment as a dependent variable:

$$(e.F^*/p + Ka) = F[\pi, i^*+f, pr, y, R, (e_{-1}.F_{-1}^*/p_{-1} + Ka_{-1}), (D_g - Bc), (Bp + Bx)_{-1}] \quad (2')$$

where $Ka_t = \Sigma Ia^*_t . e/p_t$, i.e., the cumulative flow of foreign investment in the stock market (I^*a) at the end of quarter t, since the opening of the stock market in the first quarter of 1989.

The results of the ordinary least squares estimation with quarterly data for the period 1978:2-1993:1 are presented in Table 5.5.[22]

---

[20] It should also be noted that since this is the reduced form, the values of the coefficients of wealth, inflation, and the return on external assets reflect both the impact of these variables on the structural form of the equation and the indirect effect exerted through the bond market. Thus, for example, the expected rate of return of the external assets reflects the (negative) impact of the structural form and the (positive) effect that an increase in this variable exerts through the bond market. When the domestic interest rate rises, the overall effect of the increase on the external return (reflected by the reduced form) is, therefore, less than the partial effect (reflected by the structural form, which takes the interest rate as a given).

[21] The value of this variable remains 1 after the virtual conclusion of the privatization program in 1992:3. Otherwise, the variable would not incorporate the effect of privatization on investment decisions but rather the impact of privatization through its effects on the asset markets. These effects are already implicit in the presence of the other variables that determine asset prices.

[22] The coefficients of some variables were small and not significant: the y, R, and D_2 coefficients in the interest rate equation and the $(Bp+ Bx)-1$, π, D_1, and D_2 coefficients in the external liabilities equations (2 and 2'). They are omitted from the results presented in Table 2.2.

Table 5.5. Mexico: An Estimate of the Reduced Forms of the Interest Rate and Net Foreign Liabilities, 1978:2-1993:1

Dependent variable	Constant	(Dg-Bc)	(Bp+Bx)-1	(i*+f)	π	pr	D1	R^2	DW
r	-0.263 (-4.45)	0.0014 (3.01)	0.0014 (-3.06)	0.126 (2.17)	0.250 (-10.92)	0.250 (5.80)	-0.094 (-2.48)	0.837	1.436

Dependent variable	Constant	(Dg-Bc)	(i*+f)	pr	y	R	$\dfrac{e_{-1}F^*_{-1}}{P_{-1}}$	R^2	DW
$\dfrac{eF^*}{P}$	251.07 (3.67)	0.394 (7.23)	-134.88 (-3.32)	-135.38 (-3.43)	1.06 (1.236)	-0.456 (-9.06)	0.645 (9.38)	0.976	1.729
$\dfrac{eF^*}{P}$ + Ka	167.89 (2.67)	0.438 (8.28)	-158.80 (-4.15)	-107.95 (-3.13)	1.94 (2.23)	-0.513 (-9.78)	0.693 (12.30)	0.980	1.807

The numbers in parentheses are t-statistics. R^2 is the coefficient of determination. D W is the Durbin-Watson statistic.
Source: Author's own calculations.

Capital Mobility and Deregulation of the Money Market

To begin with, the three equations are consistent with the hypothesis of imperfect capital mobility: the coefficient of the external rate of return is less than one in the interest rate equation, and the coefficient of the domestic bond supply is significant and has the expected sign in this and the other equations. The foregoing indicates that the spread between the yields of domestic and external assets (after correction of the latter for expected devaluation) is highly sensitive to the supply of government bonds, which is determined both by the fiscal deficit and by the open market operations of the central bank.

The fact that domestic and external assets are not perfect substitutes is hardly surprising since the government was subject to severe credit constraints throughout much of the period in question. Moreover, the logged coefficient in the external liabilities equations also suggests the lack of instantaneous adjustment to the desired levels, thus reinforcing the short-term sensitivity of the interest rate to supply conditions in the local bond market.

Nevertheless, the degree of capital mobility appears to have changed following deregulation of the money market. The value and significance of D1 in the interest rate equation suggests that nonresident participation in the money market since the first quarter of 1991 has significantly reduced the risk differential (or premium) between domestic and external interest rates. One result of this greater degree of capital mobility is the increased effectiveness of the central bank's open-market operations to protect the exchange rate in the short term against an *ex ante* contraction of the demand for government securities. We will return to this topic in a subsequent section.

Private Sector Flows and Portfolio Investment in the Stock Market

The external liabilities equations may shed some light on the importance of certain factors in the turnaround that has occurred since 1989 in the private sector capital account. The short-form estimation, by revealing the cumulative effects of each of the exogenous variables, is particularly useful in this regard. Consequently, Table 5.6 presents the effects of the trend observed in each of the exogenous variables since the first quarter of 1989 (assuming, in measuring each effect, that the other variables remain at their previous levels). For the purposes of comparison, the results of a similar exercise for the period 1978:2-1981:1 (i.e., during the oil boom before the massive capital flight that preceded the devaluation in early 1982) are also presented.

A number of interesting observations can be made concerning the table. The first is that all of the changes observed in the period (with the exception of the expected exchange depreciation) had a positive effect on the private sector capi-

Table 5.6. Mexico: Effects of the Observed Changes in the Exogenous Variables

	Effect on[1]		
Contribution to the change in [2]	Foreign liabilities of the private sector		Portfolio investment in the stock market
	1988:4-1993:1	1978:2-1981:1	1988:4-1993:1
Foreign interest rate	2.8	-32.4	3.9
Risk premium (exogenous)	4.0	15.2	-18.0
Expected depreciation of the peso	-100.0	-24.1	-82.0
Domestic supply of government securities	10.5	9.9	9.2
Level of economic activity (GDP)	8.6	74.9	14.4
Financial strength	74.1	-43.5	72.6
Sum of the negative effects as a percentage of the positive effects	-21.0	-86.2	-35.5
Observed change (accumulated flow in billions of dollars)	16.4	5.0	14.9

[1] The positive effects are expressed as a percentage of the sum of the positive effects, and the negative effects as a percentage of the (absolute value) of the sum of the negative effects.
[2] Equation (2') was used for estimating the effects of net private sector liabilities abroad (including portfolio investment in the stock market); the effects of portfolio investment in the stock market are obtained as a residual, given the estimated values from equation (2). Omitted are the contributions of lagged terms which reflect the (lagged) effects of the remaining exogenous variables.
Source: Author's own calculations.

tal account.[23] This reveals the extraordinary nature of the recent period. It is interesting to note in this regard that during the oil boom, the negative effects—the rise in the external interest rate, the expected depreciation, and the trend of financial wealth—almost cancel out the effect of the positive changes. This is why the flows of private capital were much smaller than they are now: during the oil boom, the growing surplus in the capital account was determined by the external indebtedness of the public sector.

Together with the extraordinary nature of the current situation, the exercise clearly suggests that the external factors, strictly speaking, did not play a significant role in the recent period. The decrease in the external interest rate and in the exogenous risk premium, as well as the improvement in the terms of trade (adjusted by the international interest rates), had a relatively minor impact: less than 7 percent of the positive effects are explained by the improvement in the external

---

[23] This ignores, for the moment, portfolio investment in the stock market. In the case of the supply of bonds, the positive effect is due to the fact that the process of reducing domestic debt began in the middle of the period under consideration and is not reflected in the point-by-point change. On the other hand, as will be seen in the next section, the model used is not the most appropriate for identifying the effects of this process.

environment. Note that during the oil boom, the improvement in the terms of trade (even when adjusted by the external interest rate) was a more significant factor than it is currently.

By far, the most important effect is the decline in private sector financial wealth (which accounts for nearly three-fourths of the positive effects). This effect is a reflection of the persistent (and growing) gap between investment and private savings in the recent period. That the capital flows from the private sector must be associated with this gap is less obvious than might at first appear. The turnaround in the capital account could have been the result of a gap between investment and public savings, partly financed by the private sector through the purchase of government bonds. This was the case during the oil boom. As Table 5.6 shows, in this period, and up to a few months before the devaluation in early 1982, the external liabilities of the private sector increased without its financial balance (savings minus investment) becoming negative. This is indicated by the negative contribution of financial wealth to the change in external liabilities in this period. Unlike the current situation, the main impetus of the private capital flows during the oil boom was the level of business activity and not a growing financial deficit in the private sector. This period was in fact a boom in which the capital flows were subject to two opposing forces: the positive effect of the surge in business activity and the effect of increased private sector financial wealth, which was negative because it stimulated demand for all types of financial assets, including external assets.

Finally, it should be noted that the determinants of portfolio investment are essentially the determinants of the other external liabilities of the private sector as well. The major differences are the larger role of the increase in business activity and the fact that the negative effects (basically depreciation expectations) offset the positive changes to a greater degree. Both observations are consistent with the longer duration of capital flows of this type.[24]

Although the exercise is informative, the limitations of the model must not be overlooked. First, the exchange rate expectations variable (which is essentially a function of a real exchange rate index) does not begin to incorporate all of the forces that shape exchange rate expectations in the short term. As explained in the following section, these expectations are so volatile that the variable used so far cannot adequately represent them. Second, the assumption that financial wealth is exogenous limits us to the observation that the persistent gap between investment and private savings has contributed greatly to the turnaround in the capital account. To overcome this obstacle, an analytical framework is needed

---

[24] The (negative) contribution of the improvement in the adjusted terms of trade is the only one in the entire exercise that fell short of expectations. Nevertheless, it is very small and the difference between the coefficients used to estimate it (those of the *pr* term in equations 2 and 2') is statistically insignificant.

wherein the capital flows and the investment and savings decisions of the private sector are determined simultaneously. This type of analysis is provided in the next two sections.

Capital Flows, Financial Markets, and Short-term Macroeconomic Policy

In the last four years, two major phases in the evolution of macroeconomic policy are discernible. Prior to the second quarter of 1992, the process of reducing the government's domestic debt was accompanied by the decline of real interest rates (and of the differential with the rest of the world), real appreciation of the peso, and the rapid accumulation of international reserves. The macroeconomic policy in this period was focused essentially on curbing inflation through strict fiscal discipline and slowing the drift of the peso with respect to the dollar.[25] The scope of measures aimed specifically at checking speculative flows was, moreover, extremely limited.[26]

In the third quarter of 1992, the surplus in the capital account continued to grow, although in the context of a reversal in the downward trend of the real interest rate and a slowdown in the accumulation of international reserves. In October 1992 the exchange rate flotation band was widened (which is the equivalent of an increase in the drift of the "ceiling" of the band from 20 to 40 centavos a day) and in November the limits on the foreign currency indebtedness of banks were expanded (representing a partial return to the limits established in April). As in the previous period, the objective of monetary and fiscal policies was essentially to reduce inflation. Real appreciation of the exchange rate continued, although at a slightly slower pace.

Recent Trend of the Exchange Rate and the Interest Rate

Since early 1989, three subperiods can be distinguished in the trend of the real rate of return on treasury certificates (CETES):

1) From early 1989 to the second quarter of 1990, when the yield remains high and stable at around 19 percent per annum;

---

[25] The drift of the peso was slowed to 80 centavos a day in May 1990, to 40 centavos in November of that same year, and to 20 centavos in November 1991, which is the equivalent of a nominal depreciation of 2.5 percent per annum.

[26] These measures consisted essentially of the establishment in August 1991 of a 50 percent liquidity requirement on the foreign exchange obligations of banks, which was replaced in April 1992 with a 10 percent cap on foreign exchange obligations (as a percentage of deposits in local and foreign currency). This limit was raised to 20 percent in November 1992. Moreover, as a result of the consolidation in November 1991 of the auction and managed exchange rates, the foreign exchange controls introduced during the debt crisis in 1982 were completely abolished.

2) From mid-1990 to mid-1992, when real rate falls constantly, until reaching approximately 3 percent per annum at the close of the period; and

3) From mid-1992 to the third quarter of 1993, when the yield suddenly increases (in the third quarter of 1992) and stabilizes at a high level of 6 to 7 percent per annum.

Throughout these three subperiods, the pace of exchange rate drift remained consistently below the rate of inflation, and the peso appreciated in real terms with respect to the dollar. The rate of appreciation was particularly high during the intermediate subperiod (when the real interest rate declined), coinciding with the slowing of the rate of drift from approximately 13 percent to 5 percent per annum in mid-1990, and then again from 5 percent to 1.2 percent per annum in late 1991.

Table 5.7 presents the quarterly trend of the expected real interest rate in the financial markets, together with the trend of the external interest rate (nominal), the expected decrease in the real value of the peso with respect to the dollar, and the spread (or risk premium) between internal and external yields, both measured in pesos. The expected rate of inflation is the rate implicit in the difference between the yields of CETES and Ajustabonos (indexed to domestic inflation). The expected nominal rate of depreciation is the rate implicit in the spread between CETES and Tesobonos (indexed to the exchange rate in dollars). These measures of exchange expectations and of inflation therefore refer to the expectations prevailing in the financial markets. Since they can only be estimated subsequent to the recent introduction of Ajustabonos and Tesobonos, the indicators could only be constructed starting with the third quarter of 1989.[27]

If the equivalence upon which this table is based is interpreted as a sign of equilibrium in the financial markets, the difference between domestic and external rates corresponds to the risk premium determined endogenously in the market. This premium, in addition to being influenced by investor perceptions of the country risk, depends (inversely) on the supply of government bonds. This is why the table also shows the quarterly trend of the real stock of government bonds held privately (by residents and nonresidents), i.e., domestic debt excluding central bank holdings of government securities.

We will now examine the behavior of the components of this equivalence in the three subperiods in question:

(1) The high real interest rate (approximately 19 percent per annum) prevailing in the initial period, up to the second quarter of 1990, was basically associ-

---

[27] The indicators of expected inflation could only be constructed up to the second quarter of 1992. For the last three quarters in the table, the real interest rate corresponds to the *ex-post* rate. It is unlikely that this limitation causes any significant distortion. During the period for which information is available, the direction of the change in the expected interest rate is identical to that of the *ex-post* rate, except for very short-term variations, and, in addition, expected inflation and *ex-post* inflation had practically converged as of the second quarter of 1992.

Table 5.7. Mexico: Interest Rate Analysis
(Percentages)

	1989:3	89:4	90:1	90:2	90:3	90:4	91:1	91:2	91:3	91:4	92:1	92:2	92:3[1]	92:4[1]	93:1[1]
Expected real interest rate	19.7	18.8	19.4	18.9	14.3	11.3	8.6	7.1	5.5	5.4	4.0	3.1	8.8	5.8	7.2
Foreign interest rate	8.5	8.2	7.9	8.0	8.0	8.0	6.8	6.0	5.8	5.0	4.1	4.0	3.3	3.5	3.2
Expected real depreciation	0.4	0.2	0.8	1.5	-0.3	-2.5	-4.7	-4.9	-4.5	-4.7	-4.5	-4.4	2.4	1.2	2.8
Differential between domestic and foreign interest rates	10.8	10.4	10.7	9.4	6.6	5.8	6.5	6.0	4.2	5.1	4.4	3.5	2.5	0.5	0.7
Change in domestic debt[1]	27.5	-6.9	8.3	25.5	13.3	-5.8	6.4	2.8	-24.4	-17.5	-34.7	-72.0	-20.0	-21.8	35.3

[1] Change in the stock of government bonds, excluding the holdings of Banco de México and development banks.
Source: Author's own calculations based on Banco de México, *Economic Indicators* (various editions).

ated with a very high risk premium (more than 10 percentage points). Although the expected rate of real depreciation is positive, it is insignificant (approximately half of a percentage point per annum). In short, in this period, the markets expected that the real exchange rate would remain stable but demanded a high risk premium to maintain the supply of government bonds.

(2) The rapid and constant decline of the real interest rate from mid-1990 to mid-1992 was associated with:

(a) the modification of exchange rate expectations, which now reveal an expected real appreciation. The change is minimal at first and then more pronounced in early 1991, coinciding with the deregulation of the money market. Compared with the average for the previous period, the change is drastic and constant: the expected real appreciation is approximately 4.5 percent per annum instead of an expected devaluation of 0.5 percent. Although the drop in the external interest rate (i^*) clearly contributed to the reduction of the domestic rate, the magnitude of this contribution is less than that of the modification of exchange rate expectations. In addition, the reduction in the domestic rate clearly began two quarters *before* the external rate started falling.

(b) the reduction of the risk premium—which was as drastic or more so than the change in exchange rate expectations—from approximately 10 to 3.5 percentage points between mid-1990 and mid-1992. In addition to the signing of the external debt restructuring agreement and the opening of NAFTA negotiations, the steady decline of the premium appears to be closely linked to the process of domestic debt reduction made possible by the enormous revenues from privatization: at the close of this period, state domestic debt (owed to the private sector and to nonresidents) had fallen 30 percent from its real value in mid-1990. Most of these amortizations occurred between mid-1991 and mid-1992, during which period the decline of the risk premium accelerated.

(3) The increase of the real interest rate in mid-1992 is associated exclusively with the reversal of exchange rate expectations in the financial markets, since both the risk premium and the external rate kept falling during this period. The reversal of expectations is again drastic: having waited (constantly for six quarters) for a real appreciation of approximately 4.5 percent per annum, the markets began expecting a real devaluation of 3 percent in the third quarter of 1992.

Finally, it should be noted that although exchange rate expectations went from stability to real appreciation and then from appreciation to real depreciation, the real *ex post* value of the peso with respect to the dollar increased constantly throughout the three periods. The swing to appreciation expectations coincides with the first announcement of a decrease in the rate of drift of the peso in May 1990, suggesting that this exchange policy had credibility in the financial markets. But this observation raises more questions than it answers: if, until mid-1990, the markets believed that the equilibrium real exchange rate was more or less the rate in effect at the time (or even a little higher), why did they not react negatively to the reduction in the rate of drift of the peso, which implied, as they in fact expected, real appreciation in the future? And why, toward the middle of 1992, did the exchange policy lose the credibility it enjoyed?

An Interpretation: The Over-adjustment of the Financial Markets

To understand the "basic mechanisms" underlying the processes of exchange appreciation and of the initial reduction and subsequent increase in the real interest rate, we will use a variant of the model developed by Branson (1985). This is a "real" model in which monetary policy plays no role and the level of GDP is at its long-term level. We will retain these assumptions throughout most of this section in order to focus attention on the behavior of asset markets and their impact on the current and capital accounts. Later, we will relax some of the assumptions in order to examine the role of monetary policy. In a subsequent section we will analyze other macroeconomic effects.

The Flow and Capital Stocks Equilibria

The model includes two equations (the flow equilibrium equation and the capital stocks equilibrium equation) and two endogenous variables (the real interest rate and the real exchange rate). The first equation concerns the equilibrium condition between investment and savings (domestic and external). Equating the current account deficit (DCC) with net imports (of exports) and assuming that net imports are determined (inversely) by the real exchange rate and that savings (A) and investment (I) are determined by the real interest rate (r):

$$DCC(er) = I(r) - A(r) \tag{3}$$

The sign of the interest rate in the savings function is uncertain because the public sector is a net debtor, and an increase in the real interest rate reduces public savings, which can cancel out the potential positive effect on private savings. The other signs are the usual ones: an increase in the real exchange rate lowers the current account deficit, and an increase in the real interest rate reduces investment. Equation (3) defines an upward curve in the (er,r) space—the I-X, as Branson calls it (see Figure 5.2)—because a reduction in the interest rate causes an increase in investment over savings and this necessitates a reduction of the exchange rate in order to maintain flow equilibrium.[28]

The second equation concerns equilibrium in the financial markets. In equilibrium, the spread between the domestic and the external rate equals the risk

---

[28] Strictly speaking, this statement is only true if the potential negative effect of the interest rate on savings (via the route mentioned above) does not cancel out the effect on investment.

Figure 5.2. Capital Flows and Capital Stocks Equilibria

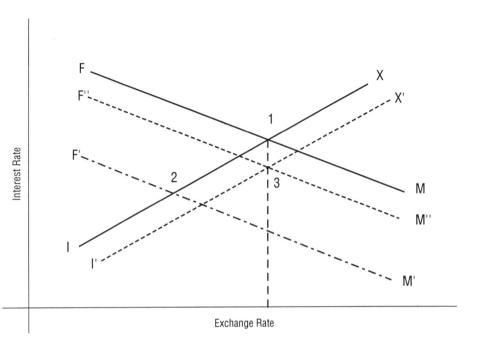

premium (μ) determined in the market by the quantity of bonds offered (government domestic debt, D_g) and an exogenous component (m_0) that reflects investor perceptions of the country risk.

$$r - (i^* + er\%^e) = \mu(D_g, \mu_0) \tag{4}$$

Expected depreciation is determined using the following expectations formation mechanism:

$$er\%^e = \delta(er - er_{-1}) + \beta(er^* - er_{-1}), \text{ with } 0<\delta<1 \text{ and } 0<\beta<1 \tag{4.a}$$

Where er_{-1} is the exchange rate at the close of the preceding period (which, therefore, is known in the markets in the current period), er is the short-term equilibrium exchange rate (obtained using the model) and er^* is the long-term equilibrium rate, i.e., the one that brings the current account to its long-term sustainable level (see below). This equation assumes that in forming their exchange rate expectations, agents in the financial markets consider both the short-term equilibrium exchange rate (*er*) and the long-term equilibrium rate (*er**). Unlike Branson, who, following in the footsteps of Dornbusch (1976), assumes that expected depreciation is only a function of the difference between *er** and *e* (and that adjustment to the short-term equilibrium rate is instantaneous), equation 4.a indicates that agents in the markets ascribe varying degrees of importance to the short and long terms (both uncertain) and that their expectations are subject to opposing forces when the short-term exchange rate moves in a direction opposite to the long-term rate.[29]

Inserting (4.a) into (4) and defining short-term equilibrium as the period in which changes in capital stocks can be ignored and the real exchange rate has been adjusted to its equilibrium level (*er$_{-1}$* = *er*) gives (4.b), which defines a downward curve (FM in Figure 5.2) in the space (*er, r*):

$$er = er* - 1/B \,.\, [r - i* - \mu(D_g, \mu_0)] \qquad\qquad (4.b)$$

For given values of the external rate and the risk premium, a reduction of the exchange rate to below its level of long-term equilibrium creates expectations of a devaluation (of the peso), which requires an increase in the real interest rate to maintain equilibrium in the financial markets. In the short term, the interest rate and the real exchange rate "clear" the commodities and financial markets, with given capital stocks. In the long term, the interest rate and the exchange rate stabilize only when the capital stocks remain stationary (with respect to the given level of GDP). In the long term, then, the capital stocks are determined endogenously.

A third equation is implicit in the other two: that of the equivalence, in equilibrium, of the current account deficit and the capital account surplus:

$$DCC(er) = F_0 + F[r,(i*+er\%),\mu] \qquad\qquad (5)$$

When the commodities market and the financial markets are in equilibrium, the endogenous capital flows (*F*, determined by the equilibrium values of the interest rate and the real exchange rate) finance the difference between the current account deficit (resulting from the equilibrium in the commodities market) and the exogenous capital flows (*F$_0$*). The long-term equilibrium exchange rate (*er**) is simply the value of *er* that makes *DCC=F$_0$*, i.e., the rate consistent with stationary capital stocks (with the exception of the exogenous flows). What we will call the long-term sustainable current account deficit is the value of *DCC* for

er=er*, or *DCC*=DCC(er*).*

---

[29] This alone explains the difference. Moreover, the notion of instantaneous adjustment to the short-term equilibrium rate would only make sense in a system with a flexible exchange rate.

Market Over-adjustment

We will now consider an initial equilibrium (point 1 in Figure 5.2), which roughly approximates the situation in mid-1989: a real exchange rate at the level generally considered long-term equilibrium (the year 1978), a current account deficit of about 2.6 percent of GDP (approximately the average of the last three decades and somewhat below that of the 1970s), and a very high real interest rate associated, as we have seen, with an exceptionally high risk premium. In mid-1990, "shocks" upset the capital stocks equilibrium in the financial markets in two ways: 1) the improvement in perceptions of the country risk (m_0) brought about by the debt reduction agreement and the opening of the NAFTA negotiations; and 2) the start of the second and more important phase of the privatization program, which, together with the fiscal adjustments of prior years, facilitated the process of domestic debt reduction between mid-1991 and 1992. Both "shocks" had the effect of shifting the *FM* curve downward and to the left (with a single exchange rate, reduction of the risk premium lowers the real interest rate); the first was a one-time occurrence, while the second continued until mid-1992. Note that, initially at least, the flow equilibrium was not disturbed, in the sense that the *I-X* curve did not shift; the reduction of domestic debt was not, in essence, the result of changes in the fiscal deficit but rather of the use of the resources generated by the sale of pre-existing public assets in the reduction of the quantity of government bonds offered.

The effect of a shift of this type in the *FM* curve, without any change in the *I-X* curve, causes a decrease in both the real exchange rate and the real interest rate, as shown in Figure 5.2. And these two phenomena are precisely what characterize the period from mid-1990 to mid-1992. At the same time, in the commodities market these changes cause an *ex ante* excess of investment over savings, which is resolved *ex post* by the increase in the current account deficit and (broadening the assumptions of the model somewhat) a surge in business activity: between the second quarter of 1990 and the second quarter of 1992, GDP grew 7.3 percent (at an annualized rate higher than that of the three previous quarters).

If the expectations formation mechanism assumed in equation (4.a) is correct, exchange rate expectations were subject to two opposing forces during the process of adjustment from point 1 to point 2. One is the expectation that the short-term equilibrium exchange rate will fall, which generates expectations of real appreciation of the peso. The other is the real appreciation itself: the fall of the real exchange rate to below its long-term equilibrium level, which has a contrary effect on expectations. This is consistent with the fact that the expected appreciation was always lower (over the course of eight quarters) than the real appreciation that actually occurred. Although the markets correctly anticipated the direction of the change in the real exchange rate, they were constantly mistaken about the magnitude thereof.

What happens in point 2, which roughly approximates conditions in mid-1992, when the financial markets attain a new short-term capital stocks equilibrium with a real interest rate lower than it was initially? Exchange rate expectations are again altered since the expectation that the short-term real exchange rate will continue falling is now inoperative and is supplanted by the perception that the exchange rate is below its long-term equilibrium level. Why? Because in point 2 the current account deficit $[DCC(er_2)]$ is larger than the long-term sustainable deficit $[DCC(er^*)]$, since $er_2 < er^*$. Moreover, the privatization program has ended and with it the debt reduction process, so that the markets expect no further reductions in the interest rate. The anticipation that under this condition the return to a long-term sustainable position requires a devaluation causes the reversal of exchange rate expectations in mid-1992. It is in this situation, in fact, that the current account deficit becomes an obsession in the financial markets.

The new long-term equilibrium depends on (a) what happens (particularly to private investment, savings, and wealth) during the process of adjustment from point 1 to point 2, and (b) the speed of the transfer from point 2 to the new long-term trajectory. In what follows we will concentrate on the latter subject and leave the former for a later section.

In the final equilibrium (point 3), the real exchange rate is the same as it was initially (er^*)[30] and, therefore, the two curves (I-X and FM) must cross at a point (er_3, r_3), so that $er_3 = er^* (=er_1)$. Does this mean that the interest rate will also return to its initial level (so that $r_3 = r_1$)? Not if the adjustment to long-term equilibrium is quick. The reason for this is that with the current level of government debt, the risk premium has fallen below its initial level. Both the smaller debt and the related decrease in the risk premium mean greater public savings and, therefore, a shift of the I-X curve to the right. Although higher than it was in the first quarter of 1992 (when appreciation was expected), the real interest rate in the final equilibrium would be much lower than it was in the first quarter of 1990, before the domestic debt reduction process. A simple calculation suggests that with the current risk premium and the external interest rate now in effect, the real interest rate in the final equilibrium (with expectations of real exchange rate stability) would be of the order of 4.5 to 5.5 percent. Although a fraction of the variation from the initial rate (which was approximately 19 percent) is explained by the decrease in the external rate, most of it is the result of the decline in the risk premium. This is the most important benefit of the process of domestic debt reduction.

This important benefit is not irreversible, however. The reason is that in the process of adjustment to the new long-term equilibrium, the very characteristics

---

[30] This does not take into account the effects (of the opposite sign) on external interest payments of the lower external interest rate, nor the larger net external debt of the private sector that initiated the process of adjustment from point 1 to point 2, nor the effects that the process of public debt reduction (external and internal) can have on exogenous capital flows.

of the long-term trajectory of the economy can take a turn for the worse. It is worth noting, first, that the process of adjustment to the final equilibrium can be delayed without this necessarily causing a balance of payments crisis. In the final analysis, the reason is that although the final equilibrium is the only one consistent with full, long-term capital stocks equilibrium, it is not the only one consistent with balance-of-payments equilibrium. To clarify this, reference must be made to equation (5), interpreting it now as the equation of balance of payments equilibrium:

$$BP = F_0 + F[r,(i^*+er\%),\mu] - DCC(er) \tag{5.a}$$

For $BP=0$ (balance of payments equilibrium, i.e, stable international reserves), equation (5.a) defines a downward curve in the space (er,r) (Figure 5.3): a decrease in the real exchange rate (which causes an increase in the current account deficit) requires an increase in the interest rate to generate the larger capital account surplus needed to close the gap in the current account. When we include the equilibrium values of er and r (er_3 and r_3) in equation (5.a), we know that the balance of payments is zero and, moreover, that the flow and capital stocks equilibria (equations 1 and 2) are also achieved: this balance of payments equilibrium corresponds to point 3. But in addition to the equilibrium values there are many other combinations (er,r) in which the balance of payments is in equilibrium—namely, all the points on the $BP=0$ curve.

Thus, it is possible to maintain equilibrium in the balance of payments at a point such as 4, with a real interest rate higher than the long-term equilibrium rate, which exactly offsets the devaluation expectations generated by keeping the exchange rate below the equilibrium rate. This is our interpretation of what happened in mid-1992: "normal" accumulation of international reserves accompanied by a real interest rate higher than the long-term equilibrium rate (approximately 7 percent instead of 4.5 percent), a real exchange rate lower than what the markets considered the long-term equilibrium rate, and constant expectations of a real devaluation that did not occur.

This explanation is consistent with events in the commodities market during the same period. The counterpart of the imbalance in the financial markets was excess supply in the commodities markets: the higher interest rate and the lower exchange rate, in contrast to the state of equilibrium, caused an *ex ante* excess of savings over investment, which could only be eliminated by lowering the interest rate and raising the exchange rate. Since this did not occur, the economy went into a recession: the quarterly average GDP in the 1992:3 to 1993:1 period was 2.3 percent below the level of 1992:2. At the same time, inflation continued to slow at a slightly faster rate than before.

What are the dynamics of these imbalances? Unless the excess supply in the commodities market generates (rapidly, which means that it must be the result of

Figure 5.3. Balance of Payments Equilibrium

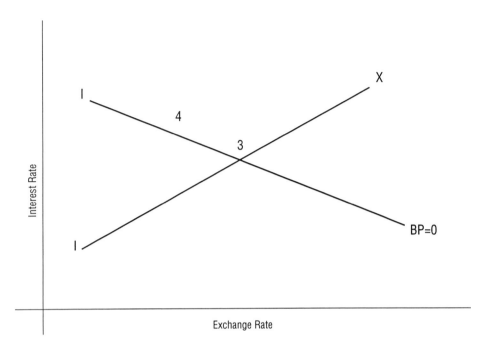

immediate deflation) the required adjustment in the real exchange rate, the persistence of the existing imbalances will change the characteristics of the final equilibrium itself: the fiscal impact involved in keeping the interest rate above the equilibrium rate—to maintain international reserves that pay a much smaller return—leads to a greater accumulation of domestic debt than would otherwise occur and, therefore, to a larger risk premium and a higher real interest rate in the final equilibrium. The danger, in short, is losing the benefits that domestic debt reduction provides. The adverse effects of this process multiply as the peso appreciates, and a higher interest rate (or a longer recession) is needed to offset the upward adjustment of devaluation expectations.

What then, if any, is the rational basis for the interest rate and exchange rate policy followed since mid-1992? Apart from the fact that the adverse effects of this policy have yet to be felt (as we have seen, the risk premium has continued falling since mid-1992), and setting aside the political constraints (which I do not believe play a decisive role), the answer must be that the authorities' opinions concerning the long-term equilibrium exchange rate differ from those prevailing in the financial markets. While the former consider the current real exchange rate sustainable, the latter do not. The only reason for agreeing with the authorities is that in the new economic environment created by the structural reform process, and given the imminence of economic integration with North America, the long-term equilibrium real exchange rate has shifted (upward) and is not what it was in mid-1989.[31] Although this topic is well beyond the scope of this study, we will touch on it in the next section. First, however, it is worth digressing briefly to compare the current situation with the one created in the period before the massive capital inflows.

Asset Flows before and after the Over-adjustment

With the end of the domestic debt reduction process and the reversal of exchange expectations, there also occurred a significant change in the pattern of the capital flows. As Table 5.8 shows, private sector purchases of external assets have increased significantly and the "errors and omissions" column (which largely reflects purchases of external assets not included in other columns) has changed sign, now indicating outflows of foreign exchange. At the same time, private sector holdings of government securities have decreased—faster than in previous quarters, although the domestic debt reduction process has already terminated—and, simultaneously, foreign investment in the money market has increased rapidly with respect to the previous quarterly flows.[32] Moreover, foreign investment in the stock market has slowed, as has the external indebtedness of the private sector, although, significantly, there is a large, positive inflow of foreign exchange in this item.[33] In short, the rate of international reserves accumulation, which slows suddenly in comparison with the previous period, retains a positive sign as a result of massive bond purchases by nonresidents (and, to a lesser extent, the increase in the foreign liabilities of businesses, either in the form of debt or share capital).

---

[31] Thus, in the interpretation we attribute to the authorities, the financial markets are in disequilibrium error because they incorrectly perceive the characteristics of final equilibrium and not because they assume (correctly) that final equilibrium is associated with a real exchange rate higher than the current one. It should be noted that both interpretations are consistent with the fact that the markets always expect a real devaluation that does not occur. Also, the error of the financial markets in this respect is one of both degree and quality: although devaluation expectations are now higher than they were in the mid-1989 to mid-1990 period, they are still too low, given the substantial difference between the real exchange rate then and the current rate.

[32] The domestic debt reduction process continued, although at a slower pace than before, in the third and fourth quarters of 1992. This reduction, however, was fully offset by the increase in the first quarter of 1993 (as a result of the sales of Banco de México bonds). For the recent period as a whole (i.e., from mid-1992 to the end of the first quarter of 1993), the reduction in public debt holdings by the local private sector is therefore associated with the sale of bonds by this sector to nonresidents and not, as was previously the case, with a reduction in the net offering of bonds by the government.

[33] This is even more true if we exclude the indebtedness of commercial banks from this item, which was affected throughout most of the second quarter of 1992 by the restrictions imposed in April of that year (and eased in November).

Table 5.8. Mexico: Movements of Financial Assets in Two Periods
(Millions of dollars)

	Average quarterly flows during the period	
	1990:3-1992:2	1992:3-1993:1
Private sector		
Foreign liabilities	1,470	732
Foreign assets	19	266
Government securities	-1,020	-2,783
Nonresidents (Portfolio investment)		
Stock market	1,313	883
Money market	789	3,340
Banco de México		
International reserves	1,572	749
Domestic credit [1]	-1,034	- 818
Errors and omissions [2]	101	-816

	Average quarterly flows during the period	
	1978:2-1981:1	1981:3-1982:1
Private sector		
Foreign liabilities	537	1,525
Foreign assets	189	913
Government securities	157	-211
Public foreign debt	923	4,760
Banco de México		
International reserves	134	-90
Domestic credit [1]	1,375	-420
Errors and omissions [2]	112	-2,006

[1] Change in the monetary base minus the change in international reserves.
[2] A negative sign indicates an outflow of reserves.
Source: Author's own calculations based on SHCP (1993); Banco de México, *Economic Indicators.*

This pattern of asset flows—in which nonresidents keep accumulating public debt, local companies keep borrowing abroad and, at the same time, the rest of the private sector moves away from the bond market toward external assets—is unfortunately reminiscent of the final quarters of the oil boom in the early 1980s (see the lower part of Table 5.8). Although there are disturbing similarities in the current situation, there are also significant differences between the two experiences. These differences explain why the current situation has been, and continues to be, more manageable in the short term.

In the first place, the change in the composition of the current account deficit has important implications. At the end of the oil boom, the counterpart of the external deficit was an excess of public investment in relation to public savings, while most of the external debt was public. Financing the overwhelming deficit therefore involved paying a growing risk premium. Eventually, the current account deficit (and the associated real exchange rate) became unsustainable in the short term. At present, the external deficit is associated with an excess of investment over private sector savings. Although the current account deficit is unsustainable in the medium term, the sector that has to finance it is not the largest debtor (in fact, the private sector retains a surplus in its net external assets position). Consequently, it does not have to pay a growing risk premium in the short term.

As noted in a previous section, the main impetus of private capital flows during the oil boom was the growth of business activity, whereas the increase in private financial wealth had the opposite effect. When GDP stopped growing in the first quarter of 1982, the greatest deterrent of private sector demand for external assets was removed. This made the situation even more unmanageable. Recently, the financial wealth of the private sector has been contracting and, consequently, so have the financial assets that can be moved abroad. The net financial assets of the public sector, however, have increased as a result of the privatization process.[34] Proof of this is the large amount of international reserves. As a result, the authorities' short-term ability to sustain the exchange rate is higher than in the previous episode.

Deregulation of the money market made the situation more manageable. First, as mentioned above, the greater degree of capital mobility made monetary policy more effective in terms of protecting the exchange rate in the short term, in the sense that it lowered the cost of the rising interest rates so as to eliminate the balance of payments deficit. In addition, this deregulation brought with it new methods of public borrowing—foreign indebtedness through "domestic" debt—which are still viable.

---

[34] The trade-off, of course, is that the public sector is poorer in terms of physical assets; but this, in and of itself, is not relevant to the present discussion.

There is, finally, a fourth (possible) difference that we have already alluded to. This is the diagnosis made in the two instances. During the oil boom, the rise in external interest rates in 1980-81 was perceived as temporary. The high oil prices following the additional increase of 1979-80, on the other hand, were viewed as permanent. This diagnosis proved to be incorrect. The recent instability of the flows could be nothing more than a temporary phenomenon, if it merely reflects uncertainties (primarily about the success of NAFTA) that will dissipate if the authorities are consistent in the application of their macroeconomic and structural reform policies.[35] In this case, the authorities would be right to protect the current exchange rate. We have already seen that the results thus far raise serious doubts about such a diagnosis. But the subject must be approached directly: To what extent is the current real exchange rate sustainable? To what extent can the related current account deficit be financed?

Domestic Savings, Direct Foreign Investment, and Long-term Growth

As noted in the preceding section, the recent capital inflows can be viewed largely as a process of over-adjustment by financial markets to the positive "shocks" experienced since 1989-90. No matter how much the economic outlook may have improved as a result of these shocks, the over-adjustment seems to have caused a medium-term problem in the real exchange rate.

As we have also seen, the long-term viability of the current real exchange rate is closely linked to the question of whether maintaining past investment and growth rates will not require a real exchange rate as high as in the past. One of the following conditions may be sufficient for responding affirmatively to this question: (1) an improvement has occurred in the historic relationship between growth and the current account deficit (either as a result of increased competitiveness or a greater capacity for domestic savings) so that in order to maintain a given investment rate the economy now generates smaller current account deficits; or (2) the level of the financeable deficit has increased, even if (1) does not hold true.

This section addresses several aspects in relation to the above matters: (a) an analysis of the recent trend of investment and private savings and its correlation with the macroeconomic impact that the capital flows have had on the recent adjustment of the financial markets; and (b) a more specific analysis of the trend of DFI and its future role in the investment process.

---

[35] For an interpretation stressing these aspects, see Banco de México, *Annual Report* (1992).

The Adjustment in the Commodities Market and the Savings and Investment Process

What happened in the commodities market during the adjustment to a lower interest rate and a lower real exchange rate? What were the macroeconomic effects of the drastic price changes in the asset markets? What, in particular, was the reaction of investment and private savings to these changes?

Table 5.9 shows the gap between investment and domestic savings (the current account deficit) in the 1989-92 period, divided into its private and public components. The first observation suggested by the table is that the rise in the current account deficit was actually related to an increase in the private sector financial deficit. The widening of this gap was in turn the result of the growth of investment and the decrease in savings. Following is an analysis of the trend of these components.

Growth of Private Investment

The decline in the real interest rate, and probably also the exchange appreciation caused by its effect on the relative price of imported capital goods, elicited a very dynamic response from private investment, which, properly deflated, increased 3 percentage points of GDP in only three years. The private investment data from the national accounts shown in Table 5.9 refer to new investment, as is appropriate when measuring the contribution of the private sector to the country's capital formation. Nevertheless, in view of the privatization of public enterprises on the scale that occurred in 1991 and 1992, it may be more useful to take the restriction of private sector wealth as the starting point for an analysis of the sector's performance in terms of the overall acquisition of capital assets.

Table 5.9 uses the restriction of private sector wealth to show the uses and financing sources for the acquisition of capital assets. A number of comments can be made about the table. First, a large and growing percentage of the upturn in the acquisition of capital assets is explained by such acquisitions on the part of foreign companies (through DFI and external indebtedness) or by the increase of foreign investment in the stock market during the period. Since the foreign investment consisted primarily of purchases of new capital assets, the proper comparison in this case is with new investment. Based on the figures in Tables 5.9 and 5.10, it can be stated that almost two of the three percentage points of GDP by which new private investment increased are explained by the growth of DFI (plus the external indebtedness of foreign companies). The rest of the investment consists of the acquisition of capital assets by the national private sector, less the amount financed through the sale of securities to foreigners. As shown in the table, to finance the acquisition of these assets, the local private sector relied on three sources: its flow of domestic savings, foreign loans, and reduction of nonmonetary financial assets.

Table 5.9. Mexico: Investment and National Savings: Totals by Sector, 1989-92
(Percentage of GDP at constant 1980 prices)[1]

	1989	1990	1991	1992
Private sector				
Investment [2]	12.6	13.1	14.1	15.6
Savings [3]	13.6	9.2	9.4	5.0
Investment minus savings	-1.0	3.9	4.7	10.6
Public sector				
Investment	5.2	5.8	5.5	4.7
Savings [3]	3.5	7.4	6.5	6.7
Investment minus savings	1.7	-1.6	-1.0	-2.0
Total				
Investment[2]	17.8	18.9	19.5	20.4
Savings	15.8	15.8	13.6	11.6
Investment minus savings	2.0	3.1	5.9	8.8
Statistical discrepancy[4]	1.30	1.5	2.2	0.2
Total interest				
(Public sector)[5]	13.6	10.4	5.8	4.2
Real interest				
(Public sector)[5]	9.6	5.2	3.5	3.1

[1] Both investment and savings are deflated by the implicit price of fixed capital formation. (For that matter, so is foreign savings—investment minus national savings.)
[2] Includes changes in inventories.
[3] Adjusted by the inflationary component of public sector payments.
[4] The difference which exists between financial information and balance of payments information.
[5] As a percentage of nominal GDP.
Source: Author's own calculations based on Banco de México, *Annual Report* (1990 to 1992, table on flows of financial funds) and *Economic Indicators.*

The third could be considered a nonrenewable source, i.e., a reduction of physical assets that occurred only once. If we subtract the amount of this reduction from both sides of the uses/sources equation, we obtain the new investment that could have been financed without privatization. The difference between this and new investment is the flow of domestic savings that was diverted (only once) to finance purchases of pre-existing public assets. Interestingly, there was absolutely no displacement effect: On average in 1991-92, the decrease in financial asset holdings was greater than the increase in the acquisition of pre-existing capital assets. The displacement effect that occurred in 1991 was more than off-set by the repurchase of domestic public debt by the government in 1992.

Table 5.10. Mexico: Financing the Acquisition of Capital Assets, 1989-92
(Percentage of the total acquisition of assets)

	1989	1990	1991	1992
Acquisition of preexisting assets[1]	3.1	2.5	22.0	20.8
New investment	96.9	97.5	78.0	79.2
Acquisition of capital assets (total)	100.0	100.0	100.0	100.0
Investment of foreign enterprises[2]	10.0 (10.3)[6]	11.3 (11.6)[6]	16.2 (20.8)[6]	16.0 (20.2)[6]
Foreign investment in the stock market	2.0	7.3	14.8	9.3
Acquisition of capital assets by the national private sector	88.0	81.4	69.0	74.7
Domestic private savings[3]	104.6	68.5	52.0	25.4
Foreign borrowing	2.1	19.6	15.9	5.6
Reduction of domestic and foreign financial assets[4]	-20.4	3.8	7.8	47.3
Change in monetary assets[5]	3.6	10.6	6.7	3.6

[1] Corresponds to privatization income.
[2] Direct foreign investment plus debt of enterprises with foreign participation.
[3] Adjusted for the inflationary component of the public sector interest payments.
[4] Nonfinancial. Adjusted for the inflationary component of public sector interest payments.
[5] Corresponds to the change in the monetary base (since it combines the financial and nonfinancial private sectors).
[6] As a percentage of new investment.
Note: The statistical discrepancy between the total acquisition of capital assets and their sources of financing is due both to the use of different sources of information for financing and for balance of payments, as well as to private sector financing extended by development banks and obtained with foreign debt.
Source: Author's own calculations based on Banco de México, *Economic Indicators* (1990 to 1992, national accounts, financial accounts, and balance of payments).

The increase in local private sector new investment (adjusted for the displacement effect, which, as we have seen, is negative) is thus even less than the one percentage point of GDP not explained by the rapid growth of foreign investment. More significant still is the trend in the financing of this investment: While in 1989 domestic savings financed all of the local investment (and also permitted a substantial accumulation of financial assets), in 1992 domestic savings represented less than a third of local private sector new investment. The change is drastic and continues throughout the period (Table 5.9).

The Decrease in Private Savings

This indicates that although the reaction of investment to the decline in the interest rate and exchange rate appreciation was quite elastic, the reaction of private savings and consumption was even more so. Most of the increased disparity between private investment and savings (11.6 percent of GDP) is explained by a decrease in private savings (8.6 percent of GDP).

A detailed analysis of this phenomenon is beyond the scope of this study. Although not given the importance it merits, the subject has been discussed by various authors (including this one), so that we will merely summarize the major findings of the existing studies. Much of the decrease in private savings that occurred in 1990 and that had already started in 1989 was associated with the "income effects" that the drop in the real interest rate had on the real interest earned by the private sector on its public debt holdings. This decrease involved a redistribution of income within the country, between the private and public sectors, which had no impact on aggregate domestic savings. As Table 5.9 shows, public savings in this period increased by the same amount that private savings declined. This effect, which continued in 1991 and 1992, explains most of the increase in public savings in the period and is a phenomenon that has tended to check the decline in aggregate domestic savings. It should be noted, however, that the positive effect of the drop in the real interest rate on public savings was partially offset by the effect of exchange rate appreciation on the real value of the government's receipts from petroleum exports.

The decrease in 1992 seems attributable to phenomena that are probably temporary. This is especially true of the rapid growth of durable goods consumption following the decline in the interest rate and the recovery of consumer financing after nearly a decade of severe credit rationing and the nonreplenishment of durable goods inventories.[36] Among the temporary phenomena that may have affected consumption in 1991 and 1992, mention has also been made of the "wealth effect" of the capital gains associated with the stock market boom prior to mid-1992.

The corollary of the above discussion is less optimistic than one might think. The reason is that when we adjust private savings and income for the effect of the high real interest that the private sector was collecting in 1989, we realize that private savings rates were already very low compared with the past. As a result of the temporary phenomena of the recent period, there was a reduction in the rate of private savings (and of national savings). This was apparently due to the decline of real income and of the share of private income in GDP that occurred

---

[36] The consumption of durable goods (14 percent of the increase in 1992) was clearly the most dynamic element in the recent growth of consumption. See Banco de México (1992) and, for an analysis of private savings and durable goods consumption in the eighties, Arrau and Oks (1992).

during the 1982-87 adjustment period, and because of the fiscal adjustments necessitated by the huge losses on oil exports in 1986.[37]

For the purposes of our discussion, the above has an important implication: even if national savings were to rebound to 1989-90 levels, it would not suffice for a return to past investment rates, given the historic deficits of the current account of the balance of payments. This means that the economy now requires a higher external savings rate than in the past to achieve the same rate of growth. In these conditions, the exchange rate is sustainable only if the economy is able to attract enough external capital to make current account deficits "financeable" that otherwise would not be. This brings us directly to the subject of the recent trend of DFI and its potential role as a source of permanent capital flows larger than any previously attracted by the economy.

Direct Foreign Investment and Structural Reforms

Direct foreign investment grew significantly in the recent period (Table 5.4). The question is, however, does this recovery represent a break with the past as far as the trend of foreign investment is concerned and, if so, is this change associated with the economic reforms of the period, in particular the greater receptiveness of economic policy to foreign investment?[38]

To answer these questions it will be helpful to develop a model for the determinants of this investment. The basic hypothesis—which is found in the extensive bibliography on the subject[39]—is that the flow of foreign investment is determined essentially by the expected return on capital in the recipient country. Following are the explicative variables of this rate of return used in our analysis:

(1) The size of the economy (which we measure by the level of potential GDP, Y^*), which influences the location decisions of multinational corporations (by affecting the degree of utilization of economies of scale) and, more generally, places limits on a country's ability to absorb capital from abroad;

(2) The degree of productive capacity utilization;

(3) The real exchange rate (er); its effect on the rate of return is expected to be positive since multinational corporations tend to establish themselves in the sectors that produce internationally tradable goods;[40]

(4) The "country risk" (RM), which adversely affects the expected long-term yields. Two measurements of "country risk" are used: the ratio of interest to ex-

---

[37] For an analysis of this process, see Ros (1992). Alberro (1991) presents econometric evidence on the importance of current income in the consumption function in Mexico in the eighties.

[38] At present, there is no updated, systematic exploration of this subject. The most recent study is that of Casar (1989), current to 1988.

[39] For a summary, see Helleiner (1989).

[40] See Lipsey (1988) and Edwards (1990).

port earnings (RM_1) and a nonlinear transformation of this variable: $RM_2 = 1/(1-RM_1)$. The implication of the latter measurement is that the impact of the interest/export ratio on the country risk increases as the ratio approaches one.

Our analysis of the effects of the structural reforms included a proxy of the degree of trade protection: the value of total imports subject to a prior permit (MC). Its effect on DFI can be negative or positive depending on: (a) the sector in which DFI is involved, and (b) the relative intensity of the positive (negative) effects of protection on investment in importable (exportable) sectors. Also, the effect of foreign investment policy reforms was examined by comparing the re-action of foreign investment to potential GDP in the 1960-83 and 1984-92 peri-ods, as explained below.

Included with the above variables was an indicator of short-term business activity in the countries of origin of the DFI. Its effect can be positive or negative depending on whether the "income effect" (i.e., the effect on the level of aggre-gate savings and investment) is greater than "the substitution effect" (i.e., the search for investment opportunities abroad in periods of recession). Given the importance of the United States as a source of DFI for the Mexican economy, the degree of capacity utilization in the U.S. manufacturing sector (Y/Y^*eu) was used as a proxy of this variable.

The model was estimated for the 1960-92 period. It should be noted that the indicator of DFI used was business investment *plans*. This indicator differs from DFI in the balance of payments definition, but only because of the delay between the authorization and the actual materialization of investments. One advantage of this indicator, from a strictly econometric viewpoint, is that referring to investment *plans*—part of which will be carried out in the future—eliminates some of the endogeneity problems that might otherwise arise in analyzing the determinants of DFI.

The equations estimated were, therefore:

$$DFI = a_0 + a_1 Y^*D_1 + a_2 Y^*D_2 + a_3(Y/Y^*) + a_4 er + a_5 RM + a_6 MC + a_7 Y/Y_{eu}^* + e_1$$
$$(6)$$

$$dfi = b_0 + b_1 y^*D_1 + b_2 y^*D_2 + b_3(Y/Y^*) + b_4 er + b_5 RM + b_6 MC + b_7 Y/Y_{eu}^* + e_2$$
$$(7)$$

D_1 and D_2 are dummy variables. D_1 takes the value of 1 in years prior to 1984—the year in which the reform of DFI regulations and other structural re-forms were initiated—and zero in all others, and D_2 takes the value of 1 in 1984 and subsequent years and zero in all others. Thus, a_2-a_1 incorporates the change in the reaction of DFI to potential GDP after 1984. The *dfi, y,* and y^* variables refer to the natural logarithm of the corresponding variable.

The results of the regression analysis are presented in Table 5.11. As indi-cated in the table, the coefficients of all the variables affecting the expected rate of return have the expected sign and, with the exception of the real exchange rate in one equation, are highly significant. In addition to the coefficients of potential GDP, the size and significance of the degree of productive capacity utilization and the country risk are especially interesting. The former confirms the highly procyclical nature of DFI, a finding that appears in earlier studies.[41] This is consistent with the hypothesis of over-indebtedness and suggests that the decrease of the latter since 1989 may have played an important role in the recent recovery of DFI. The coefficient of the degree of capacity utilization in the United States is negative (suggesting that the short-term substitution effect is greater than the "income effect"), although it is not significant in most of the estimates. The sign of the coefficient of the degree of trade protection suggests that the trade liberalization of the 1980s had a positive impact on the flow of DFI, although its value is significant only in the first estimate.

Finally, the values of the a_1 and a_2 coefficients suggest a structural change in the share of DFI in potential GDP starting in 1984. Insofar as this change is explained by foreign investment policy reforms since 1984, the results confirm the significance of these reforms.

The above equations can be used for a quantitative evaluation of the contribution of the different variables to DFI in 1992 (or, more specifically, to the level of DFI predicted by the equation of Table 5.11). Although necessarily flawed, this evaluation provides a better understanding of the factors involved in the recent trend of foreign investment. The results of this exercise are presented in Table 5.12, in which a precise definition is given for each of the effects.

One of the most positive effects is that of the reform of foreign investment policy, which suggests that in 1992 DFI was almost 25 percent larger than it was before the reforms were introduced in 1984. Other important positive effects (approximately 8 percent of DFI in 1992) are the decrease of the country risk—associated with the external debt reduction agreement and the decline of international interest rates—and the trade liberalization initiated in 1985.[42]

These positive effects were canceled out, however, by the effect of the change in the trend of potential GDP, which is defined as the decrease in DFI attributable to the fall of the growth rate of potential GDP from 6.4 percent per annum (in the 1960-83 period) to 1.6 percent per annum from 1984 on. It is significant, although perhaps not surprising, that this effect alone (-40.6 percent), as an absolute value, is greater than the entire positive effect of trade liberalization and the foreign investment policy reforms (35.2 percent). Moreover, real appreciation of the peso since 1988-89 has had an additional negative effect of nearly 5 percent.

---

[41] See Casar (1989).

[42] Note that the reference value of *MC* used to measure this effect is the one for 1980, before the complete reestablishment of import controls in 1981-82. The latter was an unusual event in the history of trade policy in Mexico.

Table 5.11. Mexico: Determinants of Direct Foreign Investment, 1960-92

Dependent variable	Constant	$y^*.D^1$	$y^*.D^2$	$Y^*.D^1$	$Y^*.D^2$	Y/Y^*	er	RM1	MC	Y/Y^*eu	RM2	R^2	DW
DFI	-92.892			0.0126	0.0155	1.115	0.052	-0.505	-0.141	-0.216		0.982	2.170
	(-2.172)			(11.128)	(16.466)	(3.039)	(0.787)	(-4.891)	(2.649)	(-1.456)			
	-101.669			0.0121	0.0153	1.403	0.140		-0.137	-0.327	-0.219	0.983	1.916
	(-2.437)			(11.771)	(17.459)	(3.910)	(2.061)		(-2.616)	(-2.165)	(-5.108)		
dfi	-16.441	1.765	1.823			0.061	0.010	-0.022	-0.004	-0.010		0.957	1.345
	(-5.217)	(8.001)	(8.644)			(2.834)	(2.435)	(-3.041)	(-1.320)	(-1.211)			
	-15.427	1.585	1.652			0.070	0.012		-0.004	-0.013	-0.008	0.953	1.274
	(-4.799)	(8.060)	(8.805)			(3.068)	(2.646)		(-1.386)	(-1.332)	(-2.535)		

The numbers in parenthesis are the t-statistics. R^2 is the coefficient of determination. DW is the Durbin-Watson statistic.
Source: Author's calculations.

Table 5.12. Mexico: Breakdown of DFI in 1992
(Percentages of DFI)

Positive effects	
Foreign investment policy (1)	24.9
Trade liberalization (2)	7.4
Country risk reduction (3)	8.4
Impact of recession in the U.S. (4)	1.7
Total	42.4
Negative effects	
Change in the production trend (5)	-40.6
Exchange rate revaluation (6)	-5.2
Total	-45.3

Notes:

(1) $(a_2 - a_1).Y_{92}{}^*$

(2) $a_6 .(MC_{92} - MC_{80})$

(3) $a_5 .(RM2_{92} - RM2_{87/88})$

(4) $a_7 .(Y/Y_{eu92}{}^* - Y/Y_{eup}{}^*)$

(5) $a_1 .(Y_{92}{}^* - Y_{92}{}^*h) + a_6 .(MC_{92} - MC_{80})$

(6) $a_4 .(er_{92} - er_{78})$

$Y/Y_{eup}{}^*$ = U.S. rate of capacity utilization (average for 1960-92).

Source: Author's calculations.

Finally, it is worth noting that the sum of the positive effects is very similar to the absolute value of the negative effects. This means that when all of its determinants are taken into account, there is no clear evidence that DFI was significantly changed starting in 1984.

Conclusions

The main conclusions and implications of this study can be summarized as follows:

- The massive capital inflows since 1989 were caused by a variety of factors or, more specifically, by the fact that nearly all of the determinants of capital flows, both external and internal, have, almost without exception, had a positive effect on these flows.
- The external environment was characterized by the steady decline of interest rates throughout the period, by recession in the international economy, and by the fall of the country risk premium as a result of the external debt reduction agreement and the terms of trade improvement (adjusted by the external interest rate). Although such an environment certainly contributed to the extraordinary nature of the recent period, the conclusion of this study is that these factors were not decisive in the generation of the capital inflows.
- The domestic factors include the privatization process, the deregulation of foreign investment, the opening of the financial markets and, more generally, the new institutional framework within which the economy evolved following the structural reforms of the 1980s. All of these "positive shocks" had the effect of lowering the country risk premium, and it is here that the mainspring of the capital inflows is located. These "internal shocks" affected capital flows in two ways: (a) through their effects on investor preferences for domestic or external assets, and (b) by permitting financial reorganization of the state, as in the case of privatizations, and, in particular, the financing of a rapid process of public domestic debt reduction.
- This study revealed no significant effects on investor preferences, except for the opening of the money market in early 1991—the effect of which was manifested by a surge in nonresident purchases of government securities—and DFI.
- The financial reorganization of the state, however, seems to have had a considerable macroeconomic impact. The process of public debt reduction financed by the privatization program cut the government's domestic debt in the first quarter of 1993 (in real terms) to nearly half of what it was in mid-1990. This seems to have been the most important determinant of the reduction of the risk premium and, therefore, the largest contributing factor to the fall of the real interest rate from around 19 percent

per annum in mid-1989 to approximately 3 percent in mid-1992. The latter is the tangible benefit of the privatization program. Nevertheless, the process that started the decline of the risk premium—the most obvious manifestation of which was the massive capital inflows from mid-1990 to mid-1992—was not beneficial for all of the macroeconomic balances. The shock to the economy's initial capital stock equilibrium led to overvaluation of the real exchange rate. The analysis and evidence presented in the third and fourth sections of this study clearly suggest that long-term capital flows need to reach a much greater volume than they have until now in order to overcome the economy's macroeconomic adjustment problem, which reaches back to mid-1992 and involves a real devaluation of the peso.

- In the health of the economy since the overadjustment of the financial markets there are some elements that reinforce and others that weaken the above statement. The former include the decline of domestic savings, which was a legacy of the crisis in the 1980s. Added to this are the effects of the displacement of private savings by the recent capital flows. Some of these effects are obviously temporary: the restoration, for example, of durable consumer goods financing following a decade of severe rationing. But even in the most optimistic of scenarios for the recovery of private savings after its recent fall, as far back as 1989 the economy would have required a higher external savings rate than in the past to achieve a given rate of growth. This conflict of economic policy objectives (growth/balance of payments), which existed even before the recent episode, was only heightened by the exchange appreciation that occurred from 1989 onward.

- DFI has responded very positively to the regulatory changes initiated in 1984 and, although to a lesser extent, also to liberalization of trade regulations in 1985 and 1988. Even so, its performance has been greatly hampered by the sluggish growth of the economy and, to some extent as well, by appreciation of the exchange rate. The adverse change in the trend of growth since 1982 has canceled out the positive effects of regulatory changes and trade reform. Given the current macroeconomic policy, any future increase in the permanent flow of foreign investment can only occur as a result of the possible effects of NAFTA, if it succeeds. The author makes no claims concerning these effects,[43] but cannot help thinking that

---

[43] The reason is as follows. The trend of foreign investment can be explained by its traditional determinants, without considering any of the changes expected under NAFTA (in fact, a fictitious variable with a value of 1 in the 1990-92 period was insignificant and had a negative sign in the regression analysis). This suggests either that NAFTA is irrelevant (unlikely) or (as the author is inclined to think) that in their investment decisions, foreign investors still have not internalized the effects of NAFTA.

the sustainability of the real exchange rate will be even more tenuous if it depends solely on the contribution that NAFTA might make to future flows of foreign investment.

- While we wait for NAFTA, our attention should be focused on the macroeconomic adjustment problem confronting the economy. It is a medium-term problem and not a short-term one, as was the case at the end of the oil boom in the early 1980s. The reason is that financing the enormous current account deficit no longer involves paying a rapidly growing risk premium in the short term. Moreover, monetary policy's short-term ability to protect the exchange rate has increased with the greater degree of capital mobility brought about by the opening of the money market. But the fact that the problems are not pressing is a two-edged sword: The dynamics of the current disequilibria are such that the economy's long-term outlook will be compromised if the necessary adjustment in the real exchange rate is not made. The danger is that the benefits of domestic debt reduction will be lost. The harmful effects of this process multiply as the peso keeps appreciating and a higher interest rate (or a more prolonged recession) is needed to offset growing devaluation expectations.

Bibliography

Alberro, J. 1991. The Macroeconomics of the Public Sector Deficit in Mexico during the 1980s. *El Colégio de México.* Mimeo.

Arrau, P., and D. Oks. 1992. Private Saving in Mexico, 1980-90. *Policy Research Working Papers.* Washington, D.C.: World Bank.

Banco de México. 1992. *Informe Anual.* Mexico City.

Banco de México. 1993. *The Mexican Economy 1993.* Mexico City.

Branson, W. 1985. Causes of Appreciation and Volatility of the Dollar. In *The US Dollar: Prospects and Policy Options,* Federal Reserve Bank of Kansas City.

Branson, W., and D. Henderson. 1984. The Specification and Influence of Asset Markets. In *Handbook of International Economics* 1, eds. R.W. Jones and P.B. Kenen. Amsterdam: North Holland.

Calvo, G., L. Leiderman, and C. Reinhart. 1992. Capital Inflows and Real Exchange Rate Appreciation in Latin America: the Role of External factors. *IMF Working Paper.* August. Washington, D.C.: World Bank.

Casar, J. 1989. An Evaluation of Mexico Policy Towards Foreign Direct Investment. In *Mexico and the United States, Managing the Relationship,* ed. R Roett. Westview Press.

Cumby, R., and M. Obstfeld. 1983. Capital Mobility and the Scope for Sterilization: Mexico in the 1970s. In *Financial Policies and the World Capital Market: The Problem of Latin American Countries,* eds. P. Aspe, R. Dornbusch, and M. Obstfeld. Chicago: The University of Chicago Press.

Dornbusch, R. 1976. Expectations and Exchange Rate Dynamics. *Journal of Political Economy* 84.

El-Erian, M.A. 1992. Restoration of Access to Voluntary Capital Market Financing. *IMF Staff Papers 39.* Washington, D.C.: World Bank.

Gasca Zamora, J. 1989. Fuentes para el estudio de las empresas paraestatales de México. Comercio Exterior. February.

Helleiner, G. 1989. Transnational Corporations and Direct Foreign Investment, In *Handbook of Development Economics* 2, eds. H. Chenery and T. Srinivasan. Amsterdam: North Holland.

Hufbauer, G.C., and J.J. Schott. 1993. *NAFTA: An Assessment,* Washington, D.C.: Institute for International Economics.

Kouri, P., and M, Porter. 1974. International Capital Flows and Portfolio Equilibrium. *Journal of Political Economy.* May/June.

Krugman, P. 1990. Macroeconomic Adjustment and Entry into the EC. In *Unity and Diversity in the European Economy*, eds. C. Bliss and J. Braga de Macedo. Cambridge: Cambridge University Press.

Lipsey, R. 1988. Changing Patterns of International Investment in and by the United States. In *The United States in the World Economy,* ed. M. Feldstein. Chicago: University of Chicago Press.

Lustig, N. 1992. *Mexico, The Remaking of an Economy.* Washington, D.C.: The Brookings Institution.

Lustig N., B.P. Bosworth, and R.Z. Lawrence, eds. 1992. *North American Free Trade.* Washington, D.C.: The Brookings Institution.

Organization for Economic Cooperation and Development (OECD). 1992. *México, Estudios Económicos de la OCDE.* Paris: OECD.

Ros, J. 1992. *Ajuste macroeconómico, reformas estructurales y crecimiento en México.* CEDEAL Foundation.

Secretaría de Comercio y Fomento Industrial (SECOFI). 1993. Evolución de la inversión extranjera en México durante 1992. *El Mercado de Valores.* (No. 9.) May 1, 1992. SECOFI, Mexico City.

Secretaría de Hacienda y Crédito Publico (SHCP). 1993. *El Proceso de Enajenación de Entidades Paraestatales.* Mexico City: Secretariat of Finance and Public Credit. May.

United Nations. 1993. *World Economic Survey 1993.* New York: U.N. Department of Economic and Social Development.

U.S. International Trade Commission. 1990. *Review of Trade and Investment Liberalization Measures by Mexico and Prospects for Future United States-Mexican Relations, Phase I.* Washington, D.C.: U.S. Government Printing Office.

World Bank. 1993. *Global Economic Prospects and the Developing Countries.* Washington, D.C.: World Bank.

INDEX